DYSLEXIA

DYSLEXIA
A HISTORY

PHILIP KIRBY
AND
MARGARET J. SNOWLING

McGill-Queen's University Press
Montreal & Kingston • London • Chicago

© McGill-Queen's University Press 2022

ISBN 978-0-2280-1435-5 (cloth)
ISBN 978-0-2280-1436-2 (paper)
ISBN 978-0-2280-1539-0 (ePDF)
ISBN 978-0-2280-1540-6 (ePUB)
ISBN 978-0-2280-1608-3 (open access)

Legal deposit fourth quarter 2022
Bibliothèque nationale du Québec

Printed in Canada on acid-free paper that is 100% ancient forest free (100% post-consumer recycled), processed chlorine free

The open access edition of this book was funded by the Wellcome Trust.

Library and Archives Canada Cataloguing in Publication

Title: Dyslexia : a history / Philip Kirby and Margaret J. Snowling.
Names: Kirby, Philip (Lecturer in social justice), author. | Snowling, Margaret J., author.
Description: Includes bibliographical references and index.
Identifiers: Canadiana (print) 20220274517 | Canadiana (ebook) 20220274533 | ISBN 9780228014355 (cloth) | ISBN 9780228014362 (paper) | ISBN 9780228015390 (ePDF) | ISBN 9780228015406 (ePUB) | ISBN 9780228016083 (Open access)
Subjects: LCSH: Dyslexia—History.
Classification: LCC RJ496.A5 K57 2022 | DDC 618.92/8553—dc23

For our brothers, Edmund and Roger.

Contents

Preface ix
Acknowledgements xi
Introduction: What's in a Word? Dyslexia in Historical Perspective 3

PART ONE • FOUNDATIONS
1 Dyslexia Discovered: Word-Blindness, Victorian Medicine, and Education (1877–1917) 15
2 Dyslexia Goes Global: Psychology, Childhood, and Trans-Atlanticism (1925–48) 36

PART TWO • EVIDENCE
3 Dyslexia Discussed: The Foundation and Work of the Word Blind Centre (1962–72) 63
4 Researching Dyslexia: From the Discrepancy Definition to Cognitive Neuroscience (1964–2009) 86

PART THREE • RECOGNITION: THE EXAMPLE OF BRITIAN
5 Tackling Dyslexia: Class, Gender, and the Construction of a Dyslexia Infrastructure (1962–97) 111
6 Dyslexia Legislated: Literacy, Policy, and the Achievement of Official Status (1962–2010) 134

PART FOUR • LEGACIES
7 Dyslexia Today and Tomorrow: Discourses of Dyslexia in the Twenty-First Century   163

Conclusion   183
Timeline: Fifty Key Dates   185
Notes   189
Bibliography   221
Index   253

Preface

It's sometimes said that there are two common opinions of dyslexia, held by two distinct groups. For group one, who either have dyslexia themselves or know a family member with the condition, dyslexia and its attendant challenges are recognised without equivocation. For group two, who do not have this first-hand experience, dyslexia is a less tangible entity; it may even be an example of the over-medicalization of contemporary society ('In my day, you just had trouble with reading!'). These are stereotypes, of course, but they possess some truth. Much of the campaign for dyslexia's political and societal recognition has been led by those with dyslexia in their families. The strongest views on dyslexia are often (but not always) expressed by those who feel that they or someone they love have been particularly affected by dyslexia.

Given this, it's perhaps valuable to note our personal, as well as professional, associations with dyslexia. Both authors of this book first encountered dyslexia via a family member – our brothers. Maggie, growing up in the north of England during the 1960s, remembers vividly her mother's struggle to get her younger brother's dyslexia recognized, and the distress that it caused when neither recognition nor help was forthcoming. Instead, her mother was told that she should not expect her son to be as clever as his sister. In fact, he was bright, but in a very different way to his sister; he became a property developer, and she went on to academe and clinical practice. Philip, growing up in North London in the 1990s, was also introduced to dyslexia via the efforts of his parents to find support for his brother. Because of the advocacy campaigns charted in this book, support was more forthcoming, but there were still challenges in obtaining (and maintaining) recognition from the various professionals encountered during his education.

Despite these personal connections, we have striven here to present a balanced history, which highlights not only the accomplishments of, for example, dyslexia advocacy campaigns, but also the recurring critiques of dyslexia that continue to mark discourses around the condition. This book has undoubtedly been informed by the lived experiences of dyslexia in our families, but our first duty has been to telling a fair and thorough history of dyslexia. There is plenty of emotion on both sides of the 'dyslexia debate' – understandably so – and we have sought here to move past some of this clamour.

We have one central ambition for the book: that it will prevent certain mistakes of the past from being repeated. Whether one favours the term 'dyslexia' or not – and we live in an age where 'labels' are being challenged and re-evaluated as never before – the difficulties presented in this book are real, and the support provided for them has undoubtedly improved lives. While the dyslexia debate seems set to rumble on, we hope that, through this book, readers may gain a better understanding of the different sides of dyslexia's fascinating story.

Philip Kirby and Margaret J. Snowling
London and Oxford

Acknowledgements

This project has been a long time in the making, and any list of acknowledgements can only be partial. At the University of Oxford, thank you to William Whyte, Kate Nation, Denise Cripps, Robert Evans, and Kieran Fitzpatrick – the Dyslexia Archive team. Steve Chinn was key to getting this project started. Robert Evans and Uta Frith provided careful and comprehensive comments on earlier versions of the manuscript. Lea-Sophie Steingrüber kindly provided translations of original sources in German. At McGill-Queen's University Press, Richard Baggaley deserves recognition for getting this book off the ground. Scott Howard was our excellent copy editor. Emily LeGrand put together a comprehensive index at very short notice. Thank you to the external reviewers of the manuscript for their helpful and detailed comments. The Oxford Dyslexia Archive project that inspired this book was funded by the Wellcome Trust (no. 105605/Z/14/Z) and a grant from St John's College, Oxford. Special thanks, of course, go to our interviewees, whose oral interviews form the basis of the archive, and to those who attended two steering conferences in Oxford in 2017 and 2019, which helped to keep the project on track. Naturally, any mistakes that remain, despite the generous assistance of everyone above, are the authors'.

I felt the words of my lessons slipping off, not one by one, or line by line, but by the entire page; I tried to lay hold of them; but they seemed, if I may so express it, to have put skates on, and to skim away from me with a smoothness there was no checking.
– Charles Dickens, *David Copperfield*

INTRODUCTION

What's in a Word? Dyslexia in Historical Perspective

Dyslexia is in the news again. A glance at recent headlines from around the world reveals myriad articles about the condition – including the efficacy of online dyslexia support in the wake of the COVID-19 pandemic, the story of a leading British politician (Penny Mordaunt, a former defence secretary) who recently 'came out' with dyslexia, and the experiences of an American musician recording the audiobook of her latest biography ('This was the first time I've read out loud without hesitation').[1] The popularity of the topic is unsurprising: about 10 per cent of people have some degree of dyslexia and, even for those not dyslexic, most will know someone who is.[2] Famous celebrities who have disclosed dyslexia include the entrepreneur Richard Branson; the chef Jamie Oliver; the actors Keira Knightley, Jim Carrey, and Tom Cruise; and the musicians Noel Gallagher, Tony Bennett, and Jessica Simpson (she of the audiobook recording above).

Dyslexia is the most common specific learning difficulty globally, and probably the best understood.[3] In 2009, the British Rose review of dyslexia and other literacy difficulties, prepared at the request of the then Department for Children, Schools and Families (now the Department for Education), provided a comprehensive working definition of dyslexia summarising the latest international research. Like all definitions of dyslexia, the Rose description is not without debate. However, it provides a useful starting point for this book, capturing the main difficulties faced by those with poor literacy, even if exact manifestations of dyslexia differ between individuals. In the Rose definition, prepared by the review's Expert Advisory Group:

Dyslexia is a learning difficulty that primarily affects the skills involved in accurate and fluent word reading and spelling. Characteristic features of dyslexia are difficulties in phonological awareness, verbal memory and verbal processing speed. Dyslexia occurs across the range of intellectual abilities. It is best thought of as a continuum, not a distinct category, and there are no clear cut-off points. Co-occurring difficulties may be seen in aspects of language, motor co-ordination, mental calculation, concentration and personal organisation, but these are not, by themselves, markers of dyslexia. A good indication of the severity and persistence of dyslexic difficulties can be gained by examining how the individual responds or has responded to well-founded intervention.[4]

But where did dyslexia come from? Who has been responsible for shifting dyslexia from a niche concern of a select group of doctors in the 1870s, when it was called 'word-blindness' (*Wortblindheit*, by its early German researchers), to the internationally recognised condition that it is today? What can the history of dyslexia tell us about how social groups achieve, and have achieved, political recognition for their causes?

This book tells the story of dyslexia through the records of the Oxford Dyslexia Archive, based at St John's College, Oxford. The Oxford Dyslexia Archive includes the world's largest collection of oral histories of dyslexia pioneers – including the first scientists to identify dyslexia in its modern form, the founders of some of the first dyslexia schools, and the politicians who offered initial political recognition of dyslexia in Britain and elsewhere. These oral histories are used here to explore, in particular, dyslexia's history from the 1950s, much of which has gone unrecorded. The archive also contains the records of leading dyslexia advocacy, research, and teaching organisations, providing a behind-the-scenes look at how dyslexia became embedded – politically, culturally, and socially – in high-income societies, including Britain, during the twentieth century. These records include the revealing, often touching, accounts of children, born across the last one hundred years, who have struggled with a condition that for a prolonged period society refused to recognise and possessed little understanding of.

Introduction: Dyslexia in Historical Perspective

While the British story of dyslexia is a thread that runs through the book, this story is placed in international context. It was research by British physicians in the Victorian era, inspired by German colleagues, which laid down many of the current tenets of dyslexia's definition. It was research, advocacy, and teaching in London, the Midlands, and Wales, beginning in the late 1950s, that influenced similar work across the world. However, this work intersected with that of teachers, researchers, and campaigners around the world, especially in the United States, but also Canada, Denmark, and France, amongst others. To date, little is known about the people, in Britain and elsewhere, who were behind this work: people whose stories are crucial not only for explaining how the awareness and understanding of dyslexia got where it is today, but also for suggesting where dyslexia might be headed.

A Brief History of Dyslexia

The first reference to dyslexia (as 'word-blindness') was made in 1877 by the German physician Adolph Kussmaul.[5] Six years later, the word 'dyslexia' was coined by his contemporary and countryman, Rudolf Berlin, an ophthalmologist based in Stuttgart, who published the first book-length treatment of the subject in 1887.[6] In the years that followed, the research of these two Germans was continued by a series of British physicians, whose work laid the foundations for later discussion of the condition in the United States and elsewhere. James Kerr, James Hinshelwood, and William Pringle Morgan were the prominent names in Britain at this time, and their stories – and the stories of their patients – provide a fascinating insight into why dyslexia emerged when it did, and how the first (faint) definitional lines were drawn around this new medical condition in the late nineteenth century.[7]

From the late 1910s to the early 1950s, there was a lull in British discussions of dyslexia – in part, as the wars between Britain and Germany channelled medical and psychological research elsewhere – until the dawn of what might be called dyslexia's 'golden age' from the late 1950s. In Britain, this saw the creation of the Word Blind Centre for Dyslexic Children in 1962, one of the first teaching-research centres in the world focused on dyslexia, followed by a series of parent-led organisations, including the British

Dyslexia Association (BDA) and the Dyslexia Institute in 1972. In substantial part, these emulated the model of the Orton Society in the United States, formalised in 1949 as one of the world's first organisations dedicated to better understanding of dyslexia.[8]

During the same period (the 1960s–70s), research on the condition expanded, with population studies of children's educational attainment in the Isle of Wight and London (1964–74), led by the psychiatrist Michael Rutter and the psychologist William Yule, proving especially influential. In the United States and elsewhere, researchers such as Frank Vellutino began to devote serious and sustained attention to dyslexia. Gradually, a series of dyslexia advocacy organisations, drawing on this growing evidence base of research, effected political recognition of dyslexia, with substantial state support rolling out from the 1990s onward, albeit proceeding at different rates in different countries. Today, dyslexia recognition has reached something of a peak in high-income countries, but cuts to funding for special educational needs, and the recurrent 'dyslexia debate' in which the very existence of dyslexia is disputed, suggest possible storms on the horizon.[9]

The Aims of This Book

Despite the prevalence of the condition, the history of dyslexia has attracted little scholarly attention. As of 2020, the *Oxford Dictionary of National Biography* (ODNB) mentioned dyslexia in just fifteen of over 75,000 entries on leading figures of British social and political history, with only two entries related to dyslexia specialists – a remarkably small number given the proportion of people affected by dyslexia.[10] The majority of published work on dyslexia's history has come from those involved in this history themselves, including researchers, campaigners, and teachers, who have authored their personal reflections.[11] The small amount of research on the history of the condition has focused on specific periods, such as dyslexia's emergence during the late-Victorian era, or offered succinct sketches of dyslexia's longer trajectory.[12] This body of work takes the first steps in understanding aspects of dyslexia's past – and is drawn upon throughout this book – but as yet, there has been no comprehensive account of dyslexia's history.[13] This book puts dyslexia on the map, joining historical accounts of other difficulties that affect learning, and can affect self-esteem, such as autism and attention deficit hyperactivity disorder (ADHD).[14]

As such, the book has two central aims, empirical and theoretical. First, it seeks to add dyslexia to the broader history of learning difficulties and disabilities, recording the personal recollections of those who have witnessed and contributed to dyslexia's history over the past sixty years. As we will show, dyslexia has a fascinating history that tells us much about Western social and political history from the Victorian period onward, and about how literacy has expanded across the twentieth century and into the twenty-first, who this expansion has left behind, and how those with dyslexia and their advocates have sought to adapt.

Second, through the history of dyslexia, this book reflects on how social change is accomplished. Specifically, it seeks to reiterate the importance of individual agency to theories of social change. The main historical work on dyslexia to date has theorised its emergence as part of larger, capital-driven societal shifts in the West, including the expansion of literacy and compulsory education, and hence the creation of a more economically productive workforce. In the formulation of the sociologist Tom Campbell, 'Literacy became central to [economic] production [in the early twentieth century], and dyslexia came to describe a difficulty with a key characteristic of the newly dominant style of labouring in the West'.[15] While structural changes like this have certainly been important in highlighting the problem of dyslexia, especially in schooling, and in creating the contexts for change, they do not alone explain dyslexia's emergence. The grassroots work of dyslexia advocates, teachers, and researchers, seeking to achieve dedicated state support for people with dyslexia, has also been crucial in bringing dyslexia to societal attention.

Conceptualising Dyslexia and Its History

While the Rose report provides a working definition of dyslexia and its common characteristics, the instability of the term 'dyslexia' and the contingency of dyslexia's emergence are key elements of the dyslexia story. To this end, it is important for any account of dyslexia to reflect on how the condition is to be conceptualised. Providing a point of approach is the literature of disability studies, the discipline that has considered in greatest depth the conceptualisation of physical and cognitive differences, and which informs the understanding of dyslexia in this book.

In disability studies, a key idea is the social model of disability. Through this lens, 'disability', meaning any kind of physical or cognitive difference from a commonly understood norm, is considered a socially produced and conditioned entity. 'At its core, the social model questions the parameters of normalcy, including who defines and enforces those borders, and most crucially the repercussions for those both inside and outside of these culturally drawn and fluctuating lines'.[16] Thus, the social model challenges 'medical' models of 'disability', which see difference as rooted in the body of the individual. Instead, to use a conventional example from the discipline, an individual who uses spectacles is disabled not by a particular visual impairment, but by the lack of, for example, books available in an accessible print. In this way, disability studies (the field) is reticent about medicalising physical or cognitive differences, preferring instead to differentiate between impairment (the bodily difference) and disability (the ways in which this impairment disables because of societal structures and conventions).[17]

Dyslexia is especially amenable to the social model of disability, being a difficulty associated principally with a social product: literacy.[18] In approaches to dyslexia that have employed the social model, those with dyslexia are disabled not by their own personal difficulties with reading or writing, but by the almost universal requirement in high-income countries for certain levels of literacy to obtain educational and career success.[19] Thus, for the disability studies scholar Craig Collinson, 'we should not let "dyslexia" disguise or cloak Lexism [discrimination against those with dyslexia], which is the real issue'.[20] At one extreme of this perspective, the 'biologizing' of dyslexia has been construed as part of an overly medical agenda to separate those with dyslexia from other 'normal' learners, to the detriment of the former.[21]

The social model of disability does much to show how society frames, and, in part, produces, 'conditions' like dyslexia. However, there are limits to the application of the social model to dyslexia, in isolation. Perhaps the main limitation of the social model is that, in interpreting the difference between those with and without dyslexia from a social perspective, it does not fully address the views and understandings of those with dyslexia them-

Introduction: Dyslexia in Historical Perspective

selves. As this book explores, it has often been those with dyslexia, and their advocates, who have campaigned *for* the dyslexia label, invoking medical and psychological research to achieve their aim of greater political and societal recognition. The dyslexia movement, throughout its history, has drawn attention to the social conditions that exacerbate dyslexia (such as strict exam times, poorly designed school workbooks, and a general lack of societal awareness), but it has also stressed the underlying biological reality of dyslexia. As such, this book employs a conceptualisation of dyslexia that goes beyond the either/or binary of medical/social models of disability, instead contending that dyslexia is something of both, but more than either.[22]

This more 'ambivalent' understanding of dyslexia and of what it means to have dyslexia, to borrow a characterisation from the sociologist Per Solvang, is well-captured by the oral histories in the Oxford Dyslexia Archive.[23] Three examples of interviewees reflecting on their 'diagnosis' are illustrative. For Susan Hampshire, a celebrated British actress and one of the first public campaigners for dyslexia rights, there was a slight psychological benefit in better understanding the difficulties that she faced, 'but of course it [dyslexia] was [ultimately] just a word I could use'.[24] For a former chairperson of the BDA, 'at the point of diagnosis, there is a phase of emotions that you go through: the anger, there is the acceptance, and then there is the moving forward'.[25] For a student growing up in Britain in the 1990s, there was 'a mixture of relief and I was a bit upset'.[26] Put another way, 'the moment of diagnosis is ambiguous: a point in which both difficulties are explained (at least through one [medical] model of understanding) and support becomes more forthcoming, but also an external label of disability is enshrined, beyond the control of the individual affected'.[27] This ambiguity makes charting a pathway between medical and social models of dyslexia necessary.

The Structure of This Book

This book is ordered chronologically, tracing dyslexia from its Victorian origins through to the present day, and is organised into four parts. Part 1, 'Foundations', considers the origins of dyslexia at the end of the nineteenth century; part 2, 'Evidence', addresses the development of the scientific basis for dyslexia; part 3, 'Recognition: The Example of Britain' provides a case study of dyslexia's political and societal recognition; and part 4, 'Legacies', looks at the ways in which dyslexia's past may shape dyslexia's futures. Each chapter within these sections is thematic, drawing out a key aspect of that part of the dyslexia story.

Chapter 1 considers dyslexia's Victorian beginnings. In 1896, William Pringle Morgan, a doctor from Seaford, Sussex, authored the first detailed account of a child with dyslexia in Britain, drawing on the evidence base established in Germany by Adolph Kussmaul and Rudolf Berlin. Pringle Morgan's contribution was joined by other important studies, including those of his fellow Britons, James Kerr and James Hinshelwood, who together laid the foundations for dyslexia's first science. During this period, an initial version of the influential 'discrepancy diagnostic model' was established, wherein dyslexia was identified as a marked difference between reading and general abilities. This period also saw the first suggestion that dyslexia was a developmental difficulty that might run in families and that dyslexia was related to the phonological component of language. This chapter profiles the groundbreaking work of these doctors, shows how changes in Victorian society and schooling enabled dyslexia to emerge, and considers what it was like to possess reading difficulties during this period.

By the 1920s, dyslexia research in Britain was waning. Elsewhere, though, the mantle of these early researchers was taken up by others. Chapter 2 considers several of the most important figures of the 1920s and 1930s, including Samuel Orton, Anna Gillingham, and Bessie Stillman in the United States, whose research further developed understanding of dyslexia and laid the foundations for the resurgence of interest in Britain from the late 1950s. It also examines the contributions of Edith Norrie in Denmark, who founded one of the first dyslexia schools in Copenhagen and helped instruct a new generation of specialist dyslexia teachers. Simultaneously, it looks at the experiences of growing up with dyslexia in the first half of the twentieth century, when, despite the work of these individuals, educational, societal, and political recognition of dyslexia around the world was slight. It also considers the first concerted criticism of dyslexia, notably that of the British educational psychologist Cyril Burt.

Chapter 3 explores the formation of the first dedicated dyslexia organisation in Britain: the Word Blind Centre for Dyslexic Children. In the early 1960s, a disparate group of physicians, psychologists, and academics founded the centre to bring together their interests in reading difficulty and its causes. The centre's principal director was a psychologist, Sandhya Naidoo, who published the first detailed analytical account of children with dyslexia from the perspective of psychology in 1972. The Word Blind Centre also served as a meeting place for others who became key figures in the dyslexia story, including the founders of further dyslexia organisations and specialist schools. This chapter explores how interest in dyslexia became a centralised, if not yet state-acknowledged, concern in Britain, drawing on and contributing to an emerging international interest in the condition. In addition, it considers how the Word Blind Centre laid down several gendered and classed associations of dyslexia that marked dyslexia's later history.

Chapter 4 considers the history of dyslexia's science from the period of the Word Blind Centre onward. Scientific work on dyslexia, by medical professionals, psychologists, and neuroscientists, amongst others, has intersected with dyslexia's social, political, and cultural histories. For campaigners, it has formed the bedrock of dyslexia's existence and has challenged political intransigence in recognising the condition. At the same time, dyslexia's science possesses a fascinating history in its own right, which has, gradually across the twentieth century, shone further light on a difficulty that in the Victorian period was marked by its opacity. Who has been responsible for this scientific research, and how have they undertaken it? In what directions has dyslexia's science developed over time? Emerging from the middle of the twentieth century, dyslexia science has expanded in the decades since into an international research effort to better understand the condition.

Chapter 5 explores how dyslexia was institutionalised in Britain: how an initial infrastructure of support was created. By the early 1970s, after helping several hundred pupils and providing a research base for dyslexia, funding for the Word Blind Centre expired. However, in its wake, Marion Welchman, professionally qualified as a nurse, brought together local dyslexia associations from across the country to form the British Dyslexia Association in 1972. A sister organisation, later rival, was founded the same year: the Dyslexia Institute. The early 1970s also saw the formation of several other specialist dyslexia organisations – in London and the South East, in the Midlands, and in Wales. Together, these organisations embedded dyslexia in British society, creating a research, teaching, and advocacy base upon which a dedicated advocacy movement for dyslexia rights was founded.

Chapter 6 considers the campaign for political recognition of dyslexia in Britain, which built on this expanding dyslexia infrastructure. As dyslexia awareness increased in society, so too did attempts at achieving political acknowledgement. The first lobbying was undertaken by the Word Blind Centre in the early 1960s, who were told by the then Ministry of Education that the evidence base for dyslexia was too thin to provide dedicated support. In refusing to acknowledge dyslexia, politicians and civil servants drew on the associations that had marked dyslexia's social history in Britain, including its associations with 'worried mothers' and the middle classes. Nevertheless, with concerted campaigning by the dyslexia support organisations, the advocacy movement was successful in achieving political recognition, unlocking the door to state support.

Chapter 7 considers dyslexia's present and future through three key discourses of dyslexia in the twenty-first century: first, dyslexia's place in popular culture, which, for better or for worse, is increasingly the mode through which the majority of information about the condition is disseminated; second, the resurgent claim that dyslexia is a myth without scientific foundation, legitimated by private educational psychologists willing to offer a diagnosis (for a fee); and third, the place of dyslexia in emerging debates over neurodiversity, and how best to characterise difficulties such as dyslexia. Bringing these strands together, a final section considers what the future might hold for dyslexia, and the possibility that the term might one day be replaced. This chapter illustrates how understandings of dyslexia in Western societies have now proliferated into an almost immeasurable diversity, with both positive and negative effects on those with dyslexia.

PART 1
Foundations

1

Dyslexia Discovered: Word-Blindness, Victorian Medicine, and Education (1877–1917)

Dyslexia, as the behavioural manifestation of a difference in brain development and cognitive functioning, has likely existed for far longer than modern science has imagined. It was only with the emergence of widespread literacy, though, that problems with learning to read were noticed and that the condition became prominent in society. Dyslexia is a curious phenomenon in this respect, blurring distinctions between nature and culture, the body and the environment, the medical and the social. Dyslexia manifests differently in different languages, cultures, and contexts, and could not occur in the form we understand it today outside of literate societies.[1] The scant attention paid to those with cognitive difficulties in centuries past, and an absence of records of their experiences, means that identifying people with dyslexia prior to the late nineteenth century is a perilous, likely impossible, undertaking.[2] It was only in the late nineteenth century that the symptoms modern researchers would confidently ascribe to dyslexia fully emerged.

Dyslexia can, however, be contextualised with historical accounts of reading difficulty. In the sixteenth century, St Teresa of Ávila (1515–1582), a Spanish noblewoman who entered monastic life as a Carmelite nun, lost the ability to recognise words and letters during her states of ecstasy.[3] In 1676, a German linguist, Johannes Schmidt, published the first account in Europe of a person unable to read for non-optical reasons. In all likelihood, this was because of a stroke, rather than an underlying developmental difficulty, but it marks one of the first occasions when reading was thought to be differentiable from general cognitive skills, recognised as a process in its own right and an ability that could be impaired.[4] In 1834, a Professor Lordat of the

University of Montpellier described his recovery from a speech disorder some years earlier, during which he had found it impossible to make sense of printed symbols.[5] The aetiology (underlying causes) of such acquired reading difficulties is very different from dyslexia, but together they illustrate how, from the seventeenth to nineteenth centuries, as the Enlightenment brought about immense change to scientific and medical epistemologies, bodies increasingly came to be seen as a form of machinery, judged according to their ability (or otherwise) to fulfil societally ascribed functions.[6]

Other widespread societal shifts were equally important. As late as the early nineteenth century, reading was a skill of the elites, not of the people.[7] During the latter half of the nineteenth century, this view changed with the expansion of elementary schooling in Europe and America, and with the rise of a professional class. For this newly educated stratum of society, literacy was crucial and the flexible orthographies of Chaucer and Shakespeare faded out to be replaced by consistent, agreed systems of spelling.[8] Between the mid-1600s and the mid-1800s, British literacy rates, for example, rose from around one-third of the population of males to approximately two-thirds, with a national average for women of about one-half; by the end of the century, as elementary education became widespread for both sexes, illiteracy had been mostly extinguished.[9] Following the Education Acts of the 1870s onwards in Britain, the stage was set for compulsory elementary education up to age twelve. While the quest against illiteracy proceeded at different paces in different Western countries, this general pattern of progress was similar.[10]

Thus, structural changes in British society, paralleled (sometimes prefigured) elsewhere in the world, threw the challenges faced by those with reading difficulties into stark relief. For David Pritchard, a historian of learning disability, 'When the ability to read and write is possessed by few, those who cannot read and write do not stand out. The child who would later be termed feeble-minded could successfully labour with his equally illiterate fellows. It was only when education became general that the problem of backwardness was discovered.'[11] Such educational interest was supported by an expansion of medical research at universities – initially in Germany, then in Britain, and later in the United States – which became increasingly concerned with what would now be called 'learning difficulties'.[12] According to the sociologist Tom Campbell, this shift in institutional structures and societal requirements led to the creation of a new group within the population: persons with dyslexia.[13] More specifically, Campbell cites economic change as the principal driver for the emergence of dyslexia: 'the clinical criteria that were negotiated for congenital word-blindness [in the late nineteenth and early twentieth centuries] seem to have been negotiated in relation to rationalities of government concerned with capitalising the population'.[14] For Campbell, the pathologizing of dyslexia is directly connected to the emergence of late modern capitalism.

Campbell's discussion of the emergence of dyslexia during this period remains the best elaborated, and this chapter builds on Campbell's arguments. Certainly, the emergence of dyslexia should be understood in dialogue with various societal changes from the late nineteenth century. In part, attention to those with dyslexia emerged for economic rather than altruistic reasons, with children (usually boys) from wealthier backgrounds brought to doctors by parents concerned that they would not be successful in education and so in their later careers. In this way, the identification of dyslexia by Victorian doctors represented a form of what Michel Foucault, the French philosopher, calls 'biopower': the exercise of state control over the bodies of its citizens for the state's greater (in this case, economic) purposes.[15]

However, there are limits to economic arguments for the emergence of dyslexia, which echo broader concerns with top-down conceptions of power in Foucauldian approaches.[16] While children were coming to the attention of Victorian researchers because they were encountering difficulties in education, a prerequisite for entry into productive economic life, there is little evidence that these doctors had an explicitly economic rationale for their actions. Rather, the shape of the economy at the start of the twentieth century seems more of a context for change than a driver. As later chapters will demonstrate, governments in Britain and the United States have shown a great resistance to recognising and supporting those with dyslexia across the twentieth century. Presumably, they would not have shown this reticence had they been principally concerned with shaping citizens with poor reading into economically productive citizen-workers. Indeed, Victorian researchers acknowledged, the number of children and adults with such difficulties was likely to have been drastically underestimated.[17] It is how people with dyslexia have been overlooked by government, and how those with dyslexia and their supporters have sought government attention, that provides the central thread of dyslexia's history, running against the theory that dyslexia is the product of a particular form of centralised political authority, whether economic or otherwise.

To this end, this chapter makes space for the agency of the first physicians to draw attention to dyslexia. Acting within a society that increasingly required literacy of its citizens, and from the perspective of a profession (medicine) that normally regarded its clients as in some way deficient, a close reading of these doctors' accounts suggests that they were, nevertheless, primarily concerned for their patients as individuals. Counter to medical models of disability, the reflections of these doctors show that they did not place responsibility for these difficulties on the children they assessed; rather, they had a more balanced understanding of reading difficulties and their biological bases, alongside the social factors (such as poor education) that exacerbated them. Consider, for example, this passage from James Hinshelwood, a Scottish ophthalmologist and the foremost thinker on dyslexia during the Victorian period and early twentieth century: 'It is a matter of the highest importance to recognise the cause and the true nature of this difficulty in learning to read which is experienced by these children, otherwise they may be harshly treated as imbeciles or incorrigibles and either neglected or flogged for a defect for which they are in no wise [ways] responsible. The recognition of the true character of the difficulty will lead the parents and teachers of these children to deal with them in the proper way, not by harsh and severe treatment, but by attempting to overcome the difficulty by patient and persistent training.'[18]

This chapter seeks to show how the first physicians to identify dyslexia, and the children with whom they worked, are best conceptualised as autonomous agents – negotiating and adapting to the demands of a society in which literacy was now dominant – rather than as the products of educational, economic, and social forces beyond their control. The work of these first physicians contributed to the categorisation of children with dyslexia as 'different' from others, and in this way distinguished them from 'normal' learners. Yet, without their research, dyslexia might have remained an imprecise synonym for 'feeble-mindedness', the common term for those struggling to read at the time, stalling later insights into the condition that would have a beneficial effect on the dyslexic learner.

The Education Act of 1870, 'Feeble-Mindedness', and the Context for Dyslexia's Emergence

In the mid-nineteenth century, cognitive differences in Britain and other European countries, when they were recognised at all, were generally subsumed under the primitive notion of idiocy.[19] What specialist provision existed for those with cognitive difference was restricted to those who (it was claimed) presented a danger to society, or to themselves, such as people with severe mental illness. In such cases, institutionalisation was a typical response.[20] In Britain, a more complex nomenclature of educational performance began to emerge with the Education Act of 1870, and the acts that followed. For the first time a broader spectrum of cognitive difference was encountered by the state through its educational apparatus, and this new set of difficulties could not be incorporated straightforwardly under existing terminology. Foremost amongst the new terms to be coined was that of 'feeble-mindedness': a catch-all word applied to any child deemed to be failing educationally due to a cognitive deficit, but who was potentially educable.

By the 1860s, annual funding for schools from the British government was approaching £1 million (over £100 million in 2020 values; for comparison, the 2020 education budget for the UK is a little under £100 billion).[21] Given this, large areas of the country remained without adequate schooling, and sometimes without any schooling at all. Overcoming objections from religious authorities, which had been Britain's traditional provider of schooling, a newly founded National Education League (NEL) established a campaign for free, compulsory, non-religious schooling for all children in 1869.[22] Composed principally of industrialists, a central driver of the NEL's efforts was the belief that mass education was crucial to the nation's ability to sustain its global pre-eminence in the increasingly complex manufacturing sector.[23] The NEL's campaign was successful. In 1870, the Education Act was passed: the first legislation in Britain to deal specifically with the provision of education.[24]

Crucially, the 1870 Education Act provided education at a national scale.[25] The instrument for this national rollout was the 'school board': locally elected bodies charged with building and maintaining schools in every district of the country.[26] In the words of the 1870 Education Act: 'There shall be provided for every school district a sufficient amount of accommodation in public elementary schools, available for all children resident in the district for whose elementary education efficient and suitable provision is not otherwise made ... It will place an elementary school where there is a child to be taught, whether of rich or poor parents; and it will compel every parent and guardian of a child to have it taught, at least, the rudiments of education, and that without reference to any religious creed or persuasion.'[27]

The question of whether education should be compulsory was left unresolved by the 1870 act, but the following 1876 Royal Commission on the Factory Acts did recommend that education be mandatory between the ages of five and ten years, specifically to inhibit the child labour in Britain dramatized so effectively by writers like Charles Dickens (who, as this book's epigraph shows, also understood that some children struggled with reading and spelling). Additional legislation in the 1890s raised the age of compulsory attendance at school to twelve years.[28]

While the 1870 act made no provision for children with cognitive disabilities, further acts in the 1880s and 1890s established special (or auxiliary) schools and formal education structures for children with visual and hearing impairments or with other physical disabilities.[29] As with the broader history of special education in Britain and other Western states, legislation was delayed while the costs of provision for such groups were assessed.[30] The first attention to children with learning difficulties came from the Charity Organisation Society, spurred by the increasing number of students struggling in schools since the implementation of the 1870 Education Act.[31] A subsequent report, *The Feeble-Minded Child and Adult* (1893), suggested that immediate attention was required to prevent such persons becoming an economic burden on the state.[32] 'Feeble-mindedness' was defined in the report as 'that feebleness of mind which, being congenital or originating in infancy or childhood, may be checked or alleviated by special care and education'.[33] As such, it differed from 'imbecility' and 'idiocy', relatively smaller groups that were considered to be largely ineducable.[34] After a decade of lobbying by the Charity Organisation Society and associated groups, a Royal Commission on the Care and Control of the Feeble-Minded in 1904 led to the official recognition of feeble-mindedness as an issue requiring state intervention.[35]

Until then, children with specific learning needs obtained support in a limited and piecemeal fashion. In 1892, the Leicester School Board established a special class for feeble-minded pupils; in the same year, the London School Board opened a school dedicated to children with mental and physical impairments, who were struggling in ordinary education.[36] Four years later, there existed some twenty-four special schools in London, with a total pupil cohort of nearly one thousand. By the end of the century, eight school boards across the country provided special schools for feeble-minded pupils and others for whom mainstream education was deemed inappropriate.[37]

The emergence of a new group within the population requiring 'special education' has been discussed in depth elsewhere, along with reflections on how the school, as part of an emerging bureaucratic machinery, became a key instrument in addressing what the state deemed social problems.[38] What is crucial for the purposes of understanding the history of dyslexia is how the bifurcation of children into those who could and could not be educated via mainstream education set the stage for the initial identification of dyslexia as congenital word-blindness by Victorian physicians. In the absence of widespread knowledge of the independence of dyslexia from intelligence, it is impossible to estimate how many children (and adults) with dyslexia fell under definitions of mental inadequacy relative to their peers at this time. The total number, and the quality of their experiences, no doubt varied according to a range of factors, including the severity of their reading difficulties, the particular understanding of parents and teachers (and employers), and socio-economic background. But that those with dyslexia could have escaped being classified as 'sub-normal' learners seems unlikely, except for those whose symptomology was especially mild, or who left school before their difficulties were identified, or who could otherwise avoid the classificatory systems of ordinary education, perhaps via private tuition.

This final point opens up the question of how dyslexia's emergence intersected with social class. Those with severe word-blindness, as we have seen, were likely to have been bracketed under various notions of the 'sub-normal' learner, and there was discussion of the overlap between this group and learners from disadvantaged socio-economic groups in debates surrounding the Education Acts of 1870 onward. Indeed, finding political solutions to the 'problem' of the uneducated poor was one of the central purposes of this legislation. With this interest came concomitant beliefs around the health of the body politic, and related concerns about the rate at which sub-normal learners were passing on their learning difficulties to their children.[39] The latter, of course, were of a piece with ideas of eugenics, codified in Francis Galton's 1883 book, *Inquiries into Human Faculty and Its Development*.[40] In this way, many children with dyslexia during the Victorian period and early twentieth century likely fell under a highly politicised notion of undesirable cognitive functioning. It was such notions of desirability and undesirability, though, that many of the earliest researchers of dyslexia sought to challenge, rather than reinforce.

From Stuttgart to Edinburgh: Turning Attention to Congenital Word-Blindness

In 1877, Adolph Kussmaul, a German physician and the son of a German army surgeon, coined the term *Wortblindheit* (word-blindness).[41] In doing so, he differentiated this newly recognised phenomenon, which he had observed in several of his patients, from aphasia: a condition in which the patient was unable to comprehend written words as the result of a stroke or accident affecting the language centres of the brain. Aphasia – possibly explaining the cases of Teresa of Ávila and Professor Lordat – had been a major concern of scientists and physicians since the middle of the nineteenth century, led principally by the French physician Paul Broca.[42] However, Kussmaul was the first to observe that reading difficulties could exist in their own right, distinct from those resulting from specific brain injuries. As the historians Peggy Anderson and Regine Meier-Hedde explain, 'Previous to this, most medical researchers believed that reading problems would appear only in the context of language problems with known neurological etiologies, such as stroke, mental retardation, and other medical problems.'[43] This changed with Kussmaul:

> In medical literature we find cases recorded as aphasia which should not properly be designated by this name, since the patients were still able to express their thoughts by speech and writing. They had not lost the power either of speaking or of writing; they were no longer able,

however, although the hearing was perfect, to understand the words which they heard, or, although the sight was perfect, to read the written words which they saw. This morbid inability we will style, in order to have the shortest possible names at our disposition, *word-deafness* and *word-blindness (cæcitas et surditas verbalis)*.[44]

Six years after Kussmaul's publication, his contemporary and countryman, Rudolf Berlin, an ophthalmologist and professor of medicine in Stuttgart, first used the term 'dyslexia' (*Dyslexie*).[45] He followed this a year later with a further article on the subject, before publishing a monograph in 1887, *Eine Besondere Art der Wortblindheit (Dyslexie) (A Special Kind of Word-Blindness [Dyslexia])*.[46] At his medical practice, Berlin had observed that some of his adult patients had problems with the printed word. Their difficulties, though, stemmed not from a lack of education and attendant illiteracy, but from a specific problem with reading. Building on Kussmaul's work, Berlin hypothesised that such difficulties may be the result of a physical difference in the brain, although the precise nature of this difference eluded him. Berlin coined the term 'dyslexia' ('difficulty with words') to align the diagnosis with the contemporary international medical lexicon: 'The symptom which imprints the signature on the clinical picture in question I have proposed to call "dyslexia". This expression joins the common names of alexia and paralexia; it is intended to say that the characteristic symptom consists in a difficulty in reading and at the same time to indicate that the cause of this disorder, as in alexia and paralexia, is to be sought in a material disease of the brain'.[47] One of the few biographical accounts of Berlin refers to him, poetically, as the man 'who named the ship even though he never became her captain'.[48]

The ship was, though, at sea. In Britain, a select group of physicians were encountering difficulties similar to those highlighted by Kussmaul and Berlin. Crucially, the former group cemented the idea that these difficulties appeared to be congenital, rather than acquired. In other words, they suggested that certain kinds of reading difficulties might run in families, with causes other than (or in addition to) environmental influences, thereby turning interest toward children. They also drew attention to the independence of such difficulties from broader intelligence and mental functioning. Of these British physicians, James Kerr, James Hinshelwood, and William Pringle

Morgan would come to leave a lasting legacy on dyslexia and how it was conceptualised. Their research became the cornerstone of a professional network of British medics who, for the first time, crafted a definition of dyslexia that would firmly differentiate the condition from other kinds and causes of reading and learning difficulties.

In 1896, James Kerr, a medical officer to the city of Bradford and a school doctor, authored an essay, 'School Hygiene, in Its Mental, Moral and Physical Aspects'. The essay received the Howard Medal of the Royal Statistical Society, and was published in the journal of that organisation the following year.[49] Presented as an encyclopaedia of children and their diverse learning needs, Kerr fleetingly mentioned 'a boy with word-blindness who can spell the separate letters [but has difficulty with understanding words]'.[50] Later in 1896, William Pringle Morgan, a general practitioner in Seaford, Sussex, published his own account in the *British Medical Journal*, 'A Case of Congenital Word Blindness' – squeezed between an article on 'Dermatitis Caused by Roentgen X Rays' and the announcement of a Belgian Climatological Congress.[51] Pringle Morgan's account is conventionally cited as the starting point for modern understandings of dyslexia, because of its focus, its depth, and its human dimension.[52] It was a case report based on the experiences of a child whom Pringle Morgan encountered during his clinical practice:

> Percy F. – a well-grown lad, aged 14 – is the eldest son of intelligent parents, the second child of a family of seven. He has always been a bright and intelligent boy, quick at games, and in no way inferior to others of his age ... His great difficulty has been – and is now – his inability to learn to read. This inability is so remarkable, and so pronounced, that I have no doubt it is due to some congenital defect ... He has been at school or under tutors since he was 7 years old, and the greatest efforts have been made to teach him to read, but, in spite of this laborious and persistent training, he can only with difficulty spell out words of one syllable.[53]

Pringle Morgan's account was soon joined by similar case studies by the Edinburgh-based ophthalmologist James Hinshelwood. Given that the early research of Kussmaul and others suggested that some kind of visual deficit was implicated in the problems faced by those with word-blindness (hence the name), ophthalmology was the specialism of many of the British physicians interested, sometimes passingly, in the condition, including Edward Nettleship, F. Herbert Fisher, Edward Treacher Collins, Sydney Stephenson, and Robert Walter Doyne.[54] Despite this, it was also widely recognised that the problem of word-blindness was not one of visual acuity; something else was causing these children's reading difficulties. While researchers like Hinshelwood postulated that visual memory might be affected, tests proved that those with word-blindness possessed no problem with eyesight.[55] Indeed, Pringle Morgan's account of Percy included the typical observation that 'his eyes are normal, there is no hemianopsia [impairment on one side of the visual field], and his eyesight is good'.[56] Instead, doctors attempting to explain their patients' difficulties began looking at other abilities, including general intelligence, receptiveness to oral instruction, and musicality. In this respect, Hinshelwood's first description of a child with word-blindness is of a type with Pringle Morgan's:

> A boy, aged 10 years, was brought to me by his father on Jan. 8th, 1900, to see the reason of his great difficulty in learning to read. The boy had been at school for three years, and had got on well with every subject except reading. He was apparently a bright and in every respect an intelligent boy. He was learning music a year ago and made good progress in it, his teacher expressing great satisfaction at the end of the year. In all departments of his studies where the instruction was oral he made good progress. His father, a medical man, thought that his great difficulty in learning to read might be due to some visual or cerebral defect, and therefore he brought him to me. It was soon evident, however, on careful examination that the difficulty in learning to read was due not to any lowering of the visual acuity, but to some congenital deficiency of the visual memory for words ... His father has noted that the boy never reads for amusement. As his father expresses it, 'it seems to take a great deal out of him'.[57]

Together, these researchers developed the foundational accounts of their continental contemporaries, highlighting not just the differences between aphasia and word-blindness, but refining the definition of the latter. Hinshelwood, describing word-blindness in 1895, noted the 'considerable time and labour [he had personally expended] in searching out similar cases scattered through French and German medical literature'.[58] Beyond this, he remarked that 'since Kussmaul's treatise our knowledge of the condition has been greatly increased by the numerous cases which have been reported [by Kerr and Pringle Morgan, amongst others]. It is now evident that the terms "word-blindness", "cécité verbale", and "Wortblindheit" are not sufficiently distinguished from one another'.[59] Specifically, Hinshelwood noted that 'the term "dyslexia" applied to these cases by Professor Berlin is a convenient one and I have adopted it as describing the prominent symptom [reading difficulty] in my case'.[60] The work of Kerr, Hinshelwood, and Pringle Morgan sat within a continuing interest in aphasia in Britain and elsewhere, but, for the first time, a focus was being given to congenital, rather than acquired, reading disability.[61]

Dyslexia Defined: Refining Understandings of 'Congenital Word-Blindness'

The complicated array of research during the late-Victorian period led to a series of disputes over who was the first to identify the various sub-types of reading difficulty, and when. For example, the German physician Oswald Berkhan expressed surprise that it was James Kerr's work of the 1890s, rather than his own work of the 1880s, which was cited in contemporary literature as the initial reference to congenital reading disability.[62] The difficulty of tracing dyslexia's precise origins today is compounded by several factors, including the challenges of diagnosing dyslexia retrospectively, the little remaining factual evidence pertaining to case studies, and the fact that the physicians of this period were often speculating on aetiology and, by their own admission, employing imprecise terminology.[63] With respect to Berkhan's claims, his publications of the 1880s appear to refer to individuals with broader intellectual difficulties, who would not (necessarily) fulfil modern criteria for dyslexia. The chronology presented here highlights the key research from which dyslexia emerged, but there is no straightforwardly linear research pathway into dyslexia's past.

Nevertheless, several aspects of dyslexia research at this time came to mark the condition's later history, making them important to highlight.

Dyslexia Discovered (1877–1917)

These include dyslexia's associations with (individual) high intelligence and (familial) socio-economic privilege; the focus on dyslexia's manifestation in childhood, usually drawn to the attention of experts by the child's parents; and the notion that dyslexia was a disability predicated on a language deficit, with some more prescient researchers speculating that this was specifically phonetic. Ahead of each of these, though, Victorian discussions of congenital word-blindness prefigured the most frequently recurring question in the dyslexia story: how should dyslexia be defined?[64]

Central here is a debate over word-blindness, played out in the pages of the *Lancet*, between James Hinshelwood and the English neurologist William Broadbent. An entertaining and largely good-tempered tête-à-tête between two Victorian gentlemen of medicine, the debate centred on what was meant by 'word-blindness', and whether the term was useful in a clinical setting. For Broadbent, responding to Hinshelwood's 1895 paper, 'Word-Blindness and Visual Memory', 'the employment of this term has been misleading and unfortunate'.[65] Referring to two cases from the early 1870s reported to the Royal Medical and Chirurgical (Surgical) Society, Broadbent suggested that 'the blindness for words was a part of a much larger defect, a complete loss of the faculty of naming an object at sight, and it is in order to point out this that the present note is written'.[66] The same year, Hinshelwood responded:

> Now I quite agree with Sir William Broadbent that the word ['word-blindness'] has frequently been used by writers loosely and with different meanings attached to it and therefore it has been frequently misleading. The fault, however, lies, not in the word, but in the fact that those who used it have not always a clear conception of what Kussmaul meant by it. By the term 'word-blindness' is meant a condition in which with normal vision, and therefore seeing the letters and words distinctly, an individual is no longer able to interpret written or printed language. With a clear understanding of this definition there is nothing misleading about the term, which is a most convenient one for describing a group of cases, which, however, includes several different forms. All the varieties have this point in common, that the inability to interpret written and printed language is not dependent upon any ocular defect, but upon disorder of the cerebral visual centres.[67]

This was one of the first debates over how word-blindness could (or should) be differentiated from other kinds of reading difficulty, and so how it should be specifically described. For Broadbent, word-blindness fell under the umbrella of a broader set of language difficulties, in which the patient completely lost the ability to name objects (again, this is likely to have been because of stroke or other brain injury, rather than any congenital condition). For Hinshelwood, who had published a more sophisticated taxonomy of reading difficulties than Broadbent, word-blindness affected only the skills involved in reading written and printed language. Hinshelwood went on to explore several features of (his definition of) word-blindness, including its congenital basis, which more closely resemble current understandings of dyslexia.

What is interesting here is less the technical accuracy of Hinshelwood and Broadbent's debate (as viewed from the necessarily subjective perspective of the twenty-first century) than the fact that it set the stage for a series of discussions over definition and terminology that would represent a recurring feature of dyslexia's scientific and social histories. To illustrate: Hinshelwood's (1896) opinion that 'the word ["word-blindness"] has frequently been used by writers loosely and with different meanings attached to it and therefore it has been frequently misleading' is uncannily similar to that of an educational psychologist (and leading opponent of the term), Julian Elliott, writing in 2016: 'One of the greatest difficulties in gaining a grasp of the term, dyslexia, is that it is used in so many different ways … the term dyslexia continues to be used loosely by researchers for studying reading difficulties.'[68] While this debate over the definition of dyslexia has promoted scientific exploration, it has also formed a core element of modern arguments around dyslexia's existence.

Elsewhere, early research on word-blindness laid down several other lasting tenets of the condition, which blurred categories of the social and the scientific. The case studies of Pringle Morgan and Hinshelwood are notable; Pringle Morgan's, in particular, would go on to be cited nearly a thousand times in academic literature.[69] In both cases, the child being considered came from a family of means: in Pringle Morgan's account, Percy had been 'at school or under tutors since he was 7 years old', 'quite unable to spell the name of his father's house'; in Hinshelwood's account, the boy's father was 'a medical man', and the child had been receiving private tuition in music.

In both cases, the child was intelligent: for Pringle Morgan, 'He [Percy] has always been a bright and intelligent boy'; for Hinshelwood, 'He [the anonymous 'Case 2'] was apparently a bright and in every respect an intelligent boy'. In both cases, the child was brought to the doctor by an anxious parent, concerned that their child would fall behind their classmates. As Pringle Morgan describes, 'His father informs me that the greatest difficulty was found in teaching the boy his letters, and they thought he never would learn them'; as Hinshelwood recounts, 'The boy had been at school for three years, and had got on well with every subject except reading.'[70]

Several aspects of these case studies would go on to mark the understanding of dyslexia for decades; indeed, many still do. First, they established a primary focus on children (rather than adults) with word-blindness, fostering developmental approaches to the condition. Pringle Morgan and Hinshelwood were amongst the first writers to move research away from acquired word-blindness and toward congenital difficulties, laying the groundwork for the differentiation of dyslexia from aphasia and, building on the work of researchers like Kussmaul, publicising the belief that the condition might run in families.[71] Second, they established an association between dyslexia and the child's otherwise high intelligence. This would form the basis of the discrepancy diagnostic model of dyslexia from the middle of the twentieth century onward, through which dyslexia was diagnosed only where there existed a marked difference between a child's reading skill and general abilities. Third, they linked dyslexia (in particular, parental concern with dyslexia and specialist remediation) with the middle classes. Again, this association would only increase in intensity in the following decades. As social conventions changed, it would increasingly be mothers, rather than fathers, who would bring their children with dyslexia to the attention of medical and educational professionals, but the broader association of dyslexia with worried parenthood is one that endured.

Beyond laying down these characteristics of dyslexia, early twentieth-century research on congenital word-blindness did something else: it reflected on what the condition implied about literate societies and on the arbitrariness of the preeminent system of communication in such societies. As early as 1899, Hinshelwood demonstrated an awareness of how the mechanics of the English language system disadvantaged children with dyslexia. Employing a rudimentary phonological understanding of reading difficulties,

Hinshelwood drew attention to the fact that effective reading is predicated on 'analysing the word into its constituents of letters and syllables'.[72] If this ability was impaired, he suggested, the process of learning to read was also inhibited. In this way, Hinshelwood's 1899 contribution was one of the first suggestions in research that problems in processing the speech stream, usually referred to as phonological processing, lay behind dyslexia – a theory that would not be firmly established in the science of reading until the 1970s, and that remains a cornerstone of modern definitions.[73]

The implications of Hinshelwood's comments for appraising the place of literacy in society were explicated some years later – decades before disability studies raised similar questions via the social model of disability. In 1910, at a meeting of the British Ophthalmological Society, the surgeon and ophthalmologist Edward Treacher Collins volunteered that he had seen multiple cases of word-blindness 'and had been surprised to find how common it was'.[74] Joining Hinshelwood in his progressive attitude toward children with the condition, Treacher Collins noted that children's difficulties with congenital word-blindness 'were frequently overlooked, and attributed to sheer stupidity, to the great discomfort of the child'.[75] He continued: 'If the British system of spelling had been phonetic the defect would not be nearly so noticeable. In Germany, the language there being much more phonetic, such cases were said to be far less common.'[76] Treacher Collins was ahead of his times, and such thoughtful reflection on the nature of dyslexia – and on who (or what) was responsible for its disabling qualities – would not become mainstream for several decades.

'All Very Curious': Word-Blindness in Newspapers, Periodicals, and the Popular Press

In the early twentieth century, British research on word-blindness was the most concerted in the world. Read and cited by researchers in Europe, North America, and South America, Britain became a global leader in dyslexia research.[77] In smaller countries with less developed medical infrastructures, research on the condition might coalesce around a single figure. In Hungary, for example, it was the psychiatrist Paul Ranschburg who conducted initial research on the condition in 1916 and who also pioneered the provision of

Dyslexia Discovered (1877–1917)

special education in the country.[78] British research was commented on by German researchers, who, drawing on the pathbreaking work of their compatriot Adolph Kussmaul, nevertheless followed British physicians' particular concern with congenital, rather than acquired, word-blindness.[79] Common across this expansion was an interest in the development of word-blindness in the early years of childhood. Such research set the stage for a second period in dyslexia's history from the 1920s onward, and was closely associated with the work of American physician Samuel T. Orton when psychology superseded ophthalmology as the leading field of dyslexia research.

The importance of dyslexia during the Victorian era and early years of the twentieth century was not restricted to scientific outlets and men of medicine, of course. For the kinds of reasons discussed above, it is not possible, either empirically or conceptually, to reconstruct the lives of Victorian children with dyslexia. However, there are methods through which to better understand reading difficulties and word-blindness in everyday life in the late nineteenth and early twentieth centuries, including the consultation of personal histories and of popular culture.

At Brunel University in London, the Burnett Archive holds a historical collection of autobiographies of working-class people in Britain. Within this collection, a Major Edward S. Humphries (born 1889), who served during both world wars, recalls his early life in the West Country and London. Reflecting on his education at national schools in Exeter and Plymouth, Humphries describes the difficulties that he faced in reading and spelling: 'It now seems strange that whilst I had no difficulty in learning my [multiplication] Tables and spelling simple words, I could not memorize the Alphabet.'[80] During his school career, Humphries remembers winning just a single prize: for the highest mark in his religious instruction class. His difficulties with reading and spelling appear to be one reason why Humphries pursued a military career, starting part-time work on a milk-round at age nine, full-time work at Almack's Bridge Club in London two years later, and joining the Royal Scots Regiment at the age of seventeen. Humphries's account provides an indication of how those with dyslexia fared in a society in which such difficulties were largely nebulous, their causes unknown.[81]

The same air of mystery as in Humphries's account surrounds descriptions of dyslexia in the popular press during the same period. A key source here is the British Library's British Newspaper Archive: a comprehensive record of over 700 British national and local newspapers from the early eighteenth to the mid-twentieth centuries.

Word-blindness first appears in British newspaper reportage in 1895, with accounts of Hinshelwood's paper in the *Lancet* ('Word Blindness and Visual Memory'), and a series of articles followed in the decades thereafter. The sub-titles of these newspaper reports convey a distinctly Victorian sense of curiosity about the condition, in keeping with that era's predilection for the odd and the peripheral: 'An Interesting Case [of Word-blindness]' (1895), 'An Extraordinary Case' (1896), 'A Strange Case' (1902), and 'Another Anomaly' (1919).[82] Often, accounts were detailed under columns devoted to miscellany or to 'queer' stories from the nascent medical sciences. The 'Science Notes' column (*Dover Express*, 1896) describes Pringle Morgan's account of Percy, the 'All Very Curious' column (*Hampshire Telegraph*, 1897) covers the same case, and the 'Science Jottings' column (*Illustrated London News*, 1902) offers an overview of Hinshelwood's research.[83] The 'Literary Gossip' column (London *Globe*) offers perhaps the first dyslexia joke, in 1900. Discussing the difficulty of instilling a love of national literature in Britain's youth, the anonymous writer suggests that, amongst other challenges faced by the schoolmaster, 'most boys suffer from a congenital word-blindness which permits them to pass strange words inattentively, or attach to them the weirdest meanings. [The English poet Thomas] Gray's lines – *Full many a gem of purest ray serene, The dark unfathomed caves of ocean bear* – have been known to awake in the mind of an otherwise sharp schoolboy only a vague wonder whether the "bear" was a Polar bear or a "grizzly".'[84]

In contrast to the attention of Victorian physicians to children with word-blindness primarily from wealthier backgrounds, newspapers of the time offer an indication of how children with the same difficulties fared in other social settings. Often, these accounts emerged several years after the initial publications of Kerr, Hinshelwood, and Pringle Morgan, presumably as knowledge of the condition in specialised institutions, including schools, (very) gradually expanded. Thus, the *South London Press* of 22 May 1908 reports the case of thirteen-year-old William Richard Magee, brought to Tower Bridge Police Court:

Before Mr. Rose, Wm. Richard Magee, a schoolboy, was charged, on remand, with stealing 11s. [shillings], the moneys of the headmistress of the Southwark Park School, Bermondsey. The boy used to do errands for his schoolmistress, and had access to her room. He admitted another theft of £1 [about £120 in 2020 values]. It was stated that although proficient at figures the lad suffered from the curious defect of 'word-blindness', being quite unable to discriminate between groups of letters. Mr. Wm. Westcott, Industrial School Officer under the L.C.C. [London County Council], suggested that the boy should be sent to an industrial school rather than a reformatory, and for that purpose the charge of being beyond the control of his parents should be substituted for that of felony. Mr. Rose [presiding] said he knew that some magistrates believed in juggling with the Acts of Parliament in such cases, but he did not. Where a boy was guilty of felony he ought to go to a reformatory, and the case should not be juggled with so that he could be sent to an industrial school.[85]

Here, the role of an industrial school officer in pleading Magee's case illustrates how, regardless of increasing scientific understanding, the day-to-day care of children with word-blindness, where they were diagnosed at all, fell to education authorities. To date, historical accounts of dyslexia during the Victorian period have tended to focus on science around the condition, but dyslexia was, of course, a lived reality for children and adults, even if they were unaware of why they faced such difficulties or unacquainted with the emerging terminology used to describe them.[86] In 1904, the *St James' Gazette*, a London evening newspaper, covered a recent report of the London School Board, which assessed the educational performance of the capital's schoolchildren. The author of the report was the board's medical officer, James Kerr, formerly of Bradford, whose earlier work was amongst the first on dyslexia. The *Gazette* summarised Kerr's findings thus: 'Some children … are totally word-deaf, and others are word-blind. A boy, who could do arithmetic well, was asked to write: "The drinks were ale and mead, drinks which were made in dark English forests with fermented honey." The boy wrote as follows: "la hase us erans and krsut erans was locts boath in hast Enitsh louss ins harest lacnt." The medical officer points out the need for special schools for such children.'[87]

Outside of these reports on word-blindness, the majority of newspaper coverage mentioned the condition only in passing references to research.

Frequently, these reproduced the introductions and conclusions of articles by Pringle Morgan and Hinshelwood.[88] In 1910, Hinshelwood had the opportunity to write a more detailed popular account of the condition for the newspaper the *Scotsman*. Alongside his monograph of 1917, *Congenital Word Blindness*, it was one of Hinshelwood's final publications on the topic, before he retired to the warmer climes of Menton on the French Riviera.[89] In the article, Hinshelwood provided a summary of his research on the topic. He finished, as in his earlier work, with a thoughtful reflection on children with congenital word-blindness. Like Kerr, he addressed the possibilities and practicalities of remediating their difficulties, showing how work on dyslexia was slowly shifting from identifying its chief characteristics to suggesting ways it could be ameliorated:

> It has been asserted by some authorities that congenital word-blindness is a defect for which it is impossible to do anything. It is supposed that there is some radical defect in the brain of such a nature that all attempts at education are mere waste of time. It would seem, however, that such a view is too sweeping. Probably, indeed, we may say undoubtedly, word-blindness varies in different cases. In some cases a child fails to learn to read in a class with other children, but if he can be taken from the class to receive daily private tuition from a careful teacher who makes sure of each step as she goes along, he may eventually respond to the care bestowed upon him, and learn to read quite well.[90]

Nine years later, the *Scotsman* carried the short obituary of their compatriot; at forty-seven words, it was a brief account of Hinshelwood, whose work on the condition would prove the most comprehensive for several decades.[91] Its brevity attested to the fact that no clear research field of word-blindness had emerged in Britain or elsewhere by the time of Hinshelwood's death, and that the condition was still not the object of comprehensive understanding in science, schools, or society. In this way, the importance of Hinshelwood and his Victorian colleagues would emerge only later, once the wider relevance of their research was recognised, and once 'congenital word-blindness' evolved more fully into 'dyslexia'. As a later dyslexia researcher, Macdonald Critchley, observed in the 1970s, with the passing of

Hinshelwood, 'What might be called the early history of this condition was closed ... This period had been one of description and identification. Thereafter began a stage of analysis and discussion with a considerable amount of change in orientation.'[92] Central to this change would be the expanding role of psychology in understanding dyslexia – in Britain, but in the United States especially.

Chapter 1 – Key Points
- Dyslexia was coined by the German ophthalmologist Rudolf Berlin, building on the work of his compatriot Adolph Kussmaul
- The research of these Germans was developed by British researchers, especially James Hinshelwood, William Pringle Morgan, and James Kerr
- Early research suggested that dyslexia was developmental and that it might run in families, and produced an initial version of the 'discrepancy diagnostic model'
- Dyslexia was defined in a context of expanding literacy, accelerated by the arrival of compulsory education

2

Dyslexia Goes Global: Psychology, Childhood, and Trans-Atlanticism (1925–48)

The research on dyslexia by James Hinshelwood and his Victorian contemporaries focused on describing the difficulties associated with dyslexia. It also speculated on the differences in brain structure that might lie behind those difficulties, and the possibility that the manifestation of dyslexia might be altered in different languages. But it said little about how individuals should be assisted, or about how society – schools and teachers in particular – should help those with reading challenges. From the 1920s onward, as compulsory education in Western countries broadened, work on both sides of the Atlantic shifted to consider how reading difficulties could, and should, be addressed.

While scientific understanding of the aetiology of dyslexia continued to improve during this period, it was educational strategies for addressing dyslexia that expanded most rapidly and by the greatest degree. In the case of dyslexia, the research of the American physician Samuel T. Orton, and that of his colleagues Anna Gillingham and Bessie Stillman, expanded the science of dyslexia, but was also central to innovative new forms of remediation. Their work, conducted from the mid-1920s onward, straddled medicine, education, and psychology. In its focus on children and their development, it spoke to new Western conceptions of childhood, and of childhood's relationship to educational performance, that would endure into the twenty-first century. Childhood became associated firmly with education and, via education, preparation for adult social and economic life.[1] Child subjects also populated the various emerging sub-fields of psychology (cognitive,

Dyslexia Goes Global (1925–48)

developmental, and educational), which would come to especial prominence in dyslexia research.

The history of Western psychology, the scientific study of mind and behaviour, has encountered substantial scholarly attention.[2] For the modern period, this has traced the discipline from Wilhelm Wundt's founding of the first psychology laboratory in Leipzig in 1879, through the establishment of psychology as a profession in the West in the early decades of the twentieth century, through psychology's current forms and interests.[3] Central to each of these accounts is an effort to explain how, in the words of the sociologist Nikolas Rose, new forms of psychological knowledge from the end of the nineteenth century changed the conceptualisation, regulation, and amelioration of individual and social problems – initially in the West, but increasingly globally, as the tenets of Western psychology proliferated.[4] This chapter does not rehearse this history, but rather focuses on three particular aspects of this new form of psychological knowledge: first, how psychology framed dyslexia in ways different to the medical approaches of the Victorian physicians; second, how psychology emerged as the dominant approach to understanding dyslexia in the early decades of the twentieth century; and third, what this meant for children diagnosed with reading difficulties, and for their treatment.

Again, Tom Campbell's rich work on the initial decades of dyslexia research represents the most sustained attention to the period.[5] For Campbell, commenting on why psychology superseded ophthalmology as the principle discipline for addressing dyslexia from the 1920s, a key reason was that psychologists, especially in the United States, exhibited an 'imperialistic rationale' which caused them to 'actively foster connections with schools and educationalists'.[6] Thus, 'psychology appears to have been better placed than ophthalmology to disperse its diagnosis into educational environments, as its technologies and practices were amenable to this environment'.[7] On Campbell's account, psychology's increasing attention to dyslexia sat within a context of expanding state education, and an increasing requirement for advanced literacy skills to communicate in an ever-more complex professional landscape.

Certainly, the ability of psychology to contribute to educational debates was one reason that the discipline came to prominence in dyslexia research in the early twentieth century. Its findings around cognitive development and learning styles were more easily acted upon than medicine's speculations on underlying differences in brain structure; there was not then – and there is not now – a proven medical (meaning here, physical) treatment for dyslexia. Yet, close engagement with the work of psychologists studying dyslexia during this period suggests that the suggestion of an 'imperialistic rationale' for their actions, a slightly opaque expression in this context, conveys at best part of the picture. If there was a tyranny that adversely affected children with dyslexia during the early twentieth century, it was the tyranny of literacy as the primary mode of societal communication, and the lack of institutional assistance for children in interpreting this code. Like Hinshelwood and his contemporaries, the leading dyslexia researcher of this period, Samuel T. Orton, founded his work on the premise that the dyslexic children he was encountering were being ill-treated by ignorant educational and medical establishments. His efforts to increase knowledge of dyslexia were intended to benefit children with the condition, not just prove the explanatory power of an expanding psychological science. Orton was also keen to draw attention to the fact that it was the arbitrary customs of the English language, rather than an individual impairment, per se, that disabled the dyslexic learner, as Edward Treacher Collins and others had argued before him.

At the same time, some prominent figures in early twentieth-century psychology promoted a series of problematic and controversial ideas about individual differences in intelligence and the relative social desirability of certain cognitive characteristics over others.[8] These ideas included the distinction between 'feeble-minded' children and 'normal' learners discussed earlier, predicated on the notion of innate and measurable individual intelligence. Such ideas appear throughout accounts of dyslexia in the early – and indeed, later – twentieth century; they form a critical backdrop to how children with dyslexia were treated and discussed during this period.

By the late nineteenth century, the collection of statistical data enabled the better administration of society via public policy.[9] In the area of education, the intelligence quotient (IQ) test was the favoured tool to gauge the quality and level of an individual's cognitive ability. As such, IQ became the new standard against which reading difficulties would be assessed.[10] But, for those with dyslexia, intelligence testing was a double-edged sword. Rather than making concepts like feeble-mindedness redundant, intelligence testing

Dyslexia Goes Global (1925–48)

gave such notions greater tangibility.[11] Children with unidentified dyslexia were now even more firmly entrenched in a class of 'sub-normal' learners. On the other hand, for those whose reading difficulties were identified as dyslexia – of whom, necessarily, there exist better records than for those without a diagnosis – intelligence tests provided them with validation that their learning difficulties were specific, rather than general.

Expanding interest in reading difficulties across the early twentieth century was, like Victorian concerns with congenital word-blindness, driven (if not fully explained) by broader societal changes. In Britain, the expansion of schooling in the half-century following 1914 has been described as the country's 'biggest cultural accomplishment' of the twentieth century.[12] In 1910, the total number of pupils attending British state secondary schools was just over 170,000; by 1950, this had increased to 2 million.[13] In the United States, for the same age group and period, enrolment increased from 5 million to 11.8 million pupils.[14] Similar expansion in state education was seen across high-income nations in the West. The rollout of rudimentary compulsory education over the late nineteenth and early twentieth centuries, and the increasing requirement for literacy in the professions, helped highlight the difficulties of the small number of children encountered by Hinshelwood and his colleagues. The larger expansion of education across the first half of the twentieth century had a similar effect, but of concomitantly greater size. Reading difficulties were no longer an individual problem detected by a knowledgeable private physician or school doctor; they were slowly becoming a societal issue.

The rise of educational psychology, too, proceeded as Western states became more interested in education and healthcare as forms of 'population management', and countries became concerned about their economic competitiveness in a rapidly globalising marketplace. In Britain after World War I, state bureaucracies changed in form: gone were government offices, 'bundles of legal powers to be exercised in turn by individual politicians', replaced by government ministries and departments, 'in which politicians and their "departments" of expert administration jointly shaped and pursued policies'.[15] These increasingly pursued their own agendas across successive governments, rather than being reconstituted anew with each general election.[16] In the United States, federal spending in 1900 represented about 3 per cent of gross domestic product; by 1950 (after the spike associated with

World War II) it represented about 16 per cent.[17] During the same period, new areas of government engagement were pioneered across Western democracies, especially in science, medicine, and education.[18] Assessing the intellectual abilities of children, and the teaching strategies used to improve these, became core responsibilities of Western educational authorities.

In charting dyslexia's path through the first half of the twentieth century, then, we need again to strike a balance between the pioneering work of individuals and the social structures in which they were working. Despite increasing attention to what (and how) their citizens were learning, which necessarily highlighted individuals who did not learn like the majority, Western democracies were yet to specifically identify or legislate for groups such as the 'word-blind'. Rather, the wide array of learning styles that did not conform to state education's conception of 'proper' learning largely continued to be categorized under notions of sub-normality. Support for those with dyslexia remained fragmentary and uneven, with private tuition and private schooling, unavailable to the majority, leading the education profession in the understanding and amelioration of the condition. As we will see, the early twentieth century saw the foundation of the first organisations dedicated to the treatment of word-blindness, but such organisations were generally private. In the area of state education, experts such as the leading British educational psychologist Cyril Burt often exhibited a degree of scepticism toward word-blindness that would characterise official rhetoric around dyslexia for decades to come.

Nevertheless, developments in the first half of the twentieth century laid the groundwork for the expansion of interest in dyslexia from the middle of the century onward. For the first time, research outside Europe, specifically that in the United States, came to prominence, and this trans-Atlanticism would typify dyslexia research into the twenty-first century. It also introduced a cast of characters, including Samuel T. Orton, Anna Gillingham, Bessie Stillman, and the Danish pioneer Edith Norrie, whose legacies, via the organisations and programmes that they founded, continue to the present day. The work of the Victorian physicians concerned with dyslexia was prescient, often remarkably so given the limited number of case studies from which they were drawing conclusions; but it does not have as direct a connection to dyslexia today as the work of Orton, Norrie, and the other pioneers introduced here. Orton's widow, June, founded the Orton

Dyslexia Goes Global (1925–48)

Society in the late 1940s (renamed the International Dyslexia Association in 1997); Edith Norrie's pupil, Helen Arkell, founded the Helen Arkell Dyslexia Centre in 1971, which also remains active. This chapter tells the story of the teachers, researchers, and educationalists who brought dyslexia to societal and political attention.

Samuel T. Orton, Strephosymbolia, and Early Psychological Research on Dyslexia in the United States

In 1925, Samuel Torrey Orton, director of the State Psychopathic Hospital in Iowa City, published an article that crystallised American interest in dyslexia. '"Word-Blindness" in School Children' was not the first work on the condition in the United States, but it was the most comprehensive, and it laid down a series of tenets about dyslexia that would come to dominate research on both sides of the Atlantic in the years ahead.[19] By virtue of Orton's specific attention to how children were thinking, and their associated performance in the area of reading, Orton's work was amongst the first that could be considered part of the new sub-field of educational psychology. Research from this perspective aimed to understand the causes of reading difficulties, but also to develop successful forms of remedial instruction. With his co-workers, educational psychologists Anna Gillingham and Bessie Stillman, Orton pioneered new, highly structured methods of teaching children with reading difficulties, using visual, auditory, and kinaesthetic (i.e., multi-sensory) approaches that would remain staples for decades.[20]

Orton's account presented case studies of children with word-blindness of a sophistication previously unseen, including extensive reproduction of the children's written work and detailed analysis of the same. His research, funded by a two-year grant of $60,000 (approximately $900,000 in 2020 values) from the Rockefeller Foundation, was based in an experimental clinic held by the State Psychopathic Hospital.[21] Orton's clinic was amongst the first in the country – indeed, the world – to survey the educational performance of children in a defined geographical area. The work of medical officials in Britain, such as James Kerr, had offered an indication of how common dyslexia might be in a general population; Orton continued work of this type, focusing in greater depth on reading difficulties. At the clinic, children attending local schools who were deemed 'dull, subnormal, or failing or retarded in school work' (by their teachers, physicians, or representatives of the social services) were assessed by Orton and his team. In total, eighty-eight pupils who met this definition were assessed by the clinic.[22] Of these, a notable proportion (fifteen of the eighty-eight) exhibited a marked difficulty in learning to read.

In seeking to understand this group's difficulties, Orton built on research conducted on the other side of the Atlantic – not just implicitly, as in the case of Kerr's work with schoolchildren, but explicitly, via reference to the case studies of the Victorian physicians and ophthalmologists. Indeed, a trip by Orton to Britain during the early stages of his research to visit Henry Head, the distinguished English neurologist and specialist in aphasia, seems to have been important.[23] The proceedings of this meeting are now lost, but it appears likely that Head alerted Orton to the research on congenital word-blindness of his compatriots, including William Pringle Morgan and James Hinshelwood. In his article, Orton drew on the research of both, as well as Adolph Kussmaul's earlier studies in the area. The work of Hinshelwood, especially, was a key inspiration. Of those children whom Orton assessed, Orton noted that two, in particular, 'fit Hinshelwood's criteria of "congenital word-blindness"'.[24] In '"Word-Blindness" in School Children', Orton focused on one of these cases, 'M.P.': a sixteen-year-old boy who 'had submitted some extremely curious productions as written exercises in school'.[25]

M.P., like his fellow referrals to the clinic, undertook a battery of tests as part of his assessment. The first, standard for the time, was the Stanford-Binet IQ test, which differentiated between 'very superior intelligence' (a score of 120 points or more), 'superior intelligence' (110–119), 'average intelligence' (90–109), 'dull normal intelligence' (80–89), 'marginal defective' (70–79), 'moron' (50–69) and 'imbecile' (25–49).[26] On this, M.P. scored 71, giving a 'mental age' of eleven years, four months, compared to his actual age of sixteen years, two months. But Orton and his team also conducted a series of other assessments. These included: the Pintner-Patterson performance test, which assessed mental agility, but reduced bias against the hearing impaired and non-native English speakers; the Healy pictorial completion task, which tested non-verbal reasoning and problem-solving skills; the Stenquist mechanical assembly test, which assessed mechanical and three-dimensional reasoning; and the Freeman mechanical puzzle box, a jigsaw-based test similar to the Stenquist. On these, M.P. fared substantially better than on the Stanford-Binet IQ test, scoring satisfactory or above on all four.[27]

Orton's approach showed the positive and negative potential of psychometric testing for those with reading difficulties. If employed carefully, such testing could make up for bias in standard IQ tests. The latter frequently offered misleading results, because they failed to differentiate between problems taking the test (performance) and the actual abilities of the examinee (competence). Thus, in Orton's words, 'it seems probable that psychometric tests [such as the Stanford-Binet] as ordinarily employed give an entirely erroneous and unfair estimate of the intellectual capacity of these children'.[28] Orton's findings led to him abandoning the language of 'defectiveness' and 'imbecility', legacies of the Victorian approach to education. 'Because the term "defective" so constantly implies a general intelligence defect, I have consistently attempted to make use of the word "disability" in describing this difficulty. That the reading disability does not correlate with a low intelligence quotient is obvious from the psychometric ratings of our fifteen cases.'[29] While Orton was not revising terminology for all groups with learning difficulties, his approach was nonetheless remarkable in an era when the effect of language and labelling on those described was rarely considered. In his attention to the individual child, Orton's style mirrored progressive educators of the time, most obviously the American psychologist and philosopher John Dewey.[30]

To those who attended Orton's clinic, the psychological benefits of this attention, and of the more sophisticated form of assessment, were apparently substantial. Many attendees had been belittled for their supposed 'stupidity' throughout their lives, in education and elsewhere. M.R., a woman aged thirty, who attended Orton's clinic of her own volition, 'had grown up in a family of brothers and sisters who were probably above average in intelligence and dexterity, so that she had been constantly impressed both at home and in school with the feeling that she was of not quite the same status as the others of her family. The result of this atmosphere was the development in M.R. of an overpowering sense of inferiority which served as an insuperable obstacle to her own efforts.'[31]

However, this sense of inferiority changed after M.R.'s diagnosis: 'When her striking reading disability was uncovered, and it was explained to her that this did not necessarily imply a general defect of intelligence, she brightened somewhat, and when she was asked whether she, herself, felt that she was as incompetent as her family had led her to believe she replied, "*I do not!*" with the first real emotional response elicited.'[32] There is celebration of Orton's achievements here, of course, but M.R.'s sense of relief at learning the reason behind her reading difficulties is a poignant moment shared by many with dyslexia throughout its history.[33]

Orton brought greater understanding of those with dyslexia in other ways, too. Like the British ophthalmologist Edward Treacher Collins fifteen years previously, he drew attention to the arbitrariness of many of the conventions of the English language, and to their role in disabling the individual with dyslexia, quite apart from any inherent difficulties possessed by the individual. In this way, Orton prefigured social models of disability that would not emerge formally for several decades. For Orton, 'the method of writing in alternate directions and with the letters correspondingly oriented as seen in certain ancient documents indicates that our present method of dextrad [left-to-right] writing with single orientation of letters has been arbitrarily fixed by custom'.[34] In other words, those with dyslexia were set up to fail, in part, by the linguistic rules of the society in which they lived.

Some of Orton's other beliefs about the differences between dextrad and sinistrad (right-to-left) writing in the case of dyslexia, though, led to speculations that would not stand the test of time.[35] Orton believed that dyslexia was more common in left-handed writers than right-handed, and associated dyslexia with mirror-writing.[36] This led him to coin a new term for word-blindness/dyslexia: strephosymbolia. 'The prefix "strepho" has been chosen to indicate the turning or reversals as it does in the word "bustrophedon" [bi-directional writing, common in Ancient Greece] ... "Symbolon" is used in its original meaning of "word", "sign" or "token" ... Strephosymbolia thus seems nicely suited to our cases in which our analysis points to confusion, because of reversals, in the memory images of symbols resulting in a failure of association between the visually presented stimulus and its concept.'[37]

Orton's term never entered common usage, and his proposition that dyslexia was a deficit in visual perception ultimately proved dubious.[38] But Orton's recognition that reading disability stemmed from an inability to disassemble words into their smallest components, phonemes, nevertheless led to one of the first phonics-based systems of remediation for specific reading disability. Countering the orthodoxy of the contemporary 'look and say' (or 'whole-word') approach to reading instruction, which taught children words individually, usually by flash card, Orton proposed (with some circumlocution) that 'the tentative envisagement of the disability herein outlined would suggest that the logical training for these children would be that of extremely thorough repetitive drill on the fundamentals of phonic association with letter forms, both visually presented and reproduced in writing, until the correct associations were built up and the permanent elision of the reversed images and reversal in direction was assured'.[39]

Orton's dismissal of the 'look and say' approach in favour of phonics-based instruction would directly prefigure the 'reading wars', in which advocates of each method disputed the best way to teach reading.[40] Orton's support for phonics-based instruction also contributed to the world's first published instructional programme for children with dyslexia: the Orton-Gillingham-Stillman method.[41]

Female Pioneers and the First Instruction for Reading Disability: Anna Gillingham, Bessie Stillman, and Edith Norrie

Born in 1878, Anna Gillingham spent the first years of her life on a Sioux reservation in South Dakota where her father was an Indian Agent. A precocious student, she attended Swarthmore and Radcliffe colleges, before earning a master's degree at Teachers College at Columbia University in New York in 1910. Between 1905 and 1936, Gillingham worked at the Ethical Culture School in New York where she was a school psychologist, one of the first in the United States. There, she encountered children with a 'baffling difficulty': otherwise academically able, they were struggling with reading and spelling.[42] With her close friend Bessie Stillman, a teacher of language skills, Gillingham believed that children with this difficulty struggled to retain whole words. Together, Gillingham and Stillman 'set about developing a sequential, alphabetic-phonetic ... multisensory program. The alphabet was used as the tool with which children formulated meaningful syllables.'[43] In this way, their proposal for reading remediation aligned with that of Samuel Orton.

The professional relationship of the three – Orton, Gillingham, and Stillman – began in the 1920s. Familiar with Orton's work, Gillingham exchanged correspondence with the physician while he was at the State Psychopathic Hospital in Iowa. When Orton moved from Iowa to a private practice in New York in 1929, they met in person.[44] By then, Gillingham had accrued enough academic credit to apply for a doctorate, which she did, at Columbia University. Orton endorsed her application, informing Columbia that he would serve as her supervisor. But Gillingham's application was refused, reportedly on the basis of her gender. Dissuaded from pursuing a doctorate, but not from helping children with dyslexia, Gillingham secured a position as a research fellow in language disabilities at the New York Neurological Institute in 1932, where she could continue to work with Orton. There, she described the purpose of her research with Orton and Stillman: 'to organize remedial techniques in reading and spelling in conformity with Dr. Orton's neurological explanation. Miss Stillman had retired and was working with individual cases at Fieldston [School, New York] and helping me to organize the remedial technique.'[45] The first edition of the manual that emerged from their research, *Remedial Training for Children with Specific Disability in Reading, Spelling and Penmanship*, was published in 1946.[46]

The Orton-Gillingham-Stillman programme pioneered a multi-sensory approach to reading instruction, engaging visual, auditory, and kinaesthetic skills. Gillingham had been inspired by a 1910 visit to Germany, where schools widely employed multi-sensory teaching.[47] The programme stemmed from Orton's recommendation at the end of his 1925 article, '"Word-Blindness" in School Children': 'it would seem as if methods could be devised which will teach those with outstanding cases [of specific reading disability] to read, as well as shorten the period of emotional stress in cases of lesser severity. It is obvious that to be effective such methods must be developed in consonance with a sound neurologic background and be adequately controlled by careful observation and experiments in training.'[48] At its core, the Orton-Gillingham-Stillman programme employed a sequential system of reading instruction: its purpose was to teach children the fundamentals of word formation before they addressed whole words. Gillingham and Stillman, building on Orton's recommendation, were rigorous in the programme's construction:

They sorted, with computer-like efficiency, the words of our language containing various single phonograms [a symbol representing a vocal sound], those containing diagraphs [two letters forming a single sound] and diphthongs [two vowels constituting a gliding sound], and those which followed a certain pattern of syllable division. They developed spelling rules and located exceptions to them, determined which spellings of vowel sounds occurred with the greatest frequency in our language, and then developed procedures for mastering non-phonetic words ... Gillingham and Stillman worked with the precision of engineers erecting a building, beginning with a firm foundation, block by block, testing and retesting their methodology. As surely as lives could be lost if a building were poorly constructed, the contribution of a mind could be lost if a child were unable to process his own language.[49]

In the decades that followed, the programme was implemented in centres and schools across the United States. The manual, still in print, was revised several times (it is currently in its seventh edition); following Stillman's death in 1947, the year after the first edition, Gillingham insisted that Stillman be included as co-author on all future editions.

As well as marking the first dedicated instruction for those with reading disabilities, and cementing the pre-eminent place of educational psychology in addressing dyslexia, Gillingham and Stillman's work represented something else: for the first time, women were coming to prominence in dyslexia research. In this way, Gillingham and Stillman's response to Orton's call for a programme of remedial instruction illustrates, in microcosm, how the social dynamics of the field of reading disability, at least in certain locations, were shifting. In Britain in 1921, the psychologist Lucy Fildes had published perhaps the first account of word-blindness by a female researcher.[50] In 1932, a colleague of Orton's at the State Psychopathic Hospital in Iowa, Marion Monroe, published *Children Who Cannot Read*, in which she developed Orton's theories.[51] In the cases of Gillingham and Stillman, interest in the area stemmed from their meeting children with specific reading disability in schools, as teaching was one of the few professions that women could enter in the early twentieth century.[52] It was also via teaching that a female pioneer of dyslexia remediation on the opposite side of the Atlantic, and a contemporary of Gillingham and Stillman, first encountered the condition: Edith Norrie.

Edith Norrie was born in Copenhagen, Denmark, in 1889; her father was a physician and her mother a nurse. At school, Norrie struggled with reading and spelling; she had dyslexia, several years before the work of the Victorian physicians first alerted specialists to the condition in children. To compensate, Norrie developed her aptitude for music. She learned to play the piano and to sing to concert standard, performing at venues across Copenhagen and on Danish national radio. Rather than pursuing music at the expense of literacy, Norrie sought to teach herself reading and spelling, too – the impetus for these efforts being the difficulty she faced in writing love letters to her fiancé. To this end, she 'began to work out techniques that could improve her spelling. Among other things, she dissolved words into their basic [syllabic] form, then mastered the various inflections of them.'[53] After qualifying as a teacher in 1935, Norrie founded the Ordblinde Instituttet (Word-Blind Institute) in 1939 by converting a large private house in Hellerup, a suburb of Copenhagen.[54] It was one of the first centres in the world dedicated to the remediation of dyslexic difficulties.

Norrie's devotion to the cause was substantial; it could also be alienating. Her loyalty to her own methods ultimately led some of the teachers at the Ordblinde Instituttet to move on, founding their own school in the late 1940s. Nevertheless, Norrie's efforts to devise an instructional system for those with dyslexia resulted in a lasting contribution: the Norrie letter-case, a box-set of letters and common letter combinations, which enabled the user to break down words into their constituent phonetic elements. At first, she used this only herself; later, she developed a formal version that could be used by the pupils at the Ordblinde Instituttet. In contrast to the Orton-Gillingham-Stillman programme, Norrie's letter-case was based on her own experiences as a person with dyslexia, rather than a systematic survey of reading difficulties in children. However, in its emphasis on phonics-based instruction, and its requirement for multi-sensory engagement, Norrie's approach was similar to that of the Americans. It was also influential. Into the 1960s, the Ordblinde Instituttet remained one of the only dyslexia centres in existence, visited by educationalists from around the world who were interested in learning more about the condition and how it could be treated. Norrie's letter-case was reissued in the 1970s by her former pupil, Helen Arkell, founder of the Helen Arkell Dyslexia Centre in Britain.[55]

Following the lead of Gillingham, Stillman, and Norrie, the role of women in dyslexia research and teaching expanded in the decades ahead. One reason for this was that women were relatively well represented in the teaching profession, where children with dyslexia were to be encountered. A further contributory factor was the rise of parent groups and associations from the 1930s. Across Western states, parents were taking greater responsibility for their children's education; their interest in schooling did not end, as it had traditionally, at the school gates.[56] Given the centrality of literacy to professional success, the mothers of children with word-blindness, in particular, began to hold schools to account and seek ways to ameliorate their children's difficulties. Like Norrie, these mothers were often from middle-class backgrounds. Where state-provided education was inadequate to their needs, as it often was, they leveraged professional contacts and private sources of capital to build an early infrastructure of support for those with dyslexia that would emerge more fully in the 1960s and 1970s.

In professional psychology, there were further reasons for women like Anna Gillingham to be working in clinical and school settings, rather than in academic institutions: 'For most of the twentieth century, female psychologists were expected to work with children and families, domains that men thought suited women's "natural" capacities.'[57] 'Women predominated in clinical and school psychology, as lower-rank employees administering psychological testing, because male academic psychologists regarded these occupations as inferior to their own.'[58] Because of this, 'a two-tiered labour-market in Psychology existed: high-paid academic positions for men, lower-paid applied positions for women'.[59]

In the case of word-blindness, gender inequalities thus mapped onto other divides. Psychologists in formal academic settings, mostly male, sometimes adopted a cynicism toward dyslexia that those who worked directly with children in school settings, often female, did not. There were also geographical divisions: the tide of psychological understanding of dyslexia did not rise uniformly across Western, or even anglophone, countries. In Britain, despite the pioneering work of Hinshelwood and his contemporaries, there was a lull in interest in dyslexia between the 1920s and 1950s, in part because the attention of psychology was focused on the difficulties faced by the returning servicemen of two world wars.[60] One of the few British psychologists who did engage with word-blindness during this period, Cyril Burt, adopted a significantly more sceptical position on the topic than the more progressive attitudes of Orton, Gillingham, Stillman, and Norrie.

Cyril Burt, the Heritability of Intelligence, and Early Scepticism of Word-Blindness

Cyril Burt was born into a medical family in London in 1883. After attending a state elementary school, Burt was educated at the King's School in Warwick, then Christ's Hospital School in London. He later attended Jesus College, Oxford, where he read classics, but also developed interests in philosophy and psychology. Burt's curiosity in these subjects was cultivated by William McDougall, professor of psychology, whose work considered the heritability of intelligence amongst other topics.

In 1907, McDougall recruited Burt to assist with a survey of the mental characteristics of the British population proposed by Francis Galton. During this research, Burt came into contact with Charles Spearman and Karl Pearson, both sympathetic to social Darwinism and the eugenicist project that Galton had done much to initiate. Their views heavily influenced the young Burt.[61] In 1909, Burt published the results of his experimental tests of intelligence – findings that led him to believe that intelligence was principally hereditary in origin.[62] In his later career, he developed a more class-focused strand to his work, suggesting that intelligence was correlated with occupational level, and that this correlation was passed down through generations. After his death, investigators suggested that some of his data had been falsified and many of his findings exaggerated.[63] During his lifetime, he was one of the most celebrated academic psychologists in the country.[64]

Burt's work crystallized a number of prominent ideas in Britain and other Western states during the early twentieth century. These included the beliefs that social class was, in large part, a product of innate differences in intelligence; that determining who performed below average educationally was important in ensuring the health of society, rather than as a means to help the individual; and that psychology, via intelligence testing and other methods, could serve the state as a mode through which the mental abilities of the population could be gauged and, if necessary, regulated. Burt's work promoted and extended these ideas. Appointed Britain's first educational psychologist by a governmental body, the London County Council, in 1913, Burt's suggestion that intellectual differences between social classes were inherent informed British educational policy in the decades immediately following World War I.[65] By 1920, Burt, building on the work of Spearman and others, believed that he had developed a way of accurately measuring innate intelligence, and employed this in his research for educational authorities.[66] In this sense, Burt 'effectively established Psychology's function as an administrative technology in the U.K.'[67]

Burt also showed an especial interest in word-blindness. As early as 1920, following Hinshelwood and others, he noted that while word-blindness was, 'in the literal sense, a mental defect ... since congenital word-blindness does not directly affect general mental efficiency, but is by definition specific and localised, it does not to my mind constitute deficiency in the technical sense'.[68] By 1935, he had decided that, because it did not relate to general abilities, the concept was largely useless, with specific reading difficulties a product of poor teaching and unfocused students. If students were suitably intelligent, Burt proposed, 'practically all the cases commonly diagnosed as suffering from "congenital alexia" (disability in reading due to inborn defect in the centre for words seen or words heard) could be converted to normal readers with six to eighteen months' special training'.[69] In other words, dyslexia was something of a ruse; an excuse for poor performance in reading, easily cured by the trained professional. This cynicism toward the concept marked Burt's later research on the condition, including his most comprehensive publication on reading difficulties, 'Teaching Backward Readers' (1946):

> With children who suffer from *special* disability in reading, i.e., who are not notably backward in intelligence or in other subjects, the first step should be to discover the chief cause (or causes) in each individual case. For them there is no one best method. Psychiatrists outside child guidance centres are still rather prone to diagnose such cases in terms of one or other of the alleged varieties of 'congenital aphasia'.

Most frequently the child is declared to be suffering from 'congenital word-blindness'; and the parent or teacher is told that 'there is little use trying to train non-existent brain structures'. Nearly every educational psychologist has had cases referred to him in which this verdict has been pronounced; and it now seems pretty well agreed that, provided adequate and appropriate teaching can be arranged, practically all such cases will respond as well as their intelligence and other abilities will permit.[70]

But what was this appropriate teaching? 'On the whole', Burt continued, 'it would seem that the best method for teaching dull and backward readers is one which is predominantly visual (the so-called "look-and-say" or "whole word" method) ... The kinaesthetic [method] by itself proves less satisfactory; the alphabetic, decidedly poor; the phonic, the least effective of all.'[71] Thus, Burt's recommended strategy exhibited a curious ignorance of the more sustained research and recommendations around reading disability of Orton, Gillingham, and Stillman in the United States, and even of the work of his Victorian compatriots. As their work, and the Orton-Gillingham-Stillman approach, described, phonics-based instruction seemed the most appropriate for those with dyslexia, whose reading difficulties stemmed from a problem breaking down words into their constituent elements. Later research would show that such instruction was indeed efficacious for the dyslexic child.[72] The attention of Burt to word-blindness thus had a deleterious effect on research of the condition, especially in Britain, which generally failed to continue the progress made by Hinshelwood and others.

Central to Burt's critique of word-blindness was the implicit contention that it was a kind of pseudo-pathology, over-diagnosed by poorly trained psychiatrists ('Nearly every educational psychologist has had cases referred to him in which this verdict has been pronounced').[73] Undoubtedly, some of these verdicts were erroneous, but Burt carried out no systematic effort to understand how prevalent such 'false positives' were. Burt's most concerted critique of dyslexia came toward the end of his career in 1966, when he issued a 'counterblast to dyslexia' reiterating the points above.[74] Such arguments found especial resonance in the decades ahead as parents, often mothers, came to the fore in dyslexia teaching, advocacy, and (to a lesser extent) research. Parents' status as 'non-experts' with vested interests, along with their gender, made them easy targets for this line of argument, which increasingly came from policymakers and civil servants eager to avoid the economic cost of providing dyslexia support.

Burt's work also reflected something else: the darker side of psychological interest in cognitive functioning during this period. In contrast to more progressive psychologists, Burt's descriptions of children with specific reading disability were riddled with condescending terminology. While initial European and American interest in children's development emerged, in part, from a concern with helping individuals, it emerged too from an interest in 'bettering' society at large. As the historian Bonnie Evans has recounted, 'Early-twentieth-century models of social development were created at a time when marked social hierarchies were assumed to be the norm, and an air of superiority prevailed amongst intellectuals who deemed themselves eligible to determine this hierarchy, often drawing from evolutionary sciences to do so.'[75] Burt himself was a eugenicist who published in the *Annals of Eugenics* and the *Eugenics Review*.[76] While, unlike other eugenicists of the time, he generally considered any differences in intelligence between races and between sexes environmental, his views on differences between social classes were predicated on nature not nurture – feeble-mindedness he believed to be an inherited trait. In 1912, he described a test comparing two groups of socially differentiated pupils:

> The children tested at the Preparatory School were nearly all sons of men of eminence in the intellectual world – university professors, college lecturers and tutors, Fellows of the Royal Society, and bishops. The children at the Elementary School were mainly sons of small tradesmen. Calculations showed that, with two exceptions, the average performances of the Preparatory boys were all superior to those of the Elementary boys; in most cases superior even to those of the cleverest groups of the Elementary boys ... We have already seen that proficiency at such tests does not depend upon opportunity or training, but upon some quality innate. The resemblance in degree of intelligence between the boys and their parents must, therefore, be due to inheritance. We thus have an experimental demonstration that intelligence is hereditary.[77]

There were several reasons for Burt's focus on children in his research. The size and scope of compulsory schooling by the 1940s meant that this was the first place that differences in intellectual performance emerged. Burt's belief that, at least for some specific conditions such as congenital word-blindness, specialist tuition could be beneficial, also meant that it was important to identify learning difficulties as early as possible (and it showed, too, that there were perhaps limits to his belief that differences in ability were innate). In addition, there were the more troubling requirements of societal expediency:

> For reasons of rights, responsibilities, and cost, the British state never, in fact, had either the will or the ability to apply psychology as a tool of effective regulation over a broad swathe of the adult population [in the first half of the twentieth century]. Even when it came to those more exposed within an institutional setting, where such ideological and economic objections were weaker – the mental hospital, the prison, and the army – advances were slow. The position of children, however, was fundamentally different. It was society's responsibility to provide them with care; it was not yet their right to resist. Moreover, the emergence of a universal elementary education system and an expanding secondary system provided what was a unique opportunity to reach out at a formative stage to a cross-section of the population as a whole. Unsurprisingly, work on the advance of psychological regulation leans heavily on the example of the child, drawing attention in particular to mental testing and child guidance.[78]

Indeed, one of the practical applications of Burt's work in Britain was the creation of child guidance clinics: state-funded institutions to which children with an array of 'problems', including feeble-mindedness, neuroticism, and word-blindness, were referred.[79] In the 1920s, the first child guidance clinics opened. In 1932, 'the City of Oxford [one of the first local authorities to involve itself in the area], with the approval of the Board of Education, opened an educational clinic for the purpose of examining children for, among other things, mental deficiency'.[80] The child guidance movement fostered new understandings of childhood and parenting that would linger into the second half of the century. 'Standardised testing, descriptions of "normal" developmental stages, and a general belief that parents (particularly mothers) could and did produce most pathology in children were necessary prerequisites for the Child Guidance movement's existence.'[81] In this way, child guidance 'carried within it (and reflected) a growing cultural misogyny, gradually leading to a pervasive attitude that "professionals" were far more trustworthy than ordinary mothers'.[82] It also problematized children who did not conform to statistical norms of educational performance.

Anxiety and Adaptation: Growing Up Word-Blind in the First Half of the Twentieth Century

The work of Samuel Orton, Anna Gillingham, and Bessie Stillman in the United States, and of Edith Norrie in Denmark, demonstrated a greater sensitivity to how children experienced dyslexia, and what this difficulty meant for them in their everyday lives. Their work was underscored by a belief that children with dyslexia were not responsible for their difficulties, and that the duty of society was to help those with the condition, rather than to ignore or denigrate them. On the other hand, influential figures like Cyril Burt in Britain, who also sought treatment for those with word-blindness, possessed more traditional attitudes; for Burt, the responsibility for poor educational performance was placed squarely on the shoulders of those who were struggling. Each of these experts distinguished those with dyslexia from 'normal' learners, but the motivations for their actions were different. The geographical diffusion of these figures – and the fact that, in the case of Burt, his views were considerably less progressive than earlier Britons who had worked on the topic – shows that tracing a singular history of dyslexia is problematic. Having dyslexia has meant something quite different, at different times, in different places; and the prospects for those with dyslexia – in education, in employment, in general life – have varied according to a range of contextual factors.

Nevertheless, the story of dyslexia is not a full one unless it offers an indication of what it was like to experience dyslexia at different points in the past. Such biographies can be only illustrative, especially in earlier decades when records are scarcer (and the difficulty of diagnosing dyslexia retroactively more substantial), but they add texture to the frequently 'top-down' understandings of the first dyslexia researchers.

As with the Victorian period, it is easier to uncover first-hand accounts of dyslexia from the professional classes during the early twentieth century than it is to excavate more prosaic experiences of the condition. In part, of course, this is because those who were formally diagnosed, and who were able to publish their own encounters with dyslexia, frequently came from more privileged backgrounds or grew up to enter the same. In the case of Ronald Hall, a senior employee at the British Foreign Office, his 1945 account of growing up with word-blindness during the first decades of the twentieth century was published in the *British Journal of Ophthalmology* (showing that, even by the mid-1940s, the legacy of the early ophthalmological interest in the condition, while dwindling, remained). It includes a vivid description of the psychological repercussions of the condition, at an age when children's ability to perform like their peers often seems crucial to them:

> Having suffered from word blindness as a child and, incredible as it may seem looking back, being unable to read up to the age of fifteen … I can speak from experience when I say what a terrible handicap this is for a child. Although in World War No. 1, I spent over three years at the Front, I can truthfully say that I never during those years experienced a fraction of the stark terror that I did as a boy at school during English lessons lest I should be called upon to read aloud and reveal to the whole class that I could not do so. Every possible device I could I used to kill time so that my turn to read aloud might not come before the lesson ended. I asked every possible question and then every possible question about the answer. Sometimes these tactics just saved me but not always. There must be many children who are to-day living a similar nightmare existence for a child's sensitivity and fear of ridicule are limitless.[83]

Hall's parents were not uninterested in his plight, but their power to assist was limited: 'In my childhood my parents did what they could to help me, taking me to an ophthalmologic surgeon who prescribed glasses, but these produced no effect whatever. It was also suggested that I should read words written in very large type but this also proved of no assistance.'[84]

Instead, Hall developed his own method of phonics-based remediation: 'All words must be analysed or broken down into their smallest parts and then synthesised again by associations.'[85] This enabled Hall to pass into the top branch of the civil service, where his career was apparently successful. Hall's tale of triumph over adversity was cited approvingly in the pages of the *Lancet*, amongst other publications.[86]

But even where parents sought to help, assistance was limited by a lack of widespread recognition of the condition. This was true even for persons who attended elite schools. Helen Arkell was born in the Netherlands in 1920. Her father, Emil, was a member of the Norwegian diplomatic service, and her mother, Dorothy Latham, was English, born in the Surrey village of Frensham. Following his posting to Holland, Arkell's father was ordered to Berlin, then Copenhagen. While living in Copenhagen, Arkell attended a French convent school. Indeed, it was the internationalism of her childhood that meant Arkell's dyslexia was initially misdiagnosed, attributed to her peripatetic upbringing and consequent exposure to multiple languages rather than any innate difficulty with language: 'I was very bad at school. I read very inadequately and very, very slowly and my writing was atrocious. I found putting my thoughts on paper was extremely difficult. It was luck that it wasn't a conventional school because everybody thought "oh, poor thing, she's mixed up with her languages", so nobody blamed me for it.'[87]

Despite the sympathy extended by her teachers, the emotional repercussions for Arkell of going undiagnosed were substantial. Indeed, her experiences were highly similar to the experiences of Hall, several decades earlier, on the other side of the North Sea: 'It was desperate being told to do a page of homework, to read it, and then write about it. I used to wake up at night and put a couple of hours in to try and keep things turning over. Not that it was very successful, but I was trying to compensate in some way … One of my abiding memories is being told to read a poem in Norwegian. The nuns thought they were being kind to me and I stood up with everyone looking at me and all I can remember is a blur. I couldn't see letters or words at all and that made me feel absolutely awful.'[88]

Arkell's dyslexia was only formally diagnosed when she was thirty. Arkell had moved to England, but her sister, Binkie, remained in Denmark. 'I remember very clearly one letter we got [from Binkie] said, "thank goodness now we know what's wrong with Carl [Helen's cousin]: he's word-blind. They've got no idea what this [word-blindness] is, but they have a name for his difficulty."' Carl's experience at school in the 1940s had been challenging: 'He was made the class buffoon and the teachers pinned up his essays for everybody to look at.' As time went on, 'I was over there [Denmark] several times, I found that all the silly things he [Carl] did were exactly the same as I did.' By this point, Edith Norrie had founded the Ordblinde Instituttet in Copenhagen. Indeed, it was Norrie who diagnosed Carl's dyslexia: 'she had tested Carl and said he was word blind or dyslexic. I asked her to look at me, too, and she said: "yes, there's no doubt about it". I was dyslexic.'[89] Arkell went on to found the Helen Arkell Dyslexia Centre in her mother's home village, one of the earliest specialist dyslexia centres in Britain. Arkell was, it might be said, one of the lucky ones: her dyslexia had been identified and she possessed the wherewithal to do something about it.

Elsewhere, progressive private schools were also developing greater specialist instruction for children with word-blindness. Millfield, an independent school in Somerset, England, was founded in 1936 by Jack Meyer: one of the first co-educational schools in the country, with a reputation for teaching students with a range of abilities. In 1942, Millfield became the first school in Britain to help a child overcome word-blindness by that name. The child in question was Martin Attlee, son of then Deputy Prime Minister Clement. Martin later obtained a place at university, and Millfield continues to describe itself as the first school in Britain to have offered assistance to a child with dyslexia.[90]

Other children, of course, were not so fortunate, although prospects varied. The case of Louise Bartie is illustrative of those whose difficulties were identified, often sympathetically, but nevertheless went unaddressed. Born in Warwick in 1923, Louise attended St Paul's primary school in Leamington. There, she was evidently a hard worker, but her reading and spelling skills lagged. In 1932, aged nine, her school report was positive, but also expressed concern at her progress in literacy: 'Louise is very intelligent but her reading

Dyslexia Goes Global (1925–48)

and spelling are below standard.' The next year, the same problem was noted: 'Louise is a splendid worker, but must still try hard with her reading and spelling.' Louise went on to secondary school, but her struggles led to disengagement from her studies. She would register at school in the morning, then change into a spare set of clothes and cycle to Leamington for the day. After school, she would find out from friends what the day's classes had involved so that she could relay this to her mother. Louise later joined the Post Office as a telephonist, where her reading and writing skills mattered less. She volunteered to work in London during World War II, and later became a Post Office manager responsible for infrastructure projects. Her dyslexia was not identified until after she retired. Like many of her generation from less wealthy backgrounds, she found ways to adapt, rather than recognition and support.[91]

The prospects for children with dyslexia from a broader range of backgrounds were about to change, though. In Britain, the 1944 Education Act widened access to formal state education, and for the first time local education authorities had responsibility for those with learning difficulties.[92] The tripartite system of education instituted by the Education Act – 'grammar schools for the most able, based on "intelligence tests", secondary modern schools for most pupils, and secondary technical schools for those perceived to have technical or scientific ability' – was designed to increase opportunities for all learners, despite its rootedness in the IQ-calibrated policy proposals of educationalists such as Cyril Burt.[93] The act increased the school-leaving age in Britain to fifteen and, in 'ensuring secondary education for all according to age, ability, and aptitude ... for the first time constructed a full national system of education'.[94] Perhaps more pertinently, it reflected the formation of a welfare state in which individual difficulties came to be seen as something that society should help ameliorate. A 'golden age' of dyslexia research and support was set to begin.

Chapter 2 – Key Points
- By the 1920s, British research on dyslexia was waning and American research came to the fore
- In the United States, the most prominent dyslexia researchers and

teachers were Samuel T. Orton, Anna Gillingham, and Bessie Stillman, whose systematic multi-sensory methods of teaching would prove highly influential
- In Denmark, Edith Norrie founded one of the first specialist dyslexia schools in the late 1930s
- The first half of the twentieth century also saw denunciations of dyslexia from educational psychologists such as Cyril Burt

PART 2
Evidence

3
Dyslexia Discussed: The Foundation and Work of the Word Blind Centre (1962-72)

Building on the late nineteenth-century studies of the German physicians who initially identified *Wortblindheit*, researchers in Britain, Denmark, and the United States sketched the first contours of a dyslexia community in the opening half of the twentieth century. This community led research on reading difficulties, with the latter coming under the terms word-blindness, alexia, reading retardation, and reading disability, as well as dyslexia. Toward the middle of the twentieth century, the first groups dedicated to better understanding the cognitive profile of dyslexia emerged and the interests of reading researchers around the world began to coalesce. This was not yet the start of what might be called a dyslexia infrastructure; it was restricted to individual research and teaching centres. However, it was the first step in moving dyslexia from a niche scientific concern into a difficulty that could be treated at scale.

In Denmark, as we have seen, the Ordblinde Instituttet was created in 1939 by Edith Norrie to assist children with word-blindness, and in the United States the Orton Society was founded in 1949 by June Orton. Building on the legacy of her husband Samuel Orton, and that of his colleagues Anna Gillingham, Bessie Stillman, and others, the society trained specialist teachers and published instructional materials for those requiring assistance with specific reading difficulties. From 1956, it began an annual publication to disseminate its research, the *Bulletin of the Orton Society*.[1] One of its early vice-presidents (1959–65) was Sally Childs, a pioneer of dyslexia support in the United States and an inspiration for Marion Welchman, later founder of the British Dyslexia Association.[2] During the 'reading wars' of the 1950s and 1960s (and beyond), which pitted proponents of the 'look-and-say' or 'whole word' approach to reading instruction against advocates of phonological methods, the society largely remained out of the fray.[3] A landmark for the society came in 1982 when it changed its name to the Orton Dyslexia Society, reflecting a growing acceptance of the term, which the society had helped to foster, in the United States and around the world.[4] By this time, similar organisations, such as the British Dyslexia Association, were creating an international landscape of dyslexia awareness and support.

In Britain, the forerunner of the British Dyslexia Association and other specialist dyslexia organisations was the Word Blind Centre for Dyslexic Children: the first institution in the country dedicated to dyslexia assessment and assistance, and one of the first of its type in the world. It was also a pioneer in other respects. At a conference in London in 1962, which preceded the centre's founding, an international array of researchers, including participants from Denmark, France, and the United States, assembled to discuss unexpected difficulties with learning to read: that is, reading difficulties that could not be attributed to poor education or other factors. The conference was funded by the International Children's Aid Association (ICAA), which was founded in 1888 by the clergyman Allen Dowdeswell Graham to assist children from poor backgrounds with a variety of disabilities. The conference was perhaps the first occasion that dyslexia's international scope was gauged, including the progress that had been made in the United States and elsewhere while British engagement had stalled in the first decades of the twentieth century. The history of the Word Blind Centre, then, serves as a case study of the status of dyslexia at the beginning of the second half of the twentieth century.

In keeping with histories of dyslexia more broadly, historical reflections on the Word Blind Centre have generally been authored by those who worked at the centre or who were involved with its work, including Macdonald Critchley, Tim Miles, Sandhya Naidoo, and Alfred White Franklin. In the sole scholarly account of the centre, William Whyte identifies two major themes of the centre's work: (1) its role in offering an initial classification of dyslexia, that is, in attempting to build an evidence base for dyslexia's existence; and (2) its focus, for a variety of reasons, on middle-class pupils rather than those from more disadvantaged backgrounds.[5] For Whyte, this makes the legacies of the centre complex: 'The London Word Blind

Dyslexia Discussed (1962–72)

Centre for Dyslexic Children achieved much in its short existence. It formed a focus for further work and a seedbed for other organisations. It helped those children who attended it. The research it supported was widely read and would inspire other researchers, as well as reassuring those already committed to the concept of dyslexia. What the Centre could not do – and could hardly be expected to do – was to overcome the many stark divisions and sharp disagreements over dyslexia.'[6]

Certainly, the Word Blind Centre never resolved the debates over how best to define dyslexia, contested principally between medical professionals at the centre and external educational psychologists critical of its work. These debates echoed the sometimes contentious discussions of Victorian researchers, as well as the criticisms of dyslexia by Cyril Burt, who had retired in 1950 but remained an influential voice in British educational psychology, and continued to publish until his death in 1971. In addition, the demographic profile of the children assisted by the centre led to unhelpful beliefs that dyslexia was a kind of middle-class con – perpetrated by anxious parents wishing to explain and so justify the poor academic performance of their children, and to divorce their children's reading difficulties from general intelligence.

However, there is a more optimistic view of the centre and of its accomplishments. The disputes over the existence of dyslexia that took place between members of the Word Blind Centre and educationalists were rife with vested interests. Educational psychologists, especially those allied to local and national governments, were wary of what they saw as an incursion by doctors and academic psychologists into their sphere of influence – 'special education', as it was later known. Education officials were concerned that recognition of dyslexia would require them to expend huge sums on support, given their statutory duties (under the Education Act of 1944) to provide appropriate schooling to all pupils. Undoubtedly, parents of children at the centre had vested interests. Nevertheless, the evidence for dyslexia produced by the Word Blind Centre was not the creation of parents; it was the product of experts whose principal concern was maximising children's welfare.

Central here are questions of power and of perspective. If one examines the Word Blind Centre from the point of view of all children struggling with reading during the 1960s, its work, conducted by a medical and academic elite, predominantly helping children from better-off backgrounds, can seem parochial, even biased. Similar claims of class bias have been made about other social movements of the 1960s, including those for gender equality and for disability rights, often led initially by middle-class academics, activists, and charities.[7] However, the practical necessities of how civil society organisations and campaigns for minority rights were formed cannot be overlooked. At least at first, these were the only groups of individuals with the power and influence to get campaigns aimed at social justice off the ground. Later, when the movements were better embedded into society, with a larger support base, they could broaden their objectives, seeking to ensure that all those who required assistance were helped. In this way, the bourgeois nature of the Word Blind Centre was indicative of the society in which it was created, rather than a part of its design.

A more instructive perspective to adopt when considering the centre's formation and work is one that looks at contemporary provision for special educational needs. At the point of the creation of the Word Blind Centre, there was almost no provision for reading disabilities in state education.[8] Although the Word Blind Centre comprised individuals from medicine and academia, the Word Blind Centre was not funded by a major hospital or university; it was funded by the ICAA, a charity. While this gave it a royal stamp of approval (Princess Margaret was president of the ICAA), it did not entitle the Word Blind Centre to dedicated state funding or to the recognition of central government. In the broader landscape of medicine and education, it was a minor entity, its accomplishments predicated on the work of its small, modestly paid, but passionate staff.

Setting the Stage: Alfred White Franklin, the Word-Blindness Conference, and a New Dyslexia Centre

Born in London in 1905, Alfred White Franklin was the second son of Ethel and Philip Franklin – the latter a Harley Street surgeon, specialising in otorhinolaryngology (conditions of the ear, nose, and throat). Despite an early interest in classics, White Franklin followed his father into the medical profession, studying medicine at the University of Cambridge, before returning to London and being appointed assistant physician at St Bartholomew's

Dyslexia Discussed (1962–72)

(Barts) and Queen Charlotte's Hospitals in 1935 and 1937, respectively. White Franklin, who came to specialise in paediatrics, retained his affiliation with the two hospitals across his career and into his retirement as honorary consultant to both. It was during White Franklin's clinical work at the hospitals that he first encountered children with reading difficulties without an obvious cause, and that his interest in word-blindness began.[9]

As we have seen, during the first decades of White Franklin's career, from the early 1940s to the late 1950s, little was known about dyslexia in Britain; the early impetus of the Victorian researchers had been largely lost. To gauge the extent of dyslexia research, White Franklin used his connections at the ICAA, where he was chairman, to fund a conference on 'Word-Blindness or Specific Developmental Dyslexia'. The conference, which took place at Barts Hospital on 12 April 1962, was organised by White Franklin with several colleagues: Thomas Ingram, of the Department of Child Life and Health at the University of Edinburgh; George Meredith, a psychologist at the University of Leeds; and Wilfrid Sheldon, a physician at Great Ormond Street Children's Hospital.[10] White Franklin described the conference's purpose: 'To ventilate what is known and thought about the diagnosis and treatment of specific developmental dyslexia, a condition that is diagnosed in children and adults and therefore is diagnosable. The condition is known and accepted as a rare one in the severe forms that so adversely affect school progress, the attitude to learning, the general behaviour and the emotional development of the sufferers.'[11]

Representing the first major conference on dyslexia, speakers attended from across the world – from America, James Roswell Gallagher, a lecturer in paediatrics at Harvard Medical School, and Donald Shankweiler, research fellow at the National Institute of Health in Bethesda, Maryland, whose later research on dyslexia's causes would prove particularly influential; from Denmark, Ingrid Riis-Vestergaard of Edith Norrie's Ordblinde Instituttet in Copenhagen; and from France, Suzanne de Séchelles, a leading speech and language therapist based in Paris. As the background of these speakers showed, dyslexia was of increasingly worldwide concern, and at the Word-Blindness Conference the interests of these international researchers were brought together for the first time.

From Britain, speakers included several who would become influential in the dyslexia world in later decades, including: Macdonald Critchley, a physician at the National Hospital for Nervous Diseases in London and himself a driving force behind the creation of the Word Blind Centre; Tim Miles, a psychologist at the University College of North Wales, who would go on to become a leading figure in dyslexia research and awareness; and Maisie Holt, a clinical psychologist at Barts, who had been informally treating children with word-blindness for several years. All three were also appointed to the Word Blind Committee. In total, as many as 350 attendees came to the conference; so many that they 'almost literally jammed the doors'.[12] Evidently, there was a substantial demand to know more about unexplained reading difficulties.

In his opening remarks, White Franklin noted the diversity of professional backgrounds from which speakers and attendees came. Dyslexia was no longer the sole preserve of medics, as it had been during the Victorian period, even if medicine was still the field that had brought the conference together: 'Now this is an extraordinary thing to me that people representing so many different disciplines – this, I think, is now the word we use for jobs – have been gathered together; it's an astonishing and very hopeful thing. We have here neurologists, paediatricians, Medical Officers of Health, psychiatrists, psychologists, Social Workers, various professors concerned with language and education, apart from school teachers and just some plain parents.'[13]

White Franklin's final reference, which understandably riled some of the 'plain parents' who attended, spoke to the beginning of a new era in the history of dyslexia: parental efforts to obtain educational and political support via the foundation of organisations such as the British Dyslexia Association. Indeed many of those who would help to start such organisations were in the audience, but, for the time being, the diverse range of professionals whom White Franklin had enlisted led the way in the understanding of and debate around dyslexia.

This plurality of professions was both a help and a hindrance to the immediate cause of achieving better dyslexia support. While it demonstrated the breadth of interest in the topic, rivalries and disputes between professions both continued and expanded the rifts demonstrated in Victorian discussions of the condition, such as the debate between the ophthalmologist James Hinshelwood and the physician William Broadbent over the definition of word-blindness, contested in the *Lancet*. At the Word-Blindness Conference, disputes mirrored contemporary fractures in the world of 'child development' – an interdisciplinary field concerned with the biological, psychological, and emotional changes of childhood, and how these could be influenced to best equip children for adult life. As William Whyte has argued, in the context of the Word Blind Centre's formation: 'Psychologists and psychiatrists differed on diagnosis and on treatment [across issues of child development]. At a major conference [the British Psychological Society's Annual General Meeting] in 1951, it was not only noted that their interactions were characterised by "tension, and at times bitterness", but also that they were often "remarkably rude to one another". There was likewise a "long-standing professional antagonism between doctors and psychologists", who similarly doubted the professional competence of one another. Teachers, too, competed for authority; as did educational psychologists.'[14]

In this way, although they had all come to learn more about dyslexia, a dividing line emerged at the conference between attendees who were more medically minded and those who were more educationally minded, the latter including psychologists involved in state education. In part, such differences mapped onto class divides, with the medical professionals frequently possessing more markers of professional esteem. Commenting on the rivalry between these two groups, Whyte suggests,

> This division was long-standing because it was more than merely academic. It was both professional and personal. It was to do with class and with status. As Adrian Wooldridge has argued, educational psychology 'only managed to win a marginal position in English professional life' in the mid-twentieth century and educational psychologists 'failed to command the rewards which they felt were commensurate with their intellectual ability and professional dedication'. They tended to come from more working- and lower middle-class backgrounds than their medical rivals. They were less likely to have attended public school or the ancient universities. Most spent time as teachers before they became academics. Almost none were elected fellows of either the British Academy or Royal Society – and there were for many years very few Chairs in psychology in Britain to which they might be promoted.[15]

Tim Miles, a psychologist at the University College of North Wales, who would later go on to found the Bangor Dyslexia Unit and develop the Bangor Dyslexia Test with his wife, Elaine, has recorded his introduction to the Word Blind Centre.[16] His recollections show how this first move toward the formation of a dyslexia infrastructure in Britain was premised on White Franklin's cultivation of diverse professional networks, but also that these connections came with existing animosities and interdisciplinary rivalries. With reference to these disputes, Miles recalls the general tenor of discussion at the Word-Blindness Conference:

> The conference was a decidedly stormy one. There was a foretaste of the heated and not always very courteous arguments which were to rage about the concept of dyslexia for the next 20 years. I remember one educationalist [Dr J.C. Daniels] warning us that if we used this esoteric term 'dyslexia' we would be 'tying a ball and chain' on our teachers. I think he was somehow under the impression that if educational difficulties had a neurological basis there was nothing one could do to remediate them. When a mother complained that her child had not received suitable help, an attempt was made (in a letter written to me after the conference) to discredit her evidence by saying that she was 'a psychiatric patient'. The letter also implied that if I libelled educational authorities by implying that they were incompetent I might find myself taken to court.[17]

There is much to unpack here. First, as Miles says, debates over dyslexia's existence would prefigure similar discussions in the decades that followed. Miles's hope that these would last twenty years, though, proved optimistic; such debates continue to the present day. In the early 1960s, a substantial evidence base for dyslexia was only beginning to emerge, and scepticism about its existence was commonplace. Principally, this scepticism came from educational psychologists who, like Cyril Burt in the 1940s, believed that dyslexia was an example of over-pathologizing by the medical profession, which the competent educational psychologist could attribute to poor teaching and so remedy.[18] As Sandhya Naidoo recalls of J.C. Daniels's contribution, 'He thought that the problem of reading difficulty lay in the teaching methods adopted.'[19] While there were exceptions, such as Anna Gillingham in the United States, an educational psychologist who acknowledged and refined the concept of dyslexia, educational psychology in the 1960s remained generally critical of 'word-blindness'.

Second, the complaint of a mother that her child's difficulties were being ignored, and the subsequent dismissal of her concerns, foreshadowed a major aspect of dyslexia's social history: the efforts of parents (usually, but not always, mothers) to obtain specialist support for their children, and the sometimes gendered rebuttal of the same. This reflected a further fracture at the conference between professionals and non-professionals, with the former often dismissing the opinions of the latter, because they considered their opinions subjective and/or predicated on their emotional connections to children with dyslexia.

Third, the letter that Miles received following the conference, presumably from an educational official, reflected the particular reticence that British educational authorities had toward dyslexia – both at the time and later.[20] It was these authorities who, in the decades ahead, would take the lead in stalling progress toward dyslexia recognition and treatment. To do so, they would often cite the disputes in dyslexia science that the Word-Blindness Conference illustrated so clearly.

However, despite – or perhaps because of – the tensions of the 1962 conference, a new era in dyslexia understanding and provision was about to begin. In his closing comments, White Franklin remarked on the disagreements between professions, and between individuals, that the conference had highlighted. To explore the concept of word-blindness further, and to create (he hoped) a widely accepted evidence base for its existence, White Franklin proposed the creation of a new centre dedicated to dyslexia: the Word Blind Centre for Dyslexic Children.

The Foundation of the Word Blind Centre: Sandhya Naidoo and an Evidence Base for Dyslexia

To finance the new centre, White Franklin and his colleagues appealed to the ICAA for further funding beyond that provided for the Word-Blindness Conference. There were several reasons for the ICAA's accession. To start, they had a track record in the area. In 1958 and 1962, the ICAA had opened two of the first schools in the country dedicated to serious speech and language problems: John Horniman School in West Sussex and Edith Edwards House School in Surrey, respectively. In addition, this was a field, reading disability, which clearly required attention at a broader scale.[21] In 1947, 16,000 children were referred to speech therapists in England and Wales; by 1957, 50,000 children; by 1967, 70,000 children.[22] Other children, reporting similar difficulties, were sent to child guidance clinics, which nevertheless struggled to provide adequate remediation. 'The I.C.A.A. had chosen a field in which it really could make a difference. There was a demonstrable, if intractable, problem and a growing awareness that state provision was not adequately addressing it.'[23]

Despite this, the Word Blind Centre's start was inauspicious. Finding a suitable site in London, where the greatest number of pupils could be seen and the majority of the Word Blind Committee were based, proved difficult. After several proposals fell through, the centre began life in the basement of the ICAA's main offices in Kensington.[24] In 1965, it relocated to Coram's Fields, Bloomsbury, where the surroundings were only slightly more serviceable. A small school building, planned for demolition, was loaned to the centre by the Institute of Child Health at Great Ormond Street Hospital, with which the Word Blind Committee had connections.[25] The main building was a converted lavatory block – 'loos', as Sandhya Naidoo recalled them – supplemented by temporary buildings (pre-fabricated units or 'pre-fabs', common in Britain after World War II) where children could be assessed and taught.[26] Many of those who later worked there remembered, wryly, their first sight of the centre, which was nevertheless officially opened by Princess Margaret, president of the ICAA, escorted by White Franklin.[27] The site, though, was appropriate in other respects, with a history related to children's welfare. Coram's Fields was named after the philanthropist Thomas Coram, who founded the London Foundling Hospital there in 1739. That hospital's mission was to take care of the many abandoned and destitute children living in London.

The Word Blind Centre's first director, appointed in 1963, was Alex Bannatyne, a psychologist from New Zealand, who specialised in both neuropsychology and educational psychology. One of Bannatyne's first tasks was to settle on a name for the new institution. He suggested that the centre drop the term 'word-blind' in favour of dyslexia alone. The Word Blind Committee demurred, arguing that the former term still held currency, and so a compromise was reached: the unit would be called the Word Blind Centre for Dyslexic Children, a name that well illustrated the moment when ophthalmological explanations for dyslexia were being superseded.[28] By the time of the closure of the Word Blind Centre, 'word-blindness' had fallen almost entirely out of fashion.[29]

In many ways, Bannatyne's appointment was a compromise, too. Given his expertise in both the medical and educational dimensions of dyslexia, it was hoped that he would bridge the gap between the two camps displayed so clearly at the Word-Blindness Conference.[30] At the time of his appointment, though, Bannatyne's area of expertise was not reading difficulties, and he had not spoken at the 1962 conference. Writing in 1966, at the end of his tenure, Bannatyne recalled, 'Although I have been involved in education and psychology for some twenty years, and in remedial education for some of that period, it is only in the last three or four years that I have developed an intense interest in reading disabilities in children of normal intelligence.'[31] Bannatyne did ensure that the Word Blind Centre's work was known internationally, visiting the Ordblinde Instituttet in 1965 and a series of centres in the United States subsequently. In 1966, he left the centre to take up a position at the University of Illinois. It would be left to his successor, Sandhya Naidoo, to conduct the first in-depth research with children at the Word Blind Centre, and to ensure that the venture had a lasting legacy, both in Britain and beyond.

Sandhya Naidoo was born in Glasgow in 1922 to Indian and Norwegian parents: Narendra Nath Basu Rai Choudhury and Jenny Olise Henriksen, a manufacturing furrier and a dressmaker, respectively. She graduated with an MA in education from the University of Glasgow in 1944, qualifying as a teacher in 1945 and as an educational psychologist in 1946. She married Dayanand Naidoo, a psychiatrist, in 1945, and the couple moved to London soon afterwards.[32] There, she continued her work as a teacher at a secondary modern (non-selective state) school and, 'inspired by lectures from her student days and informed by what she saw in the classroom, she developed an interest in children who failed to learn to read and the association between reading disorder and handedness'.[33] This interest extended beyond classroom hours. Teaching a class of eleven-year-olds, Naidoo found that several of them struggled greatly with reading – they clearly possessed a learning difficulty, but one that had gone undiagnosed and untreated. With the agreement of the school and the children's parents, she tutored the children outside of the classroom. For one of the pupils, this was the first dedicated support that she had received: 'No one has cared about us before', she told Naidoo.[34]

Given her experience and interests, Naidoo applied for the post of educational psychologist at the Word Blind Centre when it was advertised, later becoming director after the departure of Alex Bannatyne. It seems likely that she was alerted to the job by Oliver Zangwill, a member of the Word Blind Committee, and Naidoo's supervisor at the University of Cambridge, where she had undertaken doctoral studies between 1961 and 1964. Naidoo had also attended the 1962 conference. Naidoo recalls her introduction to the Word Blind Centre, and to the Word Blind Committee: 'When I was applying for the job [waiting for the interview] I watched and there was this trim, business-like woman getting out of a taxi. I thought, my god, if she's applying, I don't stand a chance!'[35] Naidoo did stand a chance, however – the woman was Mia Kellmer Pringle of the Word Blind Committee, a member of the interview panel, and Naidoo was duly appointed, serving as director from 1966 to 1970. The two women would later work closely, co-authoring a book on childcare.[36]

Naidoo's remit was both to research and to teach children at the centre: 'My first task was to devise a list of tests, which we could test hypotheses on, so I did that. We never charged for examinations; they were all free. I was determined that whatever we did should be free as well. Kellmer Pringle was very helpful; she stood us tests that we could use. It [testing] had to be broad. We soon realised that we had to teach children as well.'[37] Naidoo's research would be the lasting legacy of her work at the centre. In 1972, she published *Specific Dyslexia*, a report of her studies, which 'was successful in providing both a deep understanding of the individual [with dyslexia], and a more thorough understanding of the condition. Drawing on careful and wide-ranging psychological, educational, and neurological assessments she built detailed profiles of 98 boys with dyslexia, comparing their abilities against a control group'.[38] As the psychologist Kate Nation has written, 'Many of her [Naidoo's] observations have stood the test of time – in particular that dyslexia should be seen as a disorder of reading that is multifaceted, complex and dimensional. Her research documented dyslexic features in family members, pre-dating research that has since confirmed its genetic bases.[39] Naidoo's work provided a scientific foundation for dyslexia research, supplemented by other studies of the time, which the dyslexia community in Britain and beyond would build upon to achieve public and political recognition.

Naidoo's approach as director was compassionate, but direct. She realised early on that dyslexia was, or could be, a life-long problem for children who attended the centre, and that complete remediation was probably not feasible.[40] She also appreciated that the centre's resources were limited, and sought to help as many children as possible before the ICAA's funding elapsed. Her interactions with a child and his parents in the late 1960s are illustrative. Presented to Naidoo for assessment in September 1967, the boy was identified by her as having dyslexia. The boy and his parents were American, living in Britain during the academic year 1967/68, while the father was a visiting professor in London. Given his nationality, the boy's local education authority was unwilling to fund his place at the Word Blind Centre, but his parents were able to afford a place themselves. After receiving teaching over the academic year, his parents withdrew him from the centre in May 1968 for a family holiday, requesting that he be allowed to return afterwards. Naidoo replied that if the boy left, he left for good, as the waiting list for the centre was substantial.[41]

Naidoo's role as director also attested to a further shift in the gender constitution of the emerging dyslexia community. As education came to the fore in providing remediation, women, who formed the majority of the teaching ranks in the country, likewise came to greater prominence. At the Word Blind Centre, Naidoo's work was supported by teachers including Gill Cotterell and Helen Arkell, who would go on to play key roles in the dyslexia world. A typical day for teachers at the centre consisted of individual sessions with six children of up to forty-five minutes, with the remainder of each hour spent recording observations and progress.[42] Their work was supported by effective administration of the centre, led by the general secretary of the ICAA, Grace Rattenbury.

In 1970, as funding was wound down by the ICAA, Naidoo left the Word Blind Centre to take up a post as a senior research officer at the National Children's Bureau in London. There, she conducted broader work on the sociological, educational, and psychological aspects of childcare in Britain, including research with Mia Kellmer Pringle.[43] Her work on dyslexia, though, was not over. In addition to publishing *Specific Dyslexia* in 1972, she continued to be active in dyslexia advocacy, working with the organisations that followed the Word Blind Centre, including the British Dyslexia Association and the Dyslexia Institute. In 1974, she became the founding headteacher of Dawn House School in Nottinghamshire – a specialist school for children with severe language difficulties, administered by the ICAA.[44] This joined the ICAA's other specialist schools, Edith Edwards House School and John Horniman School. By the time of her retirement in 1983, Dawn House School had quadrupled in size, from sixteen pupils to more than sixty, and it remains one of the leading schools in Britain for children with language and communication needs.[45] The Word Blind Centre, under Naidoo's directorship, had a transformational effect on the status of dyslexia, establishing the condition as a legitimate area of scientific and educational concern.

Dyslexia's Demographics: Socio-economic Class and the Work of the Word Blind Centre

In addition to helping put dyslexia on the map, Sandhya Naidoo's work at the Word Blind Centre illustrated something else: that the emerging focus on dyslexia did not reach the full spectrum of children with dyslexia. For a variety of reasons, including the suitability of tests, the research for *Specific Dyslexia* restricted its sample to children at the centre aged between eight years, and twelve years, eleven months. It focused on boys, who were more commonly presented at the centre than girls, given the contemporary social emphasis on their schooling. Children were then selected if they scored at least 90 on an IQ test (the Wechsler Intelligence Scale for Children), possessed no neurological condition, had not been absent from school for a significant duration/changed school more than three times, and had no emotional disturbance.[46] Of the ninety-eight children meeting these criteria, Naidoo categorised each by their father's occupation (a common measure of socio-economic class at the time, drawing on the official classification scheme of the Registrar General for England and Wales) into five socio-economic groups: (1) professional (e.g., accountant); (2) intermediate (e.g., teacher); (3) non-manual/manual skilled (e.g., secretary/electrician); (4)

Dyslexia Discussed (1962–72)

semi-skilled (e.g., postal worker); and (5) unskilled (e.g., labourer).[47] In Naidoo's sample, over three-quarters of children came from groups one and two, the remainder from groups three and four, and none from group five. In the mid-1960s, when Naidoo was undertaking her research, nearly half of employees in the UK worked in either the primary sector (mainly agriculture and mining) or secondary sector (primarily manufacturing and construction), meaning that the Word Blind Centre's children were unrepresentative of the population as a whole.[48]

The focus on middle-class children in Naidoo's research is well illustrated by the case studies that open her report. All of them concern families who appear financially comfortable; often, the difficulties being experienced by the child were noticed because of the high educational performance of their siblings and/or their parents. Many of these children were an anomaly not because they were doing poorly, but because they were not doing as well as their high-achieving family members and peers. Describing the case of 'Martin', for example, Naidoo states that 'both parents were highly educated. There were two boys in the family, Martin being the younger. The elder brother was achieving distinction at school but father thought that Martin was perhaps, the more highly intelligent ... Compared with those who can barely read, Martin might almost be said to have no problem. But to Martin and his parents, this is little comfort. Martin is a highly intelligent lad, clearly of University calibre and he himself would like to go to University one day.'[49] At the time this was written, only 13 per cent of teenagers attended university.[50] In the focus on intelligence, there are parallels here with the Victorian case histories of William Pringle Morgan and James Hinshelwood.

Naidoo's case studies also indicated what the fate of children at state schools might be if their families could not afford specialist instruction for them at places like the Word Blind Centre. Throughout these accounts, there is a willingness from schools to help the centre where they can – usually by providing detailed reports of pupils' histories of reading and general academic progress. Thus, Naidoo writes appreciatively of the 'very full reports' that she received from schools, helping to contextualise the reading difficulties of the children under her care.[51] At the same time, the schools were clearly struggling with how best to help their pupils. Of 'Margaret', a girl of eleven years and six months, Naidoo writes, 'At school it was recognized that she was a bright child and that she was much handicapped by the dyslexia.

But although Margaret's need for considerable help was acknowledged, there were staff shortages and her teacher was now at a loss to know how to help.'[52] Even those children who were sent to child guidance clinics received little useful support. Of 'Simon', a boy of ten years, Naidoo writes that he 'received as much help as the school and clinic could give but he was, none the less, a depressed child making little if any headway in reading'.[53]

What explained the socio-economic background of children at the centre? Middle-class parents perhaps had better awareness of the centre and its work than other groups; once their child had been referred by a doctor or other professional, they were also better able to facilitate the child's travel to lessons, and to pay for the same if needed. Where they did not or could not pay for lessons, middle-class parents often possessed the resources to lobby their local education authorities to fund their child's place. Staff at the Word Blind Centre, including its first director, Alex Bannatyne, were aware of this demographic trend, and that it could be hazardous to the reputation of dyslexia and the centre.[54] In their view, it might lead to accusations that dyslexia was a middle-class excuse for poor academic performance, a concern that was prescient. Nevertheless, there was little that could be achieved by the Word Blind Centre to change this pattern of recruitment. Their resources were insufficient to engage with pupils who were not brought to them; they could provide support to parents lobbying local education authorities on their children's behalf, but they could not undertake this lobbying themselves. Rather, the centre's central purpose was to ensure that the children whom they did see received the best teaching possible.

However, even within the relatively narrow socio-economic stratum with which the Word Blind Centre engaged, children and parents came with a diversity of experiences; and the differences in home life between children were sometimes stark. At one end of the spectrum, as we have seen, children came from professional homes where parents were able to afford termly fees, even when a local education authority did not provide support. At the other end, children, including some from solidly middle-class homes, had parents who struggled to provide support. In some cases, this was because one or both parents also had dyslexia, making it difficult for them to complete the various forms required to lobby their local education authority. Parents were sometimes defensive, too, especially at a time when those with learning difficulties encountered substantial ignorance and prejudice in schools and elsewhere. Thus, one case file from the Word Blind Centre notes that 'father can't read and mother is apt to pin all the blame of children's backwardness onto dad. Mother is resentful of any suggestion that her children are not normal.'[55] Joyce Hargrave-Wright, who worked with the Word Blind Centre during its early years, recalls that 'when I first starting testing [children with dyslexia], I never really saw men at all. Gradually, mum would drag along dad as well and he'd sit there. In the consulting rooms they sit with their chair back and do not really take part in it at all. Whether it's because they don't want to admit anything [their own dyslexia], I don't know.'[56] The Word Blind Centre was casting light onto an issue that had previously been left unattended, and it frequently revealed tensions in the family unit, too.

In addition to contextual factors, there is suggestion that the high proportion of children in Naidoo's study from middle-class backgrounds may have been the product of selection bias. Commenting on *Specific Dyslexia*, Whyte suggests that

> the middle-class child – and, above all else, the middle-class boy – was regarded simply as normative ... The belief that 'intellectually retarded children without an organic brain disorder never, or practically never, come from middle-class families' was so widespread that it was repeated by contemporaries even when the evidence in fact suggested quite the contrary. The process of selection for this study was biased in favour of the middle-class as a result. The criteria for inclusion prioritized performance in I.Q. tests, yet it was well understood at the time that middle-class children invariably outperformed their poorer contemporaries. The researchers also found that 'Among those excluded on the grounds of emotional disturbance, the proportion of boys from State schools was greater than those from independent schools'. As the existence and extent of 'emotional disturbance' was determined in no small part by the subjective reports drawn up by these schools, there were undeniably class-based elements even to this apparently objective judgement.[57]

Certainly, Naidoo's sample was heavily tilted toward middle-class pupils, reflecting the population (the cohort of the Word Blind Centre) from which it was drawn. Naidoo foregrounded IQ in her selection criteria because it was believed at the time that low IQ was a cause of reading difficulties, independent of dyslexia. The same was true of emotional 'disturbance'. Of course, these measures were freighted with class connotations. At the same time, Naidoo's findings indicated that the problem of dyslexia was not restricted to any particular group. Despite her small sample, Naidoo noted that it provided 'no evidence that boys in private schools are more liable to specific reading or specific spelling problems than boys attending State schools'.[58] Naidoo also commented approvingly of a statement by Maisie Holt at the word-blindness conference of 1962: 'Holt, in contrast to some of the others, pointed out that word-blindness might occur in children of any I.Q.'[59]

Nevertheless, the demographics of pupils at the Word Blind Centre generally mirrored those of the centre's staff, an august array of doctors and psychologists. Alfred White Franklin was a member of London's prestigious Athenaeum Club, whose membership was – and remains – composed of those who have achieved some kind of distinction in science or literature or the arts.[60] Oliver Zangwill was a fellow of the Royal Society and president of the British Psychological Society.[61] Wilfrid Sheldon was physician-paediatrician to the Royal Household of Queen Elizabeth II between 1952 and 1971, and was knighted for his services in 1959.[62] Teachers at the centre mostly came from backgrounds that had enabled them to pursue their interest in reading disorders, including at university, which placed them in an educational elite. While Sandhya Naidoo insisted that at least initial assessments should be provided free, nascent dyslexia provision in Britain at the Word Blind Centre was a largely middle-class preserve.

The Closure of the Word Blind Centre: Loose Ends, Legacies, and Future Directions for Dyslexia

The Word Blind Centre had always been intended as a temporary venture. Initial funding was for five years, but was extended by the ICAA after high demand for the centre's services and after further lobbying by White Franklin and others. There was, though, a limit to the ICAA's resources. The centre

Dyslexia Discussed (1962–72)

was wound down from 1971, with pupils transferred from the Bloomsbury site to another in London.[63] Funds were finally exhausted by 1972.

Sandhya Naidoo viewed the closure in a bittersweet light, highlighting in *Specific Dyslexia* the accomplishments of the centre, but also the distance yet to travel in achieving widespread support for children with dyslexia. Reflecting in 1972, she wrote,

> The Centre has closed and the staff dispersed. Happily plans for further help have been made for most of the children. Those who have taken part in this enterprise may be allowed to combine with gratitude for the opportunity to serve, a modicum of pride in having gained more recognition and secured more sympathy and help for a group of disadvantaged pupils. They all share disappointment that the day has not yet dawned when responsibility for providing for the special needs of this group is fully recognized throughout the education service. They must be content with the thought that they have brought that dawn a little nearer ... The psychologists, teachers, the administrative and secretarial staff at the Centre and at headquarters have certainly earned the gratitude of dyslexic children and their families.[64]

Naidoo, as we have seen, continued to work with children with language difficulties, many of whom likely possessed dyslexia, as headmistress of a specialist school.

The end of the Word Blind Centre was marked by a final conference, mirroring the conference that had heralded its opening. This was convened by Alfred White Franklin in January 1972, and was fittingly entitled, 'Dyslexia, Where Now?'[65] By this time, White Franklin's professional attentions, too, were moving elsewhere. In 1970 he retired from clinical practice, but became a pioneer in the understanding and prevention of child abuse. He was a leading figure in the Tunbridge Wells Group, a gathering of professionals who ultimately founded the British Association for the Study and Prevention of Child Abuse and Neglect. The 1972 conference represented his final professional contribution to the study of dyslexia. At the conference, White Franklin addressed what he felt were the centre's achievements, as well as its shortcomings. While White Franklin believed that the Word

Blind Centre had served to put dyslexia on the public and political radar, and had helped a great many children directly through its assessment and specialist teaching, he acknowledged that its focus on middle-class pupils had created an unfortunate association in the popular consciousness – the association warned of by Alex Bannatyne nearly a decade earlier.[66] He also admitted that the centre's lack of a clear definition of dyslexia, and an easily administered test for young children, had led to confusion about what the condition was.[67] White Franklin finished by offering an olive branch to educational psychologists, some of whom were still sceptical of the term and of the role of medical professionals in its treatment. He indicated that in the future it would be they, rather than neurologists or doctors, who would take the lead in providing support, with reading difficulties best treated by educational interventions.[68]

As to what these educational interventions should be, White Franklin and Naidoo ensured that the approaches of the Word Blind Centre were recorded with the publication, in 1971, of the instructional book *Assessment and Teaching of Dyslexic Children*.[69] This short, edited collection was produced at the request of teachers, who wanted more information on how to assist learners with dyslexia. It was based on a series of public lectures held at the centre during 1969: 'The lectures cover the problems of diagnosis, assessment, and psychological testing, and then discuss in practical detail some of the methods of training these disabled children. It is now generally accepted that true dyslexia is a relatively uncommon condition. There are thus few remedial teachers who have a sufficiently wide experience to choose the most appropriate form of treatment for these children, who present with a range of difficulties and aptitudes.'[70] The book was one of the first guides for identifying and treating dyslexia, if not a formal manual in the style of the Orton-Gillingham-Stillman method. It showed that, while Naidoo may have been correct in saying that much of the education service still viewed dyslexia with scepticism, there also existed teachers who wanted more information.

Elsewhere, those in the orbit of the Word Blind Centre went on to have various degrees of engagement with dyslexia in the years ahead. In an effort to bring greater clarity to the term, Macdonald Critchley, as president of the World Federation of Neurology between 1965 and 1973, publicised a landmark definition of dyslexia in 1968 (discussed further below). This firmly enshrined the discrepancy definition of dyslexia, identifying dyslexia as a diagnosis only when general abilities were otherwise sound.

In 1970, as the Word Blind Centre began to wind down, Critchley also published *The Dyslexic Child*, an expansion of his 1964 work, *Developmental Dyslexia*.[71] A survey of existing research rather than a research contribution in its own right like Naidoo's *Specific Dyslexia*, *The Dyslexic Child* highlighted the achievements of the Word Blind Centre. He also set the centre's work in a global context. While the United States and Britain were at the forefront of dyslexia research and provision, Critchley believed that 'outside the English-speaking world, the pace has been almost as rapid. Special discussions upon this subject have been held in Vienna, and, largely stimulated by the World Federation of Neurology, work has been forging ahead in France, Belgium, Germany, Latin America, Spain, Czechoslovakia, Bulgaria, Romania, Taiwan; as well as France and Belgium.'[72] The Word Blind Centre was both contemporaneous with, and contributory to, a new international landscape of dyslexia awareness and interest.

In research, leading contributors to the science of reading and dyslexia in the years ahead included Donald Shankweiler at the University of Connecticut, who joined other American researchers such as Norman Geschwind at Harvard Medical School and Frank Vellutino at the University at Albany in New York. Tim Miles at the University College of North Wales, and his wife, Elaine, continued to work on a screening test for dyslexia, later formalised as the Bangor Dyslexia Test, responding to White Franklin's suggestion that greater rigour was required in identifying dyslexia and in differentiating it from other reading and learning difficulties. Teachers at the Word Blind Centre, including Helen Arkell and Gill Cotterell, became leading lights in dyslexia teaching and provision in Britain. Marion Welchman, one of the 'plain parents' referred to by Alfred White Franklin in his opening address at the word-blindness conference of 1962, went on to become the driving force behind the creation of the British Dyslexia Association. Together, these individuals were at the vanguard of the dyslexia movement from the early 1970s.

Beyond those involved with the Word Blind Centre, the immediate legacies of the centre were several. In 1970, dyslexia was mentioned for the first time in a parliamentary act: the Chronically Sick and Disabled Persons Act.

In part, this reference seems to have been a reaction to the increasing number of requests for support to local education authorities by parents; requests assisted by the Word Blind Centre when children attended the same. The act stated that local education authorities should provide specialist support for children with dyslexia in schools, with the implication that, if this was not possible, special arrangements should be made elsewhere, including at venues such as the Word Blind Centre. Two years later, progress toward political recognition was hindered by the publication of the Tizard report, *Children with Specific Reading Difficulties*. This claimed that, as far as research on dyslexia was concerned, the jury was still out.[73] However, the Word Blind Centre, both through its presence and its lobbying of education officials, had at least put dyslexia on the agenda of policymakers. This foundation would be built upon by the organisations that followed in its wake.

The centre also influenced knowledge of dyslexia in the public sphere. Two weeks before the final 1972 conference, on 12 January, dyslexia was discussed on the BBC Two documentary and current affairs series *Man Alive*. At the conference, White Franklin hailed the two-part programme as a possible watershed in achieving public acceptance of the term.[74] The show's synopsis framed dyslexia in a way highly similar to Naidoo's case histories in *Specific Dyslexia*, albeit with a more sensational opening:

> Can you read this? Could you write it? Robert Payne is a bright 16-year-old – normal in every way except that he can barely read and write. He's just one of the bright, likeable children in tonight's *Man Alive*. He suffers from what some experts call dyslexia. Dyslexic children find it very difficult to learn what comes so naturally to most of us. They are not necessarily dull – indeed, many are more intelligent than average. But they often spend their school lives in misery and frustration – thought of as stupid. Is enough being done for them? Why do some experts argue that dyslexia is nothing but a label used to excuse backward children? In the first of two programmes, Jim Douglas Henry and a *Man Alive* team look at those who are frequently written off with 'could do better'.[75]

The programme was largely a talking shop, but it represented one of the first occasions when dyslexia was put before such a large audience, and by a broadcaster with global reach. By 1970, the television revolution had firmly arrived, and nearly 92 per cent of households in Britain possessed a television set, making the potential viewership of the two-part programme substantial.[76] The themes that *Man Alive* discussed – that dyslexia might be associated with high intelligence, that children with dyslexia were often written off at school as slow or indolent, that some educational psychologists disputed its very existence – remained key elements of the dyslexia story in the decades ahead.

Writing over forty years after the Word Blind Centre's closure, Tim Miles summarised the centre's work in an appropriate tribute: 'The Invalid Children's Aid Association [by way of the Word Blind Centre] had primed the pump, which was the original intention: enough had been done to convince at least a minority of people that there was something here which was worth investigating. It was for others to determine how the ideas initiated at the Centre might be developed.'[77]

Chapter 3 – Key Points
- The Word Blind Centre, founded in 1962, was one of the first specialist dyslexia centres in the world
- The centre's first director was Sandhya Naidoo, who published the first detailed account of children with dyslexia in 1972, the same year that a BBC documentary with global reach brought dyslexia to public attention
- The Word Blind Centre, and the conference that preceded it, were meeting places for an international array of dyslexia researchers
- The Word Blind Centre, and its staff, exemplified the changing class and gender dynamics of the dyslexia movement

4

Researching Dyslexia: From the Discrepancy Definition to Cognitive Neuroscience (1964-2009)

Science has been the backdrop to much of dyslexia's history. Political and social efforts at achieving recognition for dyslexia inevitably depended upon how scientists were studying dyslexia and what their contemporary findings were. Indeed, the knowledge accruing through systematic observation and experimentation has always been used to determine how dyslexia is identified and has motivated its treatment, making science a key element of dyslexia's cultural, social, and political histories. Nonetheless, scientific advances have their own story. This chapter documents the main trends in the field of dyslexia research since the pioneering work of medical specialists, such as Samuel Orton, in the early twentieth century, highlighting key findings across dyslexia's scientific history. In doing so, it distinguishes between research that has attempted to (1) understand the causes of dyslexia, and (2) apply that knowledge to assessment and teaching.[1] The medical model upon which much of this science has been based is only one way of understanding dyslexia, as we have seen, but it has been an important one in the dyslexia story.

This chapter begins with an overview of the emerging research base on dyslexia at the time of the founding of the Word Blind Centre in 1962. The centre was key to bringing the concept of dyslexia to initial public awareness, to finding ways to assist learners with dyslexia, and to providing an evidence base that dyslexia support organizations from the 1970s could bring to the attention of policymakers. In this way, the Word Blind Centre's work was oriented principally toward *applying* dyslexia's nascent science to assessment

Researching Dyslexia (1964–2009)

and teaching. At the same time, research conducted by the Word Blind Centre, and by researchers geographically proximate to the centre in London, created a foundation for what might be called more strictly *academic* research on dyslexia, directed at elucidating dyslexia's putative causes, not necessarily (although sometimes) informing pedagogy. In practice, there has often been a gap between the findings of research and their translation into educational practice, and the focus here is on the former.

This chapter does not seek to provide a comprehensive history of dyslexia research – a task that would require its own monograph. Rather, it profiles key theorists and the theories that they proposed, showing how these developed into dyslexia as the term is understood in the twenty-first century. In so doing, it takes us from the discrepancy diagnostic model, through the phonological deficit hypothesis, up to current theoretical perspectives. While our focus is on British research, the interactions between researchers in Britain and (in particular) North America were such that proper coverage requires an international perspective. This trans-Atlanticism magnified the scope and impact of dyslexia research, while introducing greater competition between researchers and, at times, disagreement. In addition, it meant that the focus of initial dyslexia research was on how dyslexia manifested in English, rather than in other orthographies – a focus that continues, in large part, to the present day.

The Foundations of a New Dyslexia Science (1960–70)

The dawn of the modern-day concept of dyslexia was in the early 1960s, contemporaneous with the emergence of research on the cognitive processes that underpin reading and learning to read – that is, the science of reading. Indeed, so many psychologists were working on reading during this period that it has been referred to as the '*via regia*' (royal road) of psychology. Many of the scientists in the field were studying visual perception and cross-modality processes, a happy coincidence that was to prove fruitful in influencing the direction of dyslexia research in a mid-twentieth-century educational landscape in which literacy skills were becoming increasingly central to successful individual outcomes.

Fuelled by the plethora of reversal errors observed by Samuel T. Orton in the reading and writing of those with dyslexia, and particularly the confusions between *b* and *d*, much of the early research on cognitive aspects of dyslexia focused on the investigation of perceptual deficits.[2] However, dyslexia researchers from the mid-twentieth century onward discovered something else – it turned out that confusions between letters such as *k/g* and *t/d* were also common in those with dyslexia, and not easily accounted for by theories positing visual perceptual problems.[3] Rather, these errors suggested to these early researchers that language difficulties, and more specifically, problems in differentiating speech sounds, might underlie dyslexia. Furthermore, since reading was an example par excellence of a task that requires mapping between visual (symbol) and auditory (sound) modalities, other early researchers argued for the importance of cross-modal transfer – that is, the ability for multiple senses to work together effectively.[4] Thus, a further theory was that the cause of such errors was a cross-modal coding deficit.

While research on the cognitive aspects of dyslexia began to take off, researchers also became interested in individual differences in dyslexia, including those in the orbit of the Word Blind Centre.[5] The neuropsychologist Elizabeth Warrington, for example, began seeing children at the National Hospital for Nervous Diseases in Queen Square, London, in the early 1960s. The spur for Warrington's interest appears not to have been the Word Blind Centre, which was located only a few hundred yards away from the hospital, but rather Oliver Zangwill, the Cambridge psychologist who sat on the Word Blind Committee and also held an honorary position in the Department of Psychiatry at the National Hospital as its first neuropsychologist. There, Zangwill held a weekly clinic, and by 1954 an associated lectureship in neuropsychology was established. (Zangwill, as we have seen, was also influential in developing Sandhya Naidoo's interest in dyslexia.) Following Warrington's graduation from University College London, she was appointed research assistant to the first post-holder of the neuropsychology lectureship, George Etlinger, and later became his successor. It was during her time as research assistant that she was introduced to Macdonald Critchley who, in his private practice in Queen Square, 'was trying to get children with dyslexia a label rather than [them] being considered "dim"'.[6] To assist his diagnosis, Critchley began sending children to see Warrington, asking her to undertake IQ tests with the children. Warrington recalls being paid five pounds per child for this responsibility, a welcome stipend at the time. More importantly, it led her to become curious as to how different manifestations of dyslexia linked to biological differences in the brain.[7]

Broadly, Warrington and her co-researchers identified two 'kinds' of dyslexia: (1) children with higher verbal than performance IQ, who typically resembled adults with 'Gerstmann syndrome', a neurological condition characterized by poor spelling and poor arithmetic with relatively better reading; and (2) children with a contrasting profile of better non-verbal than verbal skills, who more closely resembled children with childhood aphasia – that is, possible damage to the left side of the brain, which governs language and speech.[8]

However, despite the limited scope of dyslexia research at this time, both academically and geographically, certain differences in approach began to emerge between the more applied work of the Word Blind Centre and the science of Warrington and others. Most notably, there was an increasing divergence between researchers who were following their clinical observations to devise assessment protocols, and researchers who were more interested in the 'pure' academic study of dyslexia. In the former group, notable researchers included Sandhya Naidoo, Margaret Newton, and Tim Miles, all of whom were involved with the treatment-oriented Word Blind Centre.[9] In the latter group, other scientific approaches were favoured, including the neuropsychological approach of Warrington, which would later become the foundation of one of the dominant theoretical approaches to dyslexia of the 1980s and 1990s: cognitive neuropsychology.

By the end of the 1960s, considerable clinical experience of dyslexia had accumulated, and knowledge of appropriate interventions was reaching a consensus, in large part because of the work of those at the Word Blind Centre.[10] In this way, dyslexia's *applied* science was making substantial advances. There was a clear need, however, to bring greater rigour to dyslexia's *academic* science. This was to be achieved in two ways: first, through large population studies of representative samples, free of clinical bias (in other words, seeing whether studies on small groups of children could be replicated in larger groups by applying more rigorous scientific methodologies); and second, through laboratory-based experimental studies with appropriate comparison (control) groups of so-called 'normal readers'.[11] This research was contemporaneous with the work of the Word Blind Centre, but focused more on creating a concerted evidence base for dyslexia, rather than, at least in the first instance, seeking to apply this research to the struggling reader.

Epidemiology and the Isle of Wight Study (1964-74)

By the early 1960s, as we have seen, understanding of dyslexia was growing, but it remained piecemeal, and questions continued in political circles and society about its very existence. While case histories of dyslexia were increasing, and organizations like the Word Blind Centre were undertaking detailed work with small groups of children with dyslexia, there was little idea of the scope and scale of dyslexia – in science or elsewhere. To tackle this omission, in 1964, the team led by Michael Rutter and William (Bill) Yule began one of the first detailed *population* studies of reading difficulties, which also explored the value of the term dyslexia. The Isle of Wight study was one of a series of studies of the entire population of nine- to eleven-year-old children residing on that island, off the south coast of England, which investigated the prevalence of educational, psychiatric, and other 'handicapping' disorders.[12] The study offered the ideal opportunity to test out the validity of the definition of 'dyslexia' agreed by the World Federation of Neurology in 1968, to which Macdonald Critchley of the Word Blind Centre had contributed: '[Dyslexia is] a disorder manifested by difficulty in learning to read despite conventional instruction, adequate intelligence and socio-cultural opportunity. It is dependent upon fundamental cognitive disabilities which are frequently of constitutional origin.'[13]

This definition crystallised some of the differences between dyslexia's applied and research-based science at this time. While the definition could be understood by broad audiences, which was useful for those working toward greater social and political recognition of dyslexia, it lacked scientific specificity. The term 'constitutional', in particular, was an offending word for some, carrying with it the implication that there was little to be done about dyslexia, but also skirting the issue of whether or not dyslexia was genetic in origin. However, if it was valid to classify dyslexia as a specific childhood disorder with defined signs and symptoms – including speech and language difficulties, perceptual deficits, rotation and reversal errors – the children with the disorder would differ in these symptoms from other types of poor

Researching Dyslexia (1964–2009)

reader who, like them, were failing to learn to read. As such, one of the objectives of the Isle of Wight study was to determine whether dyslexia, as a specific diagnostic category, existed.

The starting point for the Isle of Wight study was to assess the children who participated on measures of intelligence (IQ) and of reading, and then to use statistical methods to estimate the relationship between intelligence and reading ability in this population. The next step was to use regression (a form of correlation analysis) to predict, for all of the children, the level of reading to be expected based on their age and IQ. Turning to individual children, it was then possible to compare the level of reading each of them attained on the reading test with that which was to be expected according to the population-based 'norm'. Hypothetically, this last step permitted the differentiation of two groups of poor readers: first, children whose level of reading was discrepant with their age and IQ (who could be defined as 'dyslexic' under the prevailing definition); and second, children who were also poor readers, but whose reading was not out of line with their age and IQ (who would not have received a dyslexia diagnosis at the time).

The findings of the study were clear: these two hypothesised groups *did* exist. Bill Yule, Michael Rutter, and their colleagues coined the term 'specific reading retardation' for the former (dyslexia) group, and the term 'general reading backwardness' for the group of poor readers who were not IQ-discrepant.[14] In other words, this first population study of reading difficulties had found evidence for dyslexia, even if it did not employ that term. Reflecting on this linguistic choice, Yule recalled that, even by the 1960s, the range of dyslexia definitions was extensive, which was why the authors of the study were reticent to employ 'dyslexia' in the Isle of Wight study.[15] That many of the underlying features of dyslexia existed, but that dyslexia itself was a nebulous term, would form a recurring element in scientific discussions of dyslexia, as well as broader societal and political debates in the decades ahead.

The Isle of Wight study's findings contrasted with those of earlier studies suggesting that there were no qualitative differences among different types of poor reader, and that any differences (for example, between those with specific and those with more general difficulties in reading) existed on a continuum or spectrum. An example of such work was that of Eve Malmquist, a Swedish teacher and psychologist, who in 1958 published her PhD thesis, 'Factors relating to Reading Disabilities in the First Grade of the Elementary School'. The study investigated the early manifestations of dyslexia after the first year of schooling, when children were being introduced to reading.[16] Building on this early work, Malmquist became an influential figure in Sweden with her focus shifting from trying to understand the causes of dyslexia to pedagogical approaches to its remediation.

The Isle of Wight study reported several other important findings, elucidating the characteristics of children with dyslexia. In terms of sex ratio, there were approximately three boys to every girl with 'specific reading retardation', while equal numbers of boys and girls were classified as 'generally backward' readers – in other words, dyslexia appeared to be significantly more common in boys than in girls. The two groups also differed in the progress that they made in reading and spelling – children with specific reading difficulties made less progress in reading and spelling over time than generally backward readers.[17] However, beyond this, differences between the two groups were relatively few: while those with specific reading retardation used more complex language, both groups had experienced speech and language problems, and a family history of reading (and speech) difficulties was common. Together, these findings suggested that, in order to understand dyslexia, it would be important to consider how problems with written language related to earlier – and perhaps ongoing – language difficulties. The findings were also consistent with a possible genetic origin of dyslexia, or, at the very least, highlighted familial traits in reading difficulties. A few years later, a similar study in inner-city London by the same research group reported approximately double the prevalence of specific reading retardation compared with that for the Isle of Wight.[18] Such differences pointed to the important and often neglected role of environmental factors in the aetiology of dyslexia; how the environment interacts with genetic factors was to become a contentious issue in later years.

The Isle of Wight study was a landmark moment in dyslexia science, albeit a slightly ironic one given its reticence to use the term 'dyslexia': it proved that some children possessed specific difficulties with learning to read. In many ways, it achieved for academic research on dyslexia what the Word Blind Centre achieved for applied research, putting dyslexia firmly on the scientific, as well as educational, map. Moreover, the Isle of Wight study set a benchmark for an expanding psychology of dyslexia in the decades ahead, to which North American researchers would make key contributions.

The Rise of the Psychological Perspective on Dyslexia (1970-80)

The science of dyslexia prospered in the 1970s, led by pioneers in the United States and building on studies like that in the Isle of Wight. By the end of the decade, the psychologist Frank Vellutino's landmark review had reinterpreted the perceptual deficit hypothesis of dyslexia, focusing attention on dyslexia as a phonological-decoding issue.[19] By this time, the pre-eminent place of psychology in addressing reading difficulties was cemented, with psychological investigations producing some of the most compelling research findings. A very simple experiment from Vellutino's reading research lab at the University of Albany, New York, illustrated his main argument and attested to the influence of psychological methods in understanding dyslexia. In this study, children with dyslexia and normal readers copied printed words of three, four, or five letters from memory, following a short exposure.[20] As expected, the children with dyslexia performed poorly on this task compared to controls, suggestive of a visual memory deficit. However, in another version of the task, the children copied words printed in Hebrew, a writing system with which neither they nor the controls were familiar. In this case, both groups performed at the same level. The researchers concluded that the problem for the children with dyslexia was one of decoding the words, rather than of remembering their visual sequence.

Even more enduring, perhaps, was work that emanated from the tradition of speech and linguistic sciences, conducted by the renowned Haskins group at Yale University from the late 1960s.[21] This work was not about dyslexia, per se, but about learning to read; nonetheless, it had profound implications for the understanding of dyslexia, testifying to the mutual support of the science of reading and dyslexia science. Careful experimentation, coupled with insights from teaching, led Isabelle Liberman, Donald Shankweiler, and colleagues to elucidate the role of the speech code in learning to read.[22] In short, they showed that, although from about four years of age a child could break up a word into syllables (e.g., butt-er-cup), it was not until later, at age five to six years, that children could tap out the single speech sounds in words (phonemes) (e.g., pin-> [p] [I] [n]). It was argued that this transition, referred to as the acquisition of phoneme awareness, was problematic for children with dyslexia, and without phoneme awareness, insight into the alphabetic principle, as required for the development of decoding skills, was not possible.[23]

These two new ideas – that of dyslexia as a verbal deficit and as a deficit in phonological awareness – together inspired a change in the theoretical framework used to investigate dyslexia in its academic science. Rather than considering dyslexia as a clinical entity, investigators began to consider dyslexia against the backdrop of models of reading development. A change in methodology was also to follow. Since dyslexia was defined by poor reading, it became obvious that care should be taken to avoid circular arguments – put simply, to guard against experimentation that simply focused on processes that were impaired *because of* poor reading, confusing cause with consequence. Crucial was the selection of appropriate comparison (control) groups.[24] Rather than recruiting children of the same age as the children with dyslexia, the change was to include a comparison group of younger children of similar reading skill – the so-called 'reading age matched' design. If a deficit could be demonstrated in children with dyslexia after their low level of reading was taken into account, then it was more likely to be a specific causal deficit. This method was, by the late 1970s, firmly established in Britain, notably in the doctoral work of Charles Hulme and Maggie Snowling, students of Peter Bryant in Oxford and Uta Frith in London, respectively.[25] By the close of the 1970s, the stage was set for research on dyslexia from a cognitive-developmental perspective.

Phonological Deficits and the Demise of the Discrepancy Definition (1980–90)

During the 1980s, the experimental approach to dyslexia was pursued by groups on both sides of the Atlantic. Of prime importance was the study of memory processes, building on one of the cardinal symptoms of dyslexia – a verbal short-term memory deficit.[26] Research also embraced naming deficits, particularly rapid naming and verbal repetition (often characterized as phonological memory).[27] More broadly, the psychologist Uta Frith, at University College London, published the first edited volume focusing on cognitive approaches to spelling (as distinct from the reading process) in 1980.[28]

The 1980s saw a growing interest in the emerging sub-discipline of cognitive neuropsychology, building on the earlier description of subtypes of acquired dyslexia in patients who had sustained stroke or head injury.[29] The first studies published within this framework referenced the then-dominant dual-route model of reading. This model posited a 'direct route' for the pronunciation of irregular or exception words and an 'indirect route' allowing the translation of print to pronunciation via the use of grapheme-phoneme rules. The separation of these two routes, or processes, was confirmed by data from neuropsychological patients. Among these patients, the direct route was selectively impaired in 'surface dyslexia'. This was defined as an ability to decode nonwords (pseudowords that conform to the rules of a language, but do not actually exist, such as 'bave' in English), but with a specific deficit in reading irregular or exception words (words that are not pronounced as one might expect from the most frequent pronunciation of the letter strings they contain, e.g., reading 'broad' as 'brode'). In contrast, the phonological route was selectively impaired in 'phonological dyslexia', wherein patients can read words accurately, but cannot decode unfamiliar words or 'nonwords'.[30] These single case studies demonstrated a so-called double dissociation between different reading processes within the same individual. Thus, in the early 1980s, Christine Temple and John Marshall at the University of Oxford described the first case of developmental phonological dyslexia in a child who could read words (by the direct route) significantly better than nonwords.[31] In contrast, the psychologist Max Coltheart and his colleagues at Birkbeck College, London, reported the case of a boy with 'developmental surface dyslexia', who could read nonwords by the phonological route easily, but could not read exception words.[32] While certainly these cases of atypical reading in children provided some validation of a cognitive model of reading, it was less clear that they broke new ground in describing the nature, causes, or developmental course of childhood dyslexia.

Indeed, the publication of these cases provoked a quiet backlash from developmental psychologists, perhaps best exemplified by the title of Uta Frith's seminal paper, 'Beneath the Surface of Developmental Dyslexia'.[33]

Other researchers focused on the lack of control groups, the failure to take account of differences in reading instruction that might encourage the use of different reading strategies, and the lack of stability of these striking reading profiles over time.[34] However, it was also apparent that, for some children with poor phonological skills, the phonological dyslexic profile was intransigent despite intervention, and this provided a vital clue as to the nature of the underlying difficulty.[35]

Drawing together experimental studies highlighting memory and naming deficits in dyslexia, with research on the reading (and to a lesser extent spelling) profile of those with dyslexia, Keith Stanovich at the Ontario Institute for Studies in Education in Canada, in a refinement of the verbal deficit hypothesis, made two critical points in the late 1980s: first, that dyslexia could be conceptualized as a core phonological processing deficit, present regardless of general cognitive ability; and second, that poor readers experienced limited print exposure.[36] Stanovich went on to hypothesize that a low level of reading experience has a negative effect on the development of verbal ability. This could in principle lead to a decrease in IQ over time in poor readers relative to their peers who read well – the so-called Matthew effect in reading, in which children who read well read more and more, increasing their achievement gap relative to poor readers.[37] While the prediction of a Matthew effect has not been upheld in precisely the form that it was cast at the time, it seems clear that these statements were instrumental in the demise of the discrepancy definition of dyslexia.[38] From then on, the use of the dyslexia label principally for those of high intelligence became untenable – ending an association implicit since the earliest Victorian case studies of children with word-blindness, such as William Pringle Morgan's description of Percy, and which had been lent further support by the definition of the World Federation of Neurology from 1968.[39]

The Dawn of Genetic Approaches to Dyslexia (1980s–)

The 1980s also saw the burgeoning of another quite different approach to the study of reading and reading disorders: behaviour genetics. It had been known for many years that dyslexia runs in families – as we have seen, Victorian medics speculated on this, and evidence was provided by the Isle of Wight study, amongst other research.[40] However, since families frequently share environments as well as genes, it was not possible to say for sure if there was a significant genetic contribution to dyslexia. For many years, the study of twins had been informative. While identical (monozygotic) twins share all of their segregating genes, non-identical (dizygotic) twins are just like normal siblings and share only 50 per cent of their genes, on average. Early studies examining concordance rates for dyslexia found that if one twin was dyslexic (the proband) then it was more likely that the co-twin would be too, especially if they were monozygotic.[41] This kind of finding – higher concordance rates for monozygotic than for dizygotic twins – provided evidence that genetic factors contributed to dyslexia.

However, reading ability is a dimension and to split the population of readers into 'dyslexic' and 'not dyslexic' has to an extent been arbitrary; reading is a trait that is continuous in the population and a key question is whether the genes that explain variability in reading across the population are the same as those which predict dyslexia. Answering this question would be one of the first steps for behaviour genetics. The 1980s also saw the confluence of what was known about the cognitive predictors of reading skills with what was known about familial factors in the aetiology of dyslexia, and this formed an early research agenda for genetic approaches that would increasingly come to prominence.

In the 1980s, a research group in Colorado pioneered a new approach to understanding the genetic basis of reading and reading disability.[42] This approach depended upon the work of the behaviour geneticists John DeFries and David Fulker and their colleagues, who developed a new statistical technique that would allow estimates of the relative influence of genetic and environmental factors on reading ability. Data from a large sample of monozygotic and dizygotic twins, who had been assessed on measures of intelligence, reading, spelling, and related cognitive tasks, provided a rich source for these analyses.[43] The logic was simple, even if the mathematical model was complicated. The model assumes that for a continuous trait (in this case, reading ability), the measured ability of the co-twins is more similar if they are monozygotic than dizygotic. Put another way, a co-twin's measured reading will be more similar to that of the proband if the twins are monozygotic (100 per cent of genes shared); if they are dizygotic (50 per cent of genes shared), the co-twin's reading skill will be closer to that of the population average.

The statistical treatment of data within the DeFries and Fulker model (and its subsequent modifications) allows the 'parcelling' of variation in reading skills between co-twins into contributions from genes and from two environmental components: environments shared between co-twins (e.g., the home environment) and so-called 'non-shared' environments specific to one twin (e.g., hospitalization or, in some cases, different schools). Estimates of the genetic contribution to reading (heritability) range from zero to one, where one would mean that all of the variation between co-twins is under the control of genetic factors. Findings from the first Colorado studies of reading as a cognitive process, led by the psychologist Richard Olson, suggested that word reading accuracy was significantly heritable, as was spelling.[44] Reading comprehension, though, depended more on environmental factors – findings which appeared to make sense given the important role of vocabulary, a skill dependent upon environmental input, on being able to read with understanding.[45] Current estimates of the heritability of reading based on meta-analyses are about 0.6 and there is no evidence of differential genetic influences at the lower end of the distribution of reading skill (dyslexia) or at the higher end.[46]

The work of the Colorado group led to another important discovery in dyslexia science. Using data from the large battery of tests that children had been given by this group, it was possible to measure the heritability not only of reading but also of its subskills (word and nonword decoding), and the heritability of the skills that were thought to be a problem for those with dyslexia. These included deficits in phonological awareness, processing speed, and verbal memory.[47] Important theoretically was the finding that not only was reading heritable, but so were the skills that underpin it – specifically, phonological skills.

Taken together, these findings provided converging evidence for the phonological deficit hypothesis of dyslexia. They also fuelled interest in the molecular genetics of dyslexia: the same group of Colorado scientists was the first to report gene markers associated with dyslexia on chromosome 15, findings that were foundational for later studies.[48] In subsequent behavioural work, the Colorado group went on to show that the genetic contribution to reading for twins with the 'phonological dyslexic' profile was higher than the contribution to reading for those with the 'surface dyslexic' profile (described above).[49] They interpreted the finding in a way that would have found favour with Samuel T. Orton some sixty years earlier, namely that there was a strong genetic component to phonological dyslexia.[50]

Studies of Children at 'Family Risk' of Dyslexia (1990-)

By the close of the 1980s, the conceptualization of dyslexia that had been established by researchers, principally but not only in the United States and in the United Kingdom, was of dyslexia as a heritable phonological deficit that compromised learning to read by affecting the development of decoding, while reading comprehension remained relatively unimpaired (except insofar as poor decoding is a bottleneck to reading for meaning). This then is a causal hypothesis.[51] To test it, two kinds of study were undertaken from the 1990s onwards. First, if poor phonology causes poor reading, then, by the law of causal precedence, phonological deficits should be present in children before they (fail to) learn to read; second, interventions to improve phonological skills should, by definition, improve reading.

With genetic studies of dyslexia as a backdrop, a new form of investigation emerged to test this theory in the 1990s, pioneered by the psychologist Hollis Scarborough at Haskins Laboratories at Yale University, and later adopted by researchers worldwide: the family-risk study.[52] The basic method of the family-risk study involves following pre-school children who are at family risk of dyslexia by virtue of having a first-degree relative (i.e., parent or sibling) with dyslexia. Later, having assessed the children's reading (and sometimes spelling), children are classified according to reading status (dyslexic versus 'normal' reader). Finally, the researchers conduct retrospective analyses to examine the precursors of dyslexia in the pre-school period, before reading instruction begins. This method had the distinct advantage of removing the bias inherent in earlier studies which recruited individuals with dyslexia following a formal clinical or educational diagnosis.[53]

Scarborough's study was small-scale, but nonetheless important. In the study, she followed thirty-four children at family risk of dyslexia from two and a half years of age to eight years of age. At age eight, some 65 per cent of this group were assessed as having dyslexia. Their early development could then be compared with that of a control group who had no family history of reading difficulty and with their contemporaries who were at family risk, but had normal skill levels in reading.

Scarborough's findings were salutary – and not what had been predicted by those who (still) adhered to the discrepancy definition of dyslexia.[54] Rather than pinpointing specific phonological deficits, these studies revealed that children who went on to be diagnosed with dyslexia experienced pre-school language difficulties beyond the phonological domain, including difficulties in the development of expressive language skills, vocabulary, and speech production. Further, and a possible key to their later emerging dyslexia, when these children started school they had poorer letter-knowledge and less well-developed phonological awareness than children in the control and family-risk unimpaired groups, who were similar in terms of socio-economic background.

Following Scarborough's work in the 1990s, family-risk studies of dyslexia burgeoned.[55] By the end of the decade, many from English-speaking communities had been published, but one of the largest was reported by Heikki Lyttinen's group in Jyväskylä, Finland, showing how dyslexia research was expanding beyond the anglophone world (or, perhaps, re-emerging beyond the anglophone world, given dyslexia's initial identification by German doctors and ophthalmologists).[56] All, including one study conducted in Britain, were converging on the findings of Scarborough: that the precursors of dyslexia were in the spoken language system.[57] In short, these studies claimed that children destined to be poor readers come to the task of learning to read with poorly developed phonological skills, but the development of their other language skills is also, on average, delayed. The next and obvious question was whether poor language, and/or poor phonological skill, was the cause of dyslexia.

Testing the Causal Hypothesis (1990-)

The best way to test a causal hypothesis is via a training study: 'if the cause of Y disorder is X, then training X should improve Y'.[58] Although there was much well-received practice concerning teaching children with dyslexia,

Researching Dyslexia (1964–2009)

there were, by the 1990s, rather few studies that had put teaching methods to a rigorous test of efficacy – that is, that had tested interventions such as those developed by the Word Blind Centre and the applied researchers who followed in its wake. Two British studies were an exception. First, in 1983, Lynette Bradley and Peter Bryant at the University of Oxford conducted a training study in which intervention was delivered to children who were identified as 'at risk' of reading failure by virtue of their poor performance on a test of phonological awareness at four and five years of age.[59] The study was set up to test whether training children's phonological awareness would lead to an improvement in these children's reading skills. There were three forms of training: training in phonological awareness (referred to in this study as sound 'organization'), training in both phonological awareness and in letter–sound knowledge, and training in semantic categorization using the same materials as the sound categorization training (this was a treated control group). A further control group was unseen (that is, they were assessed before and after the intervention, but they did not receive any special treatment from the researchers as part of the experiment). The intervention ran over a period of two years, starting when the children were six years old. At the end of the intervention, the groups who had received the version of phonological training were ahead of both control groups in reading. However, it was only the group which had received training in phonological awareness *and* letter-knowledge that made significantly more progress; their reading attainment was some eight to ten months ahead of that of the unseen control group. This was an impressive finding at a time when using phonics in mainstream reading instruction was not in vogue, demonstrating again the complex interplay of the science of reading and of dyslexia science.

Building on this work, a much larger-scale study was conducted by the psychologists Peter Hatcher, Charles Hulme, and Andrew Ellis in the mid-1990s.[60] Working with the Cumbria local education authority in the north of England, Peter Hatcher and a team of educational psychologists assessed all of the seven-year-old pupils in the council's schools and identified the 10 per cent with the lowest reading scores (only some of these children had a formal diagnosis of dyslexia). These children were then allocated one of three forms of intervention as compared to 'business as usual', or normal reading instruction (although a small number were receiving remedial assistance). Each child in an intervention group received two one-to-one sessions of intervention, twice a week, for six months, delivered by a skilled peripatetic teacher employed by the remedial advisory service. Children in the 'reading intervention' group received a graded reading programme modelled on that of the New Zealand educationalist, Marie Clay; children in the phonological awareness group received training based on the sound categorization work of Bradley and Bryant; and a third group received reading intervention integrated with phonological awareness training and activities linking reading and phonological skills.[61] Their progress was reassessed at the end of the intervention and after a further nine months.

The findings were clear: it was the group who had received the programme that combined reading intervention with phonological awareness training that had made the greatest gains.[62] Although there was a trend for the group who had received phonological awareness training to be better at phonological awareness tasks at the end of the programme, this did not translate into stronger performance in reading (or spelling). At follow-up, gains were maintained in reading, but not in spelling (which, of course, had not been the focus of the training). Together with those of Bradley and Bryant a decade earlier, these findings showed that phonological awareness training alone was not as effective in promoting reading as training that also emphasized letter–sound correspondences. As such, the data did not clinch the argument that poor phonological awareness causes poor reading. However, these studies did not rule out the possibility that poor phonological awareness was one cause of poor reading which, when accompanied by poor letter-knowledge, could lead to dyslexia. Indeed, a study by Charles Hulme and colleagues several years later came to this conclusion.[63]

Dyslexia and the Brain (1990–)

A further trend observed in the 1990s in Britain was the advent of brain-imaging studies of cognitive processes. These built on the foundation of neuropsychology and took forward some of the first investigations of the 'dyslexic brain' by Al Galaburda, professor of neurology and neuroscience at Harvard University, and his colleagues in the United States, in the 1970s and 1980s.[64] The earlier studies had revealed abnormalities in the brains of young children with dyslexia, suggestive of an unusual pattern of neuronal circuitry with a likely prenatal origin, consistent with what might be anticipated of a disorder with genetic origins. However, they did not speak to the cognitive mechanisms that might be involved in reading and impaired in dyslexia. By the 1990s, technological advances had made it possible to view not only the structure of the brain, but also how it functions using brain imaging techniques (such as positron emission tomography [PET] or functional magnetic resonance imaging [fMRI]).[65] The initial studies of developmental disorders, including dyslexia, focused on adult participants with a history of the disorders.

In 1996, a group of neuroscientists in London published one of the first brain imaging studies of dyslexia.[66] In this study, they examined five adults with dyslexia who had documented histories of dyslexia as children whilst they carried out phonological processing tasks. One task involved deciding whether pairs of visually presented letters rhymed (e.g., 'b' and 'd' rhyme, but 'b' and 'w' do not), and another task required a memory search for a target letter in a series of successively presented letters and thus engaged verbal memory. Brain processing during these tasks was compared with that during two parallel visual processing tasks. The first of these required judgements to be made about the shape similarity of pairs of unfamiliar letters from the Korean alphabet, and the other was a memory search task for Korean letters that engaged visual memory. The analysis of these data involved what is known in brain imaging jargon as 'subtraction'. In essence, by subtracting the activation involved in the visual task from that involved in the parallel phonological task, it was possible to isolate the component processes involved in the phonological aspects of the latter task.

In this small-scale experiment, performance on the two tasks was at the same level as that of normally reading adults. However, there was less activation across the left hemisphere of the brain in the people with dyslexia during both rhyme processing and the memory search task. Specifically, a region called the *insula*, which connects regions for language comprehension with speech production, received less activation in those with dyslexia. Even though the study only involved adults who had developed strategies to compensate for their poor reading over time, the authors speculated that this was the area responsible for translating between speech input and outputs – arguably, the 'seat' of phonological representations of language. Following this study, a larger study of young adults with dyslexia recorded brain activity while reading aloud in comparison with completing a task requiring the detection of graphic features in words and nonwords. Such a task automatically engages reading, albeit implicitly. Relative to a rest condition, the adults with dyslexia showed less activation than controls of similar age and IQ in the left hemisphere of the brain (specifically, in the posterior temporal cortex) when completing both tasks.[67] Interestingly, the same area had been shown in other studies to be involved in naming – another area of difficulty observed in those with dyslexia.

By the end of the twentieth century, then, a new set of hypotheses was linking the biological with the cognitive causes of dyslexia.[68] In particular, there was evidence from twin studies of a genetic basis for phonological (speech) processing and there was a plausible link with under-activation of regions of the brain that subserve speech perception and speech production in those with dyslexia. However, this was, and remains, only a hypothesis, and although it offered a parsimonious explanation for the behavioural phenotype referred to as 'dyslexia', it was not without its critics.[69] While researchers in Britain agreed that phonological impairments were an important feature of dyslexia, suggestive of deficits at the level of phonological representations, two alternative hypotheses were gaining prominence.[70] John Stein and colleagues at the University of Oxford were continuing their work describing visual deficits in dyslexia and hypothesized that these deficits originated in the magnocellular system of the brain.[71] Elsewhere, Rod Nicolson and Angela Fawcett at the University of Sheffield proffered a completely new and more general framework for dyslexia research.[72] According to their hypothesis, individuals with dyslexia fail to automatize skills because of deficits in the cerebellum of the brain – a hypothesis that continues to attract controversy.[73]

Dyslexia in the Twenty-First Century (2000–)

By the start of the twenty-first century, the science of reading had come of age.[74] Founded in 1993, the Society for the Scientific Study of Reading was flourishing; in 2000, Keith Stanovich at the Ontario Institute for Studies in Education in Canada was awarded its prestigious Distinguished Scientific Contributions Award, and its president was the psychologist Charles Perfetti, who remains one of its most eminent scientists, having contributed to theoretical advances in most aspects of reading and reading comprehension across languages from the perspective of cognition, linguistics, and neuroscience. Perfetti's theory of 'lexical quality' – the idea that having fully specified memory representations for words (their phonological, syntactic, and semantic aspects) is at the heart of reading fluency – would have gained approval from Samuel Orton, nearly 100 years earlier.[75] Furthermore, although the research of Perfetti's lab has not specifically focused on dyslexia, his theory accommodates the cardinal cognitive and behavioural features of a disorder that, by the beginning of the twenty-first century, had been the subject of some forty years of concerted institutional research.[76]

Hence, with scientific understanding of reading as the backdrop, the stage was set for two main trends in the field of dyslexia – the agenda for dyslexia research in the new millennium. First, now that the obstacles to learning to read in English were understood, it was time to consider the challenges posed by other writing systems – alphabetic and non-alphabetic.[77] Of all the alphabetic orthographies, English is the least regular and its irregularities and inconsistencies have often been blamed for dyslexia. Indeed, Victorian studies had (fleetingly) suggested that it might be easier to learn to read in more 'transparent' languages with more consistent letter–sound correspondences, such as German, a prediction upheld by later research.[78] In contrast, in Britain, at least some researchers were of the confirmed view that phonological processing impairments were at the root of dyslexia, irrespective of language, including the reading researchers Marketa Caravolas and Nata Goulandris.[79] It is now clear that across languages, including Chinese, the predictors of individual differences in reading (and in dyslexia) include symbol knowledge (in English, letters; in Chinese, characters; in some Indian languages, *akshara*) and phonological skills – though at different levels according to the nature of the system.[80] Fine-grained phoneme–grapheme correspondences underpin learning in English, whereas mappings at a coarser level are used in other languages – for example, mappings between symbols and syllables in the Korean writing system.[81] In addition, performance on a rapid naming test appears to provide a sensitive predictor of individual differences in learning to read universally.[82] Put another way, although the manifestations of dyslexia differ between languages, particularly in the early stages when children learning to read English take longer than children learning other languages, there is surprising similarity in what is known of dyslexia's likely causation.[83]

The second strand of research that emerged in the new century was interest in the strong relationships between reading and language and the similarities and differences between oral and written language problems, arguably a renaissance of Samuel Orton's views.[84] While some argued that dyslexia was the developmental outcome of pre-school language impairment, others considered language disorder a more severe form of dyslexia, and still others have asserted that dyslexia and language disorder co-occur. Longitudinal analyses hold the promise of being able to adjudicate these debates.[85]

More generally, there was growing dissatisfaction in the first decade of the twenty-first century that dyslexia should be considered the outcome of a specific deficit of the phonological system, and British researchers were continuing to explore putative deficits in the visual system and beyond.[86] While it is clear that, at the group level, the phonological deficit hypothesis provides the most parsimonious explanation of the characteristic reading and spelling difficulties that characterize the problem, there was a return to the idea of conducting case studies, such as those employed in Victorian research on word-blindness, albeit this time in a quite different form.[87] This new approach involved assembling a series of cases, providing the possibility of looking across individuals at how deficits accumulate and segregate, in order to understand how individual cognitive profiles could inform theoretical knowledge of dyslexia. Working in London in the early 2000s, the psychologist Franck Ramus and his colleagues used the case-series approach to argue for variability in dyslexia without clear subtypes and to dismiss alternative theories, a theoretical stance that Ramus would build on in subsequent research in French.[88] How, though, would this fit into a more productive framework for thinking about dyslexia?

In 2006, the psychologist Bruce Pennington, a key member of the Colorado group, published a landmark paper that would radically reframe dyslexia in research and ultimately in practice.[89] Pennington, whose work straddles several disorders (including ADHD, autism, and Down syndrome) and embraces genetics and neuroscience, was in a unique position to attempt to unify the field.[90] In his 2006 paper, he proposed that dyslexia, in common with other neurodevelopmental disorders, is the outcome of multiple defi-

Researching Dyslexia (1964–2009)

cits that accumulate toward a threshold that determines diagnosis.[91] This theory, since recast as the multiple risk framework, provides a way not only of thinking about how deficits outside of the phonological domain (e.g., broader language impairments) may play a role in the aetiology of dyslexia, but also accommodates the fact that dyslexia frequently co-occurs with features of other disorders. For instance, it is notable that many people with dyslexia show aspects of the inattentive profile of ADHD, mathematical disorder (dyscalculia), or dyspraxia.[92]

By the end of the 2000s, the argument for considering dyslexia a disorder of written language remained strong and, in Britain at least, the means for identifying it had been broadly agreed.[93] The Rose review, discussed at the beginning of this book, drew on the accumulated evidence to inform its independent report for the UK government in 2009.[94] Its synopsis of dyslexia research was that 'dyslexia primarily affects the skills involved in accurate and fluent word reading and spelling. Characteristic features of dyslexia are difficulties in phonological awareness, verbal memory and verbal processing speed'.[95]

However, while much could be agreed, there remained two contentious issues. The first was how to teach people with dyslexia (here, the Rose review suffered from a dearth of robust evidence in the face of much undoubtedly good practice); the second related to difficulties experienced by, and therefore reported by, people with dyslexia, but which frequently reflect the fact that dyslexia often co-occurs with other disorders. To clarify this issue, the review concluded that 'co-occurring difficulties may be seen in aspects of language, motor co-ordination, mental calculation, concentration and personal organisation, but these are not, by themselves, markers of dyslexia'.[96] The Rose review's recommendation that 'a good indication of the severity and persistence of dyslexic difficulties can be gained by examining how the individual responds or has responded to well-founded intervention' was destined to await further evidence of 'what works'.[97] In this way, the dialogue between academic research and its application, which has characterised dyslexia science since the mid-twentieth century, remains at the forefront of scientific and political debates around dyslexia.

To close this history of the science of dyslexia, then, we return to the typology of dyslexia research outlined at the beginning of this chapter: that of dyslexia's *applied* and *academic* science. Much of the earliest research of dyslexia, including that conducted at the Word Blind Centre from the 1960s, was undertaken alongside efforts to assist learners with dyslexia. Since then, the majority of dyslexia research has been undertaken by dedicated research labs and university-based researchers, although often with a view to how this research might inform specialist teaching. The early informality of applied dyslexia research, though, has had several legacies for state provision, with educational officials of the 1960s and 1970s often highlighting the lack of a firm evidence base to withhold recognition of, and so funding for, dyslexia support. Even as the evidence base expanded and gained scientific rigour, ongoing debates around terminology were cited by those in politics, the media, and elsewhere who remained resistant to the term.[98] Dyslexia's science, then, has been firmly entwined with dyslexia's social and political histories.

Chapter 4 – Key Points
- Scientific research on dyslexia has formed a key part of dyslexia's social, political, and cultural histories, and has provided a bedrock for advocacy efforts at achieving official recognition
- Scientific approaches to dyslexia have been myriad, and have gradually moved away from the 'discrepancy diagnostic model'
- The most widely accepted theory regarding the cause of dyslexia is the phonological deficit hypothesis, but this is not sufficient to fully account for the condition; there is now good evidence that dyslexia has a genetic origin
- Key research on dyslexia has been undertaken in the US and the UK, but dyslexia science is a global field

PART 3

Recognition: The Example of Britain

5
Tackling Dyslexia: Class, Gender, and the Construction of a Dyslexia Infrastructure (1962-97)

Scientific research has been a key resource for campaigners in validating dyslexia across its history. The work of organisations such as the Word Blind Centre, and of early researchers like Macdonald Critchley, Sandhya Naidoo, and Donald Shankweiler, provided increasing solidity to the concept during the 1960s. In the long run, campaigners built on this evidence base and the research that followed to convince policymakers to make provision for those with dyslexia. In earlier periods, when policymakers were reticent to provide state recognition, science supported campaigners in their view that dyslexia was an issue that required attention and suggested remedial approaches. Many of those involved in the dyslexia community globally, from the middle of the twentieth century onward, have straddled research and practice, either by working in research informing the development of theoretically motivated interventions, or by contributing to both dyslexia science and advocacy.

We have previously described how individual physicians, and some teachers and small-scale organisations, offered initial assistance to a limited number of people with dyslexia. Here, we consider the foundation and work of national and international dyslexia organisations: the origins of a dedicated, non-governmental dyslexia infrastructure. In Britain, the case study under consideration, this infrastructure was formed piecemeal across the 1970s and 1980s, with a concentration of resources in the South East (especially) and the South West, where the majority of campaigners resided. While some of these early organisations have changed in name and nature since that time, this initial infrastructure has remained remarkably durable into the twenty-first century.

In Britain, the efforts of civil society to galvanize help for those with dyslexia were amongst the earliest globally, and some of the most successful. As we have seen, the Word Blind Centre was the first institution in the world dedicated to dyslexia research and treatment. The methods that the British dyslexia community employed to implement initial support were reflected in the approaches of other developed nations. The British Dyslexia Association, for example, one of the largest dyslexia associations in the world, has been key in setting up similar associations in Asia, South Africa, South America, and Europe – most obviously the European Dyslexia Association, an umbrella group of dyslexia societies from twenty-one European countries.[1] Other organisations, including the Hornsby International Dyslexia Centre and the Dyslexia Institute, have influenced individuals and organisations working on dyslexia around the globe.[2]

Britain did not achieve progress for those with dyslexia alone, or uniquely. The United States, in particular, has its own story of bringing greater attention to those with reading difficulties, and the links between British and American dyslexia research, teaching, and advocacy are strong. Central here has been the work of the Orton Society (now International Dyslexia Association), which in the United States has been chiefly responsible for the public and political attention given to people with dyslexia, building on the work of the pioneering dyslexia researcher Samuel Orton.[3] The Orton Society was a key model for early efforts in Britain and elsewhere to support people with dyslexia, as well as for organisations such as the Word Blind Centre.[4] Elsewhere, the early interest in word-blindness in Germany and Scandinavia, amongst other places, continued across the twentieth century, and British dyslexia campaigners both drew on and developed this work.[5]

What explains the emergence of a dyslexia infrastructure in Britain in the mid-twentieth century? Building on the scientific research that had created an evidence base for dyslexia, the work of the organisations profiled here, and of the pioneers who founded them, was indicative of a new world of social intervention from the 1960s. In Britain, the 1948 acts following the 1942 Beveridge report – the National Insurance Act, the National Assistance Act, and the National Health Service Act – created the foundations for the modern welfare state.[6] From 1960–75, public spending on education, health, unemployment, and pensions increased annually by 5 per cent in real terms; and the proportion of gross domestic product spent on these areas increased from 11 per cent to nearly 19 per cent.[7] This spending reflected a cultural shift in the extent to which government was expected to provide social support to its citizens. In this atmosphere, groups dedicated to women's rights and disability justice proliferated, lobbying government to make Britain a fairer society. An expanding middle class, with more time and financial resources than it had previously possessed, was better able to create action groups to exert political pressure for the causes in which they believed.

Why did parents, especially, contribute to this cause? In part, economic factors stimulated a growing concern with children's literacy difficulties, especially amongst the middle classes. British manufacturing was at its peak in the early 1950s, employing two-fifths of the national workforce and producing a third of gross domestic product. In the decades that followed, this dominance rapidly declined, and the service sector expanded in Britain and across other Western nations. As a result, the importance of literacy to educational attainment and success in the workplace increased. Education was made compulsory in Britain up to the age of fifteen after the passing of the Education Act of 1944. The same legislation introduced the 'eleven-plus' examination and effectively created a two-tier education system that lasted into the 1970s. Improved academic performance at an earlier age was becoming more important to life outcomes. Children who were struggling to read and write were particularly disadvantaged, and parents with the means to do so took a greater stake in ensuring that their children adapted to literate society's demands.

The achievements of the London Word Blind Centre in the 1960s and early 1970s provided a foundation for a 'golden age' of progress in dyslexia awareness and support. To a substantial degree, the Word Blind Centre was a pioneer and a proof of concept; it indicated the scope of dyslexia in Britain, and it offered a framework for how dyslexia might be addressed. However, it remained the fact that assistance for those with dyslexia across the 1960s–80s was generally only available to middle-class families. Often, but not always, it was women of means or the upwardly mobile who led in the foundation and running of specialist dyslexia organisations.

To provide balance, this chapter also considers the outcomes for those whom the dyslexia movement could not help. Their fate was partly a reflection of the dyslexia movement's aims and limitations, and partly a reflection of the time it took successive British governments to fully acknowledge and respond to the condition. Without government support, early dyslexia organisations were left to fend for themselves – helping those that they could, where they could. Given their limited resources, and the requirement of specialist schools and tuition centres for private fees, those with dyslexia from disadvantaged socio-economic backgrounds were frequently left behind by initial dyslexia provision.

An Emerging Dyslexia Landscape: The British Dyslexia Association and the First Dyslexia Organisations (1960s-80s)

The London Word Blind Centre closed in 1972. However, by bringing together the expertise of leading dyslexia scientists and professionals, it set the stage for the fuller emergence of dyslexia in British society.[8] Foremost amongst the specialist organisations that followed was the British Dyslexia Association, which, together with its sister organisation the Dyslexia Institute, pioneered support and understanding for those with dyslexia.[9]

The driving force behind the BDA was Marion Welchman, known in Britain and beyond as the 'needle and thread' of the dyslexia community for the way that she brought together the interests of both local and international dyslexia organisations from the mid-1960s through the 1990s.[10] Born in 1915 in Penarth, Wales, Welchman studied nursing at the Cardiff Royal Infirmary, and was a practising nurse for seventeen years. Like many of those in the dyslexia movement, her interest in dyslexia, and in those with the condition, stemmed from a professional caring role coupled with the experiences of a family member. In Welchman's case, the latter was her youngest child, Howard: 'a bright boy who had incredible difficulties in learning at school', who was later diagnosed with dyslexia.[11]

Like many others in Britain, Welchman's introduction to the dyslexia world came via the Word Blind Centre, which she visited soon after its opening in 1962 seeking assistance for Howard.[12] Through her search, Welchman became connected with the American Orton Society, including the teachers

Agnes Wolff and Sally Childs, specialists in the Orton-Gillingham-Stillman method of reading instruction. Wolff was the first teacher to successfully assist Welchman's son with his dyslexia; later, Welchman and Childs created the first dyslexia teacher-training course in Britain, employing a multi-sensory approach based on the Orton-Gillingham-Stillman programme. The inaugural training course was held at Bath Technical College in 1969 with twenty-five teachers in attendance. Demand was so great that the course was repeated over the following four years.[13] Attendees included Kathleen Hickey, Bevé Hornsby, and Frula Shear – women who would make their own mark on the dyslexia world, and whose attendance attested to the close-knit nature of the dyslexia community at the time.

Alongside her organisation of teacher training, Welchman mobilised the parents of children with dyslexia, seeing this mobilisation as key to achieving social and political recognition for the condition. In this way, her efforts were crucial to the expansion of interest in, and support for, dyslexia in British civil society. In 1966, Welchman brought together a committee of concerned parents, as well as doctors, psychologists, and teachers, to found the Bath Association for the Study of Dyslexia: the first dyslexia association in the country. By 1970, Welchman had traversed Britain helping parents groups to set up similar local associations in the wake of the closure of the Word Blind Centre, and the need for a national organisation to coordinate their efforts was becoming clear.[14] The Invalid Children's Aid Association again lent support, providing office space and secretarial assistance. Alfred White Franklin of the Word Blind Centre chaired the steering committee to draw up the BDA's first constitution, and Welchman drew together the eight existing local dyslexia associations in Britain – Bath, Cambridge, Essex, North London, North Surrey, Northern Ireland, Scotland, and West Surrey – to officially create the BDA in 1972.

The BDA was instrumental in establishing the first nationwide infrastructure of dyslexia support, connecting parents groups around Britain and creating a single, concerted voice for the dyslexia community. Welchman also ensured that the organisation's ambitions and influence were global. Throughout the 1970s and 1980s, she travelled widely – to Czechoslovakia, Germany, Italy, South Africa, Singapore, and the United States – testifying to her belief that 'dyslexia is of world-wide concern'.[15] Her opinion of the British influence on dyslexia globally was characteristically bold: 'We in

Britain have been able to make a significant contribution. Our two recent international conferences have enabled a wide sharing of interests, and Brazil and Singapore have set up their own dyslexia associations using our British Dyslexia Association as a model.'[16] As we have seen, the BDA also took inspiration from American equivalents, including the Orton Society. In developing the latter's work, the BDA became a model for the civic efforts of other countries where dyslexia awareness was slight.[17]

While the BDA was the largest of the early national dyslexia organisations in Britain, it was not the only such institution. In 1973, the Dyslexia Institute was founded, principally by Kathleen Hickey and Wendy Fisher, a special needs teacher and homeworker, respectively. The reason for its creation was similar to that of the BDA. The closure of the Word Blind Centre, in the words of a founding member of the Dyslexia Institute, Joyce Hargrave-Wright, 'removed a valuable source of help for dyslexic children and their families ... [as well as] information and advice, especially for parents and teachers'.[18] The North Surrey Dyslexia Association, founded by Fisher and one of the more active of the local associations of the late 1960s, stepped in to fill the gap, providing direct aid to children and adults. Funds were raised to purchase a property in Staines, Surrey, which became the Dyslexia Institute's headquarters. The institute's initial aims were threefold: to provide remedial instruction to those with dyslexia; to serve as a source of information for parents and teachers; and to train specialist teachers. To expedite the first of these objectives, the institute created the Dyslexia Institute Literacy Programme, a multi-sensory programme like the Orton-Gillingham-Stillman method. Other, smaller organisations multiplied in the wake of the BDA and the Dyslexia Institute.[19]

The BDA and the Dyslexia Institute, which became sister organisations, laid the groundwork for dyslexia support in Britain, helping several thousand individuals over the coming decades. Their economic models, though, were contrasting. The BDA sought to ensure that its services were free at the point of use, with funding obtained by donation. In this way, it joined other dyslexia organisations that were able to provide assistance at no cost. At the intersection of dyslexia science and support, the Bangor Dyslexia Unit led by Tim Miles, the Aston Language Development Unit led by Margaret Newton (who, with Mike Thomson, developed the influential Aston Index), and the London Barts Dyslexia Clinic led by Bevé Hornsby were able to draw from resources within government-funded institutions – universities and hospitals – to deliver assistance.[20] From the early 1960s, local authorities in Britain had begun, on an ad hoc basis, to fund a small number of places for state school students at institutions such as the Word Blind Centre; from the late 1970s, the policy of 'statementing' – the creation of an official record of a child's educational needs – brought support to a greater number of pupils with dyslexia. Nonetheless, in the absence of central government recognition of dyslexia, there was a limit to what donations and non-dedicated funding streams could provide, and private fees remained a key feature of the emerging dyslexia landscape.

The Dyslexia Institute, in part because it provided more specialist instruction, became a business enterprise under the leadership of the psychologist Harry Chasty. This led to rivalry, and occasionally conflict, between the BDA and the Dyslexia Institute, which otherwise dovetailed effectively in pursuit of their common aims.[21] This reliance on private fees included not only the Dyslexia Institute, but specialist dyslexia tuition centres and schools. In 1971, the year before the establishment of the organisations above, Helen Arkell – with Joy Pollock and Elisabeth Waller, a remedial teacher and an occupational therapist, respectively – founded the Helen Arkell Dyslexia Centre. Through social connections, Arkell had been able to 'beg, borrow or steal a house in London [Fulham] and so set up there'.[22] Later, Arkell secured more substantial premises in Frensham, Surrey. Like the Dyslexia Institute, Arkell modelled her centre on the Word Blind Centre, where she had briefly worked. The Helen Arkell Dyslexia Centre was funded by charitable donations and student fees; like other dyslexia organisations, it served as a meeting ground for interested parties who would go on to create further specialist establishments.[23]

However, organisations such as the BDA, the Dyslexia Institute, and Helen Arkell's centre, and research and teaching units such as the Bangor Dyslexia Unit, could only provide part-time assistance to people (mainly children) with dyslexia. For some parents of means, further support was desired – support made available by a new type of dyslexia institution in Britain: the specialist school. Such schools sought to make up for the impact of dyslexia on children and their families in the unprepared state school classroom. They frequently provided a 'wrap-around' system that took account of the need for both specialist teaching and the improvement of self-esteem and resilience in children who, even where they had sympathetic teachers, still often struggled relative to classmates.

While Millfield school had provided specialist support for students with dyslexia like Martin Attlee since 1942, this had been as part of a general ethos of assisting learners with diverse needs. In the decades that followed Millfield's pioneering support, schools opened that specialised in helping children with language disorders, including Moor House in Surrey (1947), John Horniman School in West Sussex (1958), Edith Edwards House School in Surrey (1962), St David's College in Llandudno, Wales (1965), and Dawn House in Nottinghamshire (1974).[24] In addition, several specialist dyslexia units were created at existing schools, such as Bideford College in Devon.

By the 1980s, it was becoming clear that there was a demand for schools that specialised wholly in dyslexia. To this end, Edington and Shapwick Schools in Somerset were founded (in 1981 and 1984, respectively, before merging in 1994) by the former head of Millfield, Colin Atkinson. Other dedicated dyslexia schools included Maple Hayes in Staffordshire (1981), East Court in Kent (1983), and Mark College in Somerset (1986), located in wealthier parts of South West and South East England, where parents could afford their term fees. In addition to compensating for the lack of provision in state schools, these schools, which were generally residential, sought to counter the ignorance of dyslexia in non-specialist private schools.

In parallel, there was a growing demand for dyslexia day schools for parents who did not want to send their children away and/or for children who did not wish to leave home. One of the first dyslexia day schools was set up in London by Daphne Hamilton-Fairley, a speech and language therapist, who raised funds for her project with the support of several parents of children with dyslexia. In 1976, Hamilton-Fairley hosted a 'Spell Ball' at the Intercontinental Hotel in Mayfair, London, raising over £50,000 for the school's founding. By the early 1980s, Fairley House School had opened in Kensington, later moving to Pimlico. 'It was magic from the point of view of parent power', Hamilton-Fairley recalls, 'and how they'll fight for their children.'[25] Other specialist dyslexia day schools were founded by Sarah and Colin Agombar in London and Bath. A new organisation, the Council for the Registration of Schools Teaching Dyslexic Pupils, emerged in 1989 to keep track of and monitor the standards in this growing sector.

Tackling Dyslexia (1962–97)

As with the early histories of the BDA and the Dyslexia Institute, British specialist schools fostered global connections, often with groups and individuals in the United States. The experiences of Steve Chinn, who founded Mark College, are illustrative. Chinn first encountered dyslexia as a state secondary teacher in the 1970s, before becoming headmaster of Shapwick Senior School in the early 1980s. The school hosted international visits from specialist teachers, often American, and Chinn ultimately departed Shapwick to become headmaster of the specialist dyslexia school Chautauqua Academy in Baltimore, Maryland. There, he worked with the Orton Society, headquartered in the city, and studied with dyslexia researchers at Johns Hopkins University. Chinn used this experience on his return to Britain to set-up his own specialist dyslexia secondary school, Mark College.[26] The new dyslexia infrastructure was international, and it was growing.

Worried Mothers? Women, the Dyslexia Movement, and Helping Children Adapt to Literate Society

Dyslexia's early history was almost uniformly male. The Victorian physicians concerned with the condition were men, and the majority of their patients were boys, whose education was afforded primacy – it was they, rather than their sisters, who would go on to fill the ranks of the professions, where good literacy skills were essential. In the first half of the twentieth century, this gender balance gradually started to shift: teachers and researchers like Anna Gillingham, Bessie Stillman, and Edith Norrie were pioneers in dyslexia provision in the West. Over the 1950s and 1960s, as dyslexia increasingly came under the purview of education, the mothers of dyslexic children became central to advocating for and providing support. The majority of the main dyslexia organisations in Britain were founded and/or led by women. Others, such as the Bangor Dyslexia Unit, relied heavily on a female workforce at all levels of operation.

The increasing prominence of women in the dyslexia community sat within a context of wider social and economic change in Britain, which mirrored that of other Western nations. At the beginning of the twentieth century, under a third of women and girls over the age of ten earned a salary in Britain; by 1971, 53 per cent of women between the ages of sixteen and sixty-four were in paid employment.[27] This was partly a product of changing cultural attitudes around women's capacity to work, accelerated by women's widespread employment on the home front during the world wars, and partly a product of economic restructuring, including the expansion of the service sector and of part-time employment. In the workplace, sexual segregation gradually began to erode. Education Acts from 1944 onward, as we have seen, raised the school leaving age, and were crucial to these shifts. With children at school for longer, women, largely responsible for domestic childcare, were better able to undertake paid work outside of the home.[28] The teaching profession that was to encounter children with dyslexia was increasingly populated by women.[29]

The first women to become influential in Britain's dyslexia community, from the late 1950s, were educational psychologists. They exemplified women's changing professional roles. Sometimes, but not always, they possessed personal experience of dyslexia. Later, women with other experiences of the condition joined them, often the mothers of children with dyslexia, or those who had encountered dyslexia through the teaching and caring professions. As we have seen, for Marion Welchman, an interest in dyslexia was spurred by the difficulties faced by her son. After finding support, Welchman recalls that 'the gradual process of our son learning to read, write and comprehend was like unlocking a secret casket'.[30] For Wendy Fisher, co-founder of the Dyslexia Institute, it was the dyslexic difficulties faced by her daughter, Sophy, which triggered an initial interest. For those like Helen Arkell, following in the footsteps of Edith Norrie, it was her own difficulties with dyslexia, as well as those of her family, which led to an interest in the area.[31]

Despite their limited representation in the elite professional landscape of the time, this group of women was able collectively, often through improvisation and informal connections, to lay the foundations for the increasing institutionalisation of dyslexia in organisations such as the BDA and the Dyslexia Institute. To do so, these women grafted their labour onto formal channels of power, employed social networks, and otherwise found innovative solutions to create schools and organisations to support those with dyslexia.

In Britain, the history of the Word Blind Centre exemplifies the beginning of this shift toward female leadership. Alongside Alfred White Franklin, the centre's first Word Blind Committee, formed in 1962, included Macdonald Critchley, George Meredith, Oliver Zangwill, Mia Kellmer Pringle, and Maisie Holt. All were psychologists or neurologists who had encountered children with specific reading difficulties during their work. Mia Kellmer Pringle was head of the Remedial Education Centre at the University of Birmingham; Maisie Holt was a clinical psychologist at Barts Hospital, London, and one of the first female educational psychologists appointed by a local authority.[32] The centre's first director, Alex Bannatyne, an educational psychologist, laid the centre's foundations. His replacement, Sandhya Naidoo, another psychologist – who, in her own words, came from a family 'riddled with dyslexia' – led the centre successfully until its closure in 1972.[33]

Outside of her contributions to the Word Blind Centre, Maisie Holt worked with children with dyslexia in the Department of Psychological Medicine at Barts Hospital. After Holt's retirement in 1971, the Barts Dyslexia Clinic was formally established by Bevé Hornsby, a speech and language therapist. In the decade that followed, under Hornsby's stewardship, the clinic grew from a small corner of the Department of Psychological Medicine to a department in its own right.[34] As Maggie Snowling, who worked with Hornsby at the clinic, recalls, 'she basically just moved into Barts Hospital and took over some rooms that were vacant and started a clinic. That was how it worked in those days.'[35] While there, Hornsby, with Frula Shear, a language therapist, created *Alpha to Omega* (1974): an internationally respected phonics-based programme to teach reading, writing, and spelling to children with dyslexia and other language difficulties. Hornsby went on to become the 'grande dame' of dyslexia in Britain, and the Hornsby International Dyslexia Centre assisted a generation of children and trained a generation of teachers across Britain, Europe, and the United States.[36]

At these organisations, the principal concern was with providing remedial reading and writing support to children with dyslexia. At the same time, the direct experience of working with dyslexic children often led to a further aim: the provision of emotional support. At the Bangor Dyslexia Unit, Ann Cooke, who started as a teacher and later became the unit's director, recalls that 'there was a lot of, you wouldn't call it counselling that went on [with children], but confidence building'.[37] For Patience Thomson, former headmistress of Fairley House School, 'you are, at school, humiliated on a daily basis [if you have dyslexia], and you're bored silly if you can't read and everybody else is'.[38]

Indeed, disparaging treatment of those with dyslexia could sometimes be more direct.[39] Tim Miles, founder of the Bangor Dyslexia Unit, became interested in dyslexia after being moved by the plight of several children sent to him for examination by the local child guidance clinic from the 1940s: 'What particularly saddened me was that ignorance about dyslexia resulted not only in failure to meet dyslexic children's needs but in hurtful accusations that they were "not trying"'.[40] At the specialist dyslexia school, East Court, Bill Watkins recalls of the 1980s that 'some of them [pupils] when they came [to the school] were so damaged and bruised by their experiences at [non-specialist] independent schools or prep schools. One dear little kid, he was tiny, one of the masters had just thrown him across the room.'[41] While such treatment was rare, children and young people whose dyslexia was ignored in school often experienced a downward spiral of declining self-confidence, disengagement, and poor career prospects. Given this, a key aim of early dyslexia organisations was to meet emotional, as well as educational, needs.

The role of gender in the dyslexia movement is an interesting one for the social historian. Generally, it was mothers, rather than fathers, who took the lead in finding specialist support for their children.[42] The preponderance of women in childcare professions, and in childcare at home, meant that they were, perhaps, more attuned to the emotional needs of children who were struggling.[43] If this was the rule, though, there were certainly exceptions: at the Word Blind Centre, at university research units, at several specialist schools, male physicians, scientists, and educators demonstrated a commitment to the psychological wellbeing of children with significant reading difficulties, echoing the concerns expressed by male Victorian doctors. Nevertheless, the increasing role of women in the dyslexia movement coincided with an increasing focus on the emotional needs of dyslexic children, in addition to providing remedial language instruction.[44]

In this way, the rise of parent-led dyslexia organisations should be contextualised with the proliferation of voluntary organisations seeking to assist the vulnerable, especially medical patients, in postwar Britain.[45] In the 1950s, during the first years of the National Health Service, several female-led campaigns for an expanded consumer role in healthcare were created. These included the championing of mothers' rights to visit their children in hospitals. In the 1960s, the Patients Association (1963–present), which campaigned more formally for patients' rights, was founded by a teacher, Helen Hodgson, like many of the early dyslexia organisations. Such groups campaigned for the 'voice and choice' of consumers as the bureaucracies of welfare, including those pertaining to healthcare and to education, expanded in Britain.[46]

In addition, the history of dyslexia parallels the history of other cognitive differences, such as autism. In the case of autism, parents – usually, but not always, mothers – led efforts at providing support for, and recognition of, the condition in the West.[47] As with dyslexia, parents in the autism movement often straddled roles as parent and researcher, or parent and campaigner.[48] In the cases of both autism and dyslexia, the preponderance of 'worried mothers' was frequently invoked by critics to query the existence of these conditions.[49] For autism, the 'mother-blaming' of the 1960s and 1970s went so far as to claim that poor mothering itself precipitated the condition.[50] For dyslexia, accusations were generally not so extreme, but the notion that middle-class mothers used the label to further their children's educational success, despite low educational ability, has been a recurring element of the dyslexia story. Such arguments have also invoked a further quality of the dyslexia movement: class.

Middle-Class Bias? Socio-economic Class, Gender, and Early Criticism of the Dyslexia Community

While research on dyslexia by women such as Sandhya Naidoo, Bevé Hornsby, and Margaret Newton occurred in the traditional professional spaces of research centres and clinics, advocacy and lobbying for dyslexia rights, via organisations such as the BDA, was planned in a less formal and more piecemeal fashion. Often, local associations met at a member's house, conducting work on a voluntary basis. As such, the women who founded and led these organisations were generally, at least at first, those who could provide their labour for a modest (sometimes non-existent) wage. This meant that these women were often, but not exclusively, from more middle-class backgrounds. This characteristic of the dyslexia community set the stage for its success; it was also invoked by dyslexia's critics to critique the concept.[51]

The term 'middle class' obscures a great deal of variety and complexity. The women who founded early dyslexia support organisations included those in possession of private means, those supported by a partner's earnings, and those who worked part-time elsewhere to support their voluntary dyslexia work. Many belonged to more than one of these categories. The 'middle class', as the historian Lawrence James has noted, is a heterogeneous entity, constantly evolving and variously defined.[52] When we employ the term 'middle class' here, it is largely in keeping with contemporaneous understandings of that term, such as the official classification scheme of the Registrar General for England and Wales, which used professional status as a proxy (and which Sandhya Naidoo used in the 1960s to classify the children who attended the Word Blind Centre).

The general expansion of the middle class in Britain from the midtwentieth century was one of the reasons for the rapid increase in dyslexia interest; more and more, middle-class parents were concerned that poor educational performance would lead to later struggles for their children. The role of mothers within this middle-class milieu was crucial. The history of dyslexia shows how the purposes of middle-class mothering, while traditionally associated with childcare, were shifting in Britain by the middle of the century. In the Victorian case studies of physicians such as William Pringle Morgan and James Hinshelwood, the fathers of middle-class children with dyslexia brought them for assessment; it was fathers, rather than mothers, who took the lead in decisions regarding children's educational trajectories.[53] By the time dyslexia support organisations were formed, mothers were increasingly assuming this role, taking charge not only of general childcare, but children's educational performance. New standards for parenthood, and new gendered patterns of parental labour, were emerging.[54]

The founders of dyslexia organisations were not the only mothers in the frame. At the inaugural meeting of the Word Blind Centre, a Mrs Devon, one of Alfred White Franklin's 'plain parents', posed a question that was typical of those in attendance: 'She had fought and got her child over the first "hump" as learning to read had become known, what worried her was how her capable children would get through all the examinations on the road to an adequate career?'[55] Patient records of the Word Blind Centre show that it was normal for mothers to bring their children for assessment, the bulk of recommended tuition being funded by the families themselves. In Janice Edwards's survey of children with dyslexia growing up in Britain in the 1980s, the 'pattern that emerges is that in all of the cases studied it was the mother who took the dominant role in the initial move to get help'.[56] In interviews for the Oxford Dyslexia Archive, the central role of middle-class mothers in securing support for their children comes across repeatedly during the early – and, indeed, later – decades of the dyslexia movement.[57]

The story of Susan Hampshire, a celebrated British actress who came to international prominence in the 1960s (and who was perhaps the first celebrity in Britain to publicly disclose their dyslexia), is emblematic of how motherhood and socio-economic class could combine in the early years of the dyslexia movement.[58] As a child, Hampshire's difficulties at school were severe. In response, her mother founded a specialist school in London: 'It was she, when I was about four maybe five, [who] was worried about me, so she started this little school [the Hampshire School] for me', years before Hampshire was diagnosed with dyslexia as an adult in the early 1970s by representatives of the Word Blind Centre.[59] After her diagnosis, she 'decided to be very involved and stand up and be counted, and worked probably three or four days a week [primarily for the BDA and the Dyslexia Institute] ... talking about it [dyslexia], going on the radio, visiting schools or whatever'. Of her work, Hampshire recalls, 'That was a labour of love. I was doing it to raise money for dyslexia, it wasn't my personal profit. It didn't raise huge quantities, but it raised a lot in those days to help.'[60] Hampshire served as president of the Dyslexia Institute during the 1990s.

The socio-economic and gender make-up of the dyslexia movement had its own geography, too. Through organisations like the BDA, middle-class parents came into contact with teachers, researchers, and other parents who shared an interest in dyslexia. They then, via their various social and economic capitals, fostered these connections. While this network spanned the country, its members were generally concentrated in better-off parts of the country. At the Word Blind Centre, patient files suggest that the majority of children came from wealthier areas of London and the 'Stockbroker Belt' of England's southeast, and were generally of average or above-average intelligence.[61] For most of their duration, the BDA (Bath, later Bracknell), the

Dyslexia Institute (Staines, later Egham), and the Helen Arkell Dyslexia Centre (London, later Frensham) were located within twenty miles of one another, across the relatively wealthy Surrey/Berkshire borders. Campaigners like Joyce Hargrave-Wright were aware of this geography: 'When you look at the population in Surrey, you've got a lot of very caring parents, which you get everywhere, but they were in a position to help. They had the facilities and they were prepared to form groups and local associations and spend money, which if you're in a big city and in a poor area, it just wouldn't happen.'[62] For Lynette Bradley, a leading dyslexia researcher of the period, 'The [middle-class] parents held the school to account, that was where the difference was.'[63]

The intersection of socio-economic class, gender, and dyslexia support was to be found in other dyslexia centres, too. From the early 1960s, when the Bangor Dyslexia Unit was first established by Tim Miles (before being formalised in 1977), it relied on a predominantly female workforce willing to work for low salaries on sometimes tenuous contracts, often because they were from otherwise comfortable backgrounds. For Elaine Miles, the first director of the Bangor Dyslexia Unit's teaching service and the co-author of several books on the condition with her husband, 'finding people to join the team was not difficult ... there were several college wives [of male professors] who had been teachers, had small children and therefore did not want to commit themselves to a full-time job'.[64] Ann Cooke, later a director of the unit, recalls that 'we were all part-time and there were no contracts. We were all paid on what I call "pinkies": claim forms that you put in either every month or every half term.'[65] 'It was accepted in those days', continues Miles, 'that your husband's salary should support you, too.'[66]

The social and financial resources of the early dyslexia community were thus crucial in getting early dyslexia support off the ground, in terms of both advocacy and research. It had a downside, though: it formed the bedrock for arguments — found throughout dyslexia's history, but coming to prominence in the 1960s — that the condition was a 'middle-class myth' with no firm scientific basis. Again, such arguments blurred the boundaries between socio-economic class and gender, with accusations that dyslexia was a middle-class myth frequently going hand in hand with those that implied dyslexia was a product of over-anxious mothers.[67]

Tackling Dyslexia (1962–97)

In the political sphere, lobbying by Word Blind Centre representatives during the early 1960s was rebuffed by representatives of the Ministry of Education, who claimed that there was no conclusive evidence for the condition (explored further in the next chapter). In the mid-1970s, Mary Warnock, as chairperson of a landmark review of special educational needs, recalls being summoned by the male civil servant responsible for the committee to be told that dyslexia ought to be omitted from her inquiry.[68] Warnock included several references to dyslexia in her final report, and to organisations and persons including the BDA, the Dyslexia Institute, the Bangor Dyslexia Unit, and Bevé Hornsby, but the term 'dyslexia' was absent from the legislation that followed her report, even if the statements of special educational needs that Warnock introduced helped many pupils with dyslexia.[69] While the role of sexism in this interaction is obviously impossible to prove or disprove, certainly efforts at political recognition of dyslexia were characterised by female advocates from various professional backgrounds coming up against a disbelieving and largely patriarchal political establishment.[70]

The class and gender constitution of the dyslexia community was used to undermine dyslexia and the ability of women within the community, too. Such criticism came from many quarters, including unexpected ones. When Marion Welchman first approached the Word Blind Centre in the 1960s, looking for help for her son, she was introduced by a representative 'in a rather disdainful voice, as a "mother from Bath who thinks she may be able to do something"'.[71] Jennifer Salter, a specialist teacher who lobbied her local authority for support for her son in the 1970s, recalls being dismissed as a 'belligerent woman'.[72] In the 1970s and 1980s, especially, 'There used to be articles in the paper saying what nonsense it [dyslexia] was and how it was anxious mothers who'd rather have a dyslexic child than a stupid one and all this sort of thing.'[73] The implication of these accusations was clear: dyslexia, whether it existed or not, was being exaggerated by over-concerned, middle-class mothers, who were principally interested in justifying their children's learning difficulties.

While it was true that middle-class mothers were interested in furthering their children's educational futures, their activism brought together concerned parents across the country, whose efforts at founding organisations led to substantial, if not universal, dyslexia support. Gendered criticisms of the dyslexia community as self-interested hindered state recognition in Britain, not least because such criticisms were often made by government representatives themselves, with the ironical result that support for other, less privileged children was delayed. The work of the dyslexia community from the late 1960s created an initial infrastructure of support; an impressive achievement, given the organisational feats that it required. However, it could not reach all, or even most, of those with dyslexia, whose difficulties frequently remained an obstacle to educational and career success.

Left Behind? Dyslexia, Demography, and Reading Difficulties Outside of the Dyslexia Community

Telling the story of those with dyslexia who escaped recognition prior to state acknowledgement of dyslexia in the late 1980s presents the same issues as for the Victorian era: how are they to be identified in retrospect? Here, we follow the same approach as in the analysis of that period: we offer a contextual discussion of how children with reading and writing difficulties fared. This approach provides an indication of how literacy difficulties affected children and adults who did not receive specialist support and whom the dyslexia movement could not reach. In addition, it is possible to gain insight into the typical experiences of children with dyslexia at various points in the twentieth century via case studies of those who were diagnosed later in life. There exists, too, substantial data concerning (for example) the proportion of young people and adults with reading difficulties in young offender and prisoner populations, suggesting how a lack of diagnosis and specialist support may have contributed to adverse outcomes for some. Such an account, albeit partial, helps to sketch the limits of the initial dyslexia infrastructure in Britain.

In 1972, the same year that the BDA and the Dyslexia Institute were founded, estimates suggested that nearly fifteen thousand pupils aged fifteen in England were semi-literate – literacy being defined as the ability to read and write at a standard sufficient for daily life.[74] Reports that stemmed from these statistics, including the 1975 Bullock report on the teaching of English, omitted reference to dyslexia. The 1978 Warnock report, as discussed in further detail later, mentioned the condition, but only fleetingly. Moreover, while the process of statementing Warnock introduced meant that some children presenting with dyslexic difficulties received dedicated attention – including via state-funded places at private specialist dyslexia schools, if necessary – the process of receiving a statement was complex and usually required sustained lobbying by a child's parents. Many children who required statements did not receive them. While the organisations profiled here assisted several thousand pupils with dyslexia across the 1970s–80s, they could help only a minority of those who needed support.

Where did this leave the 'average' state school pupil with dyslexia in Britain from the mid-twentieth century? Without access to private specialist teaching or tuition, experiences naturally varied. Jennifer Salter, a specialist dyslexia teacher who later joined the BDA, recalls that her son with dyslexia was placed in the 'duds class' at a state school in the 1970s. Like many with dyslexia at the time, his difficulties were initially mistaken for low intelligence and indolence. When Salter requested greater support from the local education authority, she was told to 'realise that he's not very bright'.[75] Steve Williams, who started state schooling in South London in the 1980s, encountered similar ignorance from his school. In his case, a sympathetic teacher came to his aid: 'I remember we used to have these reading and writing tests at school and every time you finished you went up a grade, and I was miles behind all my friends … At that stage, the school, I don't think they'd even heard of dyslexia, a lot of the teachers. The headmistress didn't really believe in it. But there was a very, very good teacher there. I don't quite know how it happened, but my parents managed to arrange some additional classes with her.'[76] Specialist assistance, then, was predicated on the willingness and opportunity of parents to provide and/or organise the same. Moreover, Williams' story of two teachers with substantially different views and understandings of dyslexia, who were consequently able to offer starkly different levels of support, exemplifies why organisations like the Dyslexia Institute were so committed to providing specialist teacher training programmes.

In the early 1990s, publications began to collect the experiences of those who had grown up with dyslexia in the previous decades, but who had not received a formal diagnosis at the time that their difficulties arose.[77] Naturally, these were generally published by advocates for dyslexia rights, the intention of the collections being not only to record life stories, but also to influence contemporary policy. The most famous of these, *Every Letter Counts*, was written by Susan Hampshire, who, as we have seen, was one of the earliest celebrity campaigners for dyslexia rights. In *Every Letter Counts*, Hampshire profiled a series of adults, including fellow celebrities, laying out a common pattern of initial difficulties at school, followed by frustration but often adaptation to the demands of literacy, before the (usually) cathartic moment of diagnosis later in life.[78] More recently, Hampshire's account has been joined by a series of autobiographical reflections by adults with dyslexia growing up without a diagnosis, which tell a similar story.[79]

There is some evidence that children from black and ethnic minority backgrounds may have fared especially poorly during this period.[80] Asher and Martin Hoyles, in an account of dyslexia and the black experience in Britain, cite the example of the Afro-Caribbean poet Benjamin Zephaniah, as indicative of how dyslexia and difficulties at school were often framed by race. Zephaniah left school in 1971 at the age of thirteen unable to read or write. After a series of petty crimes, he enrolled in an adult education class organised by Greater London Council, where he was diagnosed with dyslexia. As Zephaniah recalls, 'It was then that I had a flashback to my school days and realised what had been happening to me.'[81] The inference in Hoyles and Hoyles's account is that Zephaniah's experience might have been improved had he been from a different socio-economic and different ethnic background. The dyslexia movement was composed principally of white, middle-class Britons; certainly, its work largely struggled, albeit not by design, to reach ethnic minority communities.[82]

The possibility of dyslexia being associated with criminality, as in Zephaniah's story, with children disengaged at school and struggling to succeed in life conventionally, receives further confirmation elsewhere. As we have seen, newspaper reports correlated word-blindness and criminality from the early twentieth century. In 1968, Eileen Critchley, the wife of Macdonald, published one of the first accounts of the association between dyslexia and antisocial behaviour. Sampling the London Remand Home and Classification Centre, she observed that 60 per cent of children who had engaged in antisocial behaviour experienced reading difficulties.[83] In the years that followed, further studies found an association between criminal behaviour and reading and language difficulties, including dyslexia.[84] Similar patterns were observed in other countries, including the United States, where a survey in the mid-1970s found that over 75 per cent of juvenile delinquents possessed a history of reading failure, the causes of which included dyslexia.[85] While these studies concluded that dyslexia had no direct effect on criminal tendencies, they were amongst the first to highlight the links between reading difficulties, criminality, and class, with the majority of prisoners with dyslexia from poorer families.[86]

While they were not necessarily its focus, the dyslexia community, in places, worked directly with children with dyslexia from disadvantaged socio-economic backgrounds, including young offenders. For example, Patience Thomson, later head of Fairley House specialist dyslexia school, conducted teaching sessions with young offenders in Britain during the 1970s, finding that a substantial proportion had dyslexia: 'I got so angry that they hadn't been taught properly when they were much, much younger. There were all these little things that you could do to make it easier. For instance, right-hand justification makes it much harder to read.'[87] After her retirement, Thomson used her experiences with these young offenders to create a dyslexia-friendly children's publisher in 1996: Barrington Stoke. Despite campaigns by dyslexia voluntary organisations and groups like the Prison Reform Trust, a parliamentary debate on dyslexia in the prison population did not occur until 2012.[88] The overrepresentation of prisoners with dyslexia has continued in recent decades.[89]

Of course, only a minority of those people with reading difficulties experienced such extreme outcomes; the majority faced the lesser, but still substantial, challenge of coping with the literacy demands of school and later life. The case studies above capture the sense in the Oxford Dyslexia Archive of how children at state schools fared during the 1960s–80s, when dyslexia was still little recognised and state support for dyslexia was yet to be provided. Special arrangements for examinations, such as additional time, would not be introduced until the late 1980s, the justification for its introduction being that the performance of children with dyslexia on untimed tests improved significantly, whereas the performance of children without dyslexia did not.[90] Largely, children with dyslexia at state schools and their parents were left to fend for themselves, with the best way of improving educational outcomes remaining private tuition and schooling, where this could be afforded and obtained. State schools, with lower budgets for pupil expenditure, struggled to provide specialist support.

Outside of these case histories, there undoubtedly have been children and adults with reading difficulties, whether diagnosed or not, who did not want or require assistance. Disability rights advocates from the 1960s expressed reticence about charities, which they saw as perpetuating a mentality of victimhood, even if the purpose of such charities was ostensibly benevolent.[91] In this sense, it is important to leave space here for those with dyslexia and reading difficulties who came to their own conclusions about where responsibility for their 'disability' lay, and to what extent they wanted it addressed. Their response to their difficulties may have been a knowing acceptance of the arbitrary requirement for widespread literacy in society, rather than a desire to be assisted; it may have been a refusal to engage with charities that, however well-intentioned, provided support only after a diagnosis. As one commentator on the dyslexia advocacy movement has stated: 'The downside of this admirable pursuit is that those not involved in the charity are "on the outside" ... By definition charities are the "haves" giving to the "have nots".'[92]

Elsewhere, there is suggestion that some parents in the early 1960s were reticent to have their children diagnosed, fearing that their child would be sent to a school that they (the parents) thought inappropriate.[93] Similarly, adults with dyslexia, without a legal guarantee of support from their employer until the Equality Act of 2010, may have been reluctant to divulge their condition in the workplace for fear of stigmatisation.[94] Thus, it is important to note that not all persons with dyslexia may have desired support at a time when the consequences of self-reporting dyslexia were uncertain and potentially disadvantageous. The story of initial efforts to help people with dyslexia in Britain is not just one of those who were assisted and those who missed out, but also of those who did not see the requirement, or disliked the idea, of being 'diagnosed'.

Chapter 5 - Key Points
- In Britain, the end of the Word Blind Centre heralded an important new chapter in dyslexia's history, including the founding of the British Dyslexia Association and the Dyslexia Institute
- Together with specialist schools and other enterprises, these organisations helped to embed dyslexia into British society and influenced dyslexia associations around the world
- Women played a key role in dyslexia advocacy and lobbied for better provision throughout the latter half of the twentieth century
- The intersection between dyslexia and social class left many with dyslexia absent of support, despite this 'golden age' of dyslexia awareness

6

Dyslexia Legislated: Literacy, Policy, and the Achievement of Official Status (1962–2010)

The dyslexia community in Britain, consisting primarily of parents, practitioners, and medical professionals, built an infrastructure of support for children (and, to a lesser extent, adults) with dyslexia. The facilities this provided were largely, but not exclusively, private, and included fee-paying assessment and teaching centres as well as independent schools. However, from the early 1960s, the dyslexia movement concerned itself not only with providing dyslexia support directly (which could only ever be limited in scope), but also with lobbying for political recognition of the condition. This lobbying occurred at multiple levels – from parents requesting support for their children from local authorities, to representatives of the dyslexia community talking directly to politicians and civil servants. Early solicitations to the Ministry of Education by members of the Word Blind Centre in the 1960s later expanded to encompass lobbying by the British Dyslexia Association and Dyslexia Institute from the 1970s. Educational authorities were the target of many documented advocacy efforts, because schooling was where those with dyslexia required the most assistance.

The campaign by the dyslexia community in Britain for political recognition of dyslexia again attests to the importance of individuals and individual agency in the dyslexia story. This includes the dyslexia community itself, often represented by a few key spokespersons. It also includes the political establishment that the dyslexia community was seeking to influence. How receptive particular government officials were to the concept of dyslexia, and to the arguments of the dyslexia movement, was crucial to

Dyslexia Legislated (1962–2010)

the ultimate achievement of political recognition. In Britain, certain policy-makers and civil servants expressed a marked antipathy to dyslexia, for the reasons already rehearsed – namely, that dyslexia was a middle-class excuse for poor academic performance on which they did not wish to expend limited state resources. On the other hand, progress in the campaign for political recognition was predicated on the sympathy of individuals in political power to the goals of the dyslexia movement. In this way, government recognition of dyslexia was contingent, rather than inevitable.

In emphasizing the importance of individuals, this chapter differs from existing accounts of learning difficulties, which have stressed their social construction.[1] Commonly, such accounts are based on Foucauldian approaches to bodily difference, in which responsibility for the emergence of conditions like dyslexia, ADHD, and autism, is placed principally on medical, educational, and legal authorities.[2] Thus, in the case of dyslexia, Tom Campbell has argued that a particular kind of governmental logic was responsible for its political recognition – a logic based on the requirement for economically productive workers in modern capitalist states like Britain. Similar sentiments, emphasising the role of the social in producing the 'learning-disabled' individual, are found in accounts of other cognitive differences. For example, Matthew Smith has argued that 'imperfect children, when it comes to ADHD, are not born; they are constructed'.[3] Majia Nadesan has argued that autism is not 'a biologically based psychiatric condition to be therapied, remedied, assaulted in an effort to "save" afflicted children'; rather, 'autism, or more specifically, the *idea* of autism is fundamentally *socially constructed*'.[4]

Certainly, social and political changes, including the increasing centrality of literacy to educational and professional success across the twentieth century, contributed to a landscape in which dyslexia could be recognised. However, such changes are broad and invoking them does not offer substantial explanation. Social constructionist approaches to dyslexia's emergence can serve to play down the process of recognition by political authorities in all its intricate complexity. Moreover, they risk attributing intentions to political authorities that they did not necessarily possess.

For example, Campbell has argued that the political recognition of dyslexia in Britain and the West has proceeded 'as our [economically developed societies'] linguistic capacity becomes increasingly articulated into the accumulation of capital'.[5] In this argument, dyslexia is construed as a 'technology of power that, when engaged to accredit an individual as dyslexic, also serves to carve a population from the multitude – a population of dyslexics'.[6] The enactment of political recognition, though, has not been as smooth as this suggests. In Britain, successive governments have *ignored* dyslexia; and many educational psychologists – and some teachers – have disputed, not recognised, its existence.[7] Rather, it has been those with dyslexia themselves and their advocates – persons, in other words, outside of state bureaucracies – who have argued *for* the dyslexia label. Here, we argue that the social construction of dyslexia cannot be theorised purely as due to institutional agents of 'governmentality' exerting their power to classify a person as having dyslexia. Rather, ultimate political recognition of dyslexia has emerged through a complex dialectic between campaigners and political representatives.[8]

There is also an implication in the existing literature that campaigns for political and societal recognition of cognitive differences have been problematic for those with such difficulties.[9] Drawing again on Michel Foucault, accounts have argued that such efforts have differentiated certain individuals by comparing them to a perceived norm. In the process, so the argument goes, voluntary organisations have reinforced, rather than contested, the superiority of 'normal' cognitive functioning. For example, Campbell has argued that 'educational institutions', of which organisations like the Dyslexia Institute might be examples, 'plot children's intelligence and attainment upon norms and classes are then segmented based upon these instruments'.[10]

However, the history of efforts to achieve political recognition for dyslexia in Britain does not support the view that such efforts, when taken as a whole, have been disadvantageous for those with dyslexia. In fact, the opposite may be true. The campaign discussed here has not been about cementing the 'normal' intelligence of those without dyslexia; rather, it has been about attempting to assist a disadvantaged group in society, whose difficulties have stemmed not just from going unrecognised, but from being recognised incorrectly. The views of those with dyslexia on the dyslexia label are as varied as one might expect from any group of individuals – for many, the label has been a tool of empowerment, rather than of difference.[11] The label has also been crucial in bringing the condition to the attention of

Dyslexia Legislated (1962–2010)

policymakers, and in directing eventual funding toward dyslexia in state education. Campaigners for political recognition of dyslexia have been interested in better integrating, rather than further differentiating, dyslexic learners in state education.

To support this contention, we present a detailed account of the behind-the-scenes efforts by the dyslexia community in Britain to sway political opinion on dyslexia – a campaign that was often marked by small steps toward progress and repeated disappointment, but which ultimately achieved substantial success. Our account draws on documents in the UK's National Archives and the Oxford Dyslexia Archive, including correspondence from representatives of the dyslexia movement to political officials and vice versa. It also draws from the (sometimes heated) debates between policymakers that occurred in the House of Commons, in which a small band of MPs with connections to dyslexia sought to persuade government officials to acknowledge dyslexia's existence, often at the behest of voluntary dyslexia organisations. The advocacy efforts of the first members of the dyslexia community, based at the Word Blind Centre, were unsuccessful. Later, their successors at the British Dyslexia Association and the Dyslexia Institute were able to better achieve what earlier lobbyists could not: nationwide state support for those with dyslexia.

Raising the Issue: The Word Blind Centre and Initial Efforts to Achieve Political Recognition for Dyslexia (1962–70)

The political lobbying of the Word Blind Centre was led by Alfred White Franklin, the chairman of the Word Blind Committee. In December 1962, eight months after the inaugural meeting of the committee, White Franklin wrote regarding dyslexia to the Ministry of Education, then under the leadership of Harold Macmillan's Conservative government (1959–63). He framed his letter around a preliminary report on reading delay, prepared by the ministry's medical officer, J.N. Horne.[12] Writing to the ministry's chief medical officer, Peter Henderson, Franklin wished to know whether the ministry recognised the importance of dyslexia to reading delay, given that dyslexia was not specifically referenced in Horne's preliminary report: 'He [Horne] does not appear to mention word-blindness, specific dyslexia or developmental dyslexia except to say that the [full report] aimed at determining whether the condition existed. Am I to understand that he is still sitting on the fence? ... As you know, the I.C.A.A. [Invalid Children's Aid Association, the sponsor of the Word Blind Centre] is devoting some attention to this subject, and has been eagerly awaiting the publication of this interim report'.[13]

Horne himself replied (suggesting Henderson had passed the buck), and was clearly irritated by White Franklin's conjecture: 'It is quite correct to understand that I am still "sitting on the fence", for this survey is not yet complete. Surely it is logical to conclude before reaching conclusions? ... In the course of this survey, I have been surprised at the depth of feeling expressed about some of the terms ... In due course, when the survey is completed, publication will be arranged, and the conclusions reached will be clearly stated. I hope that the I.C.A.A. will be able to defer any major action until the needs [stated in the full report] have been made obvious.'[14]

Horne's reply, though, did not deter White Franklin, who responded:

> I cannot imagine you have not made up your mind about cases that you have already seen ... I know that you are aware of the I.C.A.A'.s anxiety to help cases that have been given this diagnosis and we know that there are differences of opinion. Because I am anxious to work with the Ministry and with its employees, I have been restraining my group from taking any action until we had some idea of what the Ministry was going to be prepared to do ... From reading your report I formed the opinion that you were not accepting the concept of specific developmental dyslexia. If I have surmised correctly then we must go ahead because there is nothing to wait for ... Will you be good enough to help me over this by letting me know the answer to one simple question, – 'As far as you have got with your survey have you seen a single case which you would accept as a case of specific developmental dyslexia?'[15]

Horne replied tersely, reiterating his reticence to make (what he deemed premature) conclusions and thereby closing the correspondence: 'Your short question looks so easy to answer, but it represents too simple a concept of the underlying factors causing reading delay. For this reason my answer must be "No".'[16]

Dyslexia Legislated (1962–2010)

The year following White Franklin's letter, George Meredith, another member of the Word Blind Committee, tried again to convince Horne of dyslexia's existence, this time in person. By this time, Horne had issued his full report, which had dismissed the term dyslexia, and Meredith's efforts were similarly rebuffed, as Horne recorded in the minutes of their meeting: 'I pressed Professor Meredith as to whether he held the view that reading delay existed in a varying degree of severity, or whether at the most severe grade were a group of children who had distinctive features whereby they could be called "specific dyslexia". He replied that he held the latter view. I replied that amongst the 350 children that I had seen [for the report] I found no evidence to support this view.'[17]

In the tenor of the discussion between these professionals, there are echoes of the disputes over dyslexia between Victorian physicians like James Hinshelwood and William Broadbent, contested in the pages of the *Lancet* in 1896. There, as here, central to the debate was whether dyslexia could be differentiated from other kinds of reading difficulty. In mentioning his surprise at the 'depth of feeling' expressed by some in relation to dyslexia, Horne also alluded to what would become a cornerstone of arguments against dyslexia: that the term was more emotive than scientific, a label sought after by campaigners but not useful in a diagnostic sense or to teachers in the classroom.[18] In addition, Horne's contention that dyslexia represented 'too simple a concept' to encapsulate the complexity of reading difficulties prefigured later arguments that the dyslexia label subsumed, and so obfuscated, other causes of reading difficulty.[19]

The reticence of the Ministry of Education to recognise dyslexia, as expressed by Horne, derived principally from the belief that there was a lack of definitive research. At the time Horne was writing, this was not an entirely unfair conclusion. However, Horne also seems to have held strong convictions about dyslexia prior to White Franklin's letter. Between 10 and 13 April 1962, Horne visited Edith Norrie's Ordblinde Instituttet in Copenhagen, his visit coinciding, perhaps not unintentionally, with the first meeting of the Word Blind Committee on 12 April. Although, in a report to his superiors, Horne wrote in praise of the 'alphabet box' (Edith Norrie's 'letter case') employed at the Instituttet, which would shortly be introduced by Helen Arkell at her dyslexia centre in London, he was less enamoured of the concept of word-blindness: 'The term word-blindness is a traditional one in Denmark, but even though the Institute that I visited bears this title, the staff are not firmly adherent to the concept ... Outside the Institute [in Denmark as a whole] the term finds less favour, and ordinary schools prefer to talk of remedial reading groups ... This conflict in view echoes much of the conflict of opinion in Britain.'[20]

In addition to doubts over the evidence base for dyslexia, there is suggestion that, as ever in political decision-making, the cost of addressing the issue was an obstacle.[21] In the marginalia of a report about a meeting with representatives of the Word Blind Centre in 1963, Horne included an exclamatory note about the prospective cost of directly funding premises for, and places at, the centre. The Word Blind Centre requested of the ministry '£8,000 per year plus mortgage payments ... [s]pread over 60 children, this amounts to £3–4 per session'; Horne noted of the last figure, 'i.e. per child per day!'[22] Local authorities, too, cited the cost of providing dyslexia support as a reason not to engage with the condition.[23] Ultimately, the Word Blind Centre relied on funding from the ICAA to commence operations, as we have seen.

The reticence of the Ministry of Education to engage with dyslexia was reflected in the British parliament, and by the British government. Only one reference to dyslexia occurred in the early 1960s in parliamentary debate – in a question by the Scottish Unionist MP Henry Brewis. In February 1962, Brewis asked Macmillan's Conservative government what it was doing to help children with dyslexia.[24] It is unclear what spurred Brewis's question – like many with an interest in dyslexia at the time, it may have been the experiences of a family member, or it may have been the appeal of a constituent.[25] Either way, Macmillan's government, through the person of Kenneth Thompson MP, parliamentary secretary to the Ministry of Education, deferred their answer, stating that the ministry was still looking at evidence in the area.[26] Presumably, this was a reference to Horne's (then) ongoing research on reading delay.

Like Macmillan's Conservative government, the Labour government of Harold Wilson (1964–70) generally stalled when asked about dyslexia, arguing for the remainder of the decade that the existence of dyslexia remained debatable.[27] Notwithstanding this, there were signs that the solicitations of the Word Blind Centre were starting to make a small difference. In 1966, Wilson's Department of Education and Science – the new name of the Ministry of Education from 1964 – sponsored a research project on dyslexia by George Meredith of the Word Blind Centre, suggesting that, although his initial meeting with Horne had been chilly, Meredith had managed to garner some interest from the ministry.[28] Possibly this change of heart was accelerated by the change of government, with the Wilson administration showing a commitment to better funding for state education, principally via the expansion of comprehensive schooling. However, the interim findings of Meredith's ongoing project were ambivalent about dyslexia and oddly abstruse for someone seeking to sway political opinion, referring to dyslexia as 'a sort of syndrome'.[29] The opportunity had been missed.

The hedging in Meredith's report may have been one reason that the 1967 Plowden report, *Children and Their Primary Schools*, which mentioned Meredith's work, was ambivalent about dyslexia.[30] The Plowden report, one of the best-known British education reports, greatly upset educational traditionalists with its progressiveness, advocating a child-centred approach to teaching (as indicated by its title), greater engagement with parents, and increased opportunities for disadvantaged learners.[31] Such recommendations chimed with the aims and beliefs of the dyslexia movement. However, the Plowden report's opinion of dyslexia was decidedly cautious: 'Some of our witnesses have suggested the existence of specific developmental dyslexia (sometimes called word-blindness), a failure in reading which is thought to be due to neurological causes. There are so many possible reasons for poor reading, such as late maturation, ill-timed or poor teaching, sensory and speech defects, strephosymbolia (misperceptions of letters or numbers which usually correct themselves in time) and the emotional disturbances which may both cause, and result from, retardation in reading, that it is difficult to be sure whether specific dyslexia exists as an independent factor.'[32]

Like the Ministry of Education before it, the Plowden report invoked the lack of research consensus as a reason to ignore dyslexia – at least for the time being. However, its choice of alternative causes of poor reading, confusing factors extrinsic and intrinsic to the child and their behavioural consequences, was curious. 'Strephosymbolia', for example, was coined by the American physician Samuel T. Orton – but as an alternative term for dyslexia, not as a separate diagnostic entity from it. In other words, Plowden's list of alternative causes of reading difficulties ironically reaffirmed the centrality of dyslexia to reading delay.

In the years following the Plowden report, the evidence base for dyslexia mounted. In the early 1970s, two landmark texts on dyslexia were published – Macdonald Critchley's *The Dyslexic Child* (1970) and Sandhya Naidoo's *Specific Dyslexia* (1972).[33] These joined influential international publications on dyslexia, including articles in the American *Bulletin of the Orton Society*.[34] Dyslexia was becoming harder to ignore. For his part, Critchley, in *The Dyslexic Child*, called expressly for greater political consideration of dyslexia:

> Obviously the problem is sufficiently important to merit official recognition. Facilities are sorely needed for the early recognition of dyslexics, followed by opportunities for these children to receive individual, sympathetic, and intensive tuition, either in the classroom or in special schools, residential or otherwise. An even more satisfactory solution would be to train a corps of specialised teachers of dyslexia who could be sent to the schools in sufficient numbers to deal with children who had been screened and later accepted as victims of developmental dyslexia. The problem is one which requires the active participation of neurologists at the diagnostic stage, for differentiation is not always an easy matter.[35]

In highlighting the difficulty, but possibility, of differentiating dyslexia from other reading difficulties, Critchley was responding directly to Plowden's objections. In the same year (1970), the Education (Handicapped Children) Act made local authorities responsible for the education of all children, including those with learning difficulties.[36] The Chronically Sick and Disabled Persons Act, also enacted in 1970, and amongst the first legislation in the world to proscribe discrimination on the basis of disability, mentioned dyslexia for the first time in British law: 'It shall be the duty of every local education authority to provide the Secretary of State at such times as he may direct with information on the provision made by that local education authority of special educational facilities who suffer from acute dyslexia ... The arrangements made by a local education authority for the special treatment of children suffering from acute dyslexia shall, so far as is practicable, provide for the giving of such education in any school maintained or assisted by the local education authority.'[37]

Dyslexia Legislated (1962–2010)

This promising statement, though, was a false dawn in the overall campaign to achieve political recognition. It came with no suggestion for how dyslexia might be addressed in schools, nor even a description of the term. As a starting point for greater legislation in the area, it was also poorly timed: the act was published in May 1970, but by July the Wilson government was ousted in a surprise general election result, and Edward Heath's Conservative government (1970–74) took office. The new secretary of Education and Science, replacing Edward Short, was Margaret Thatcher. Her department would exhibit a marked antipathy to dyslexia.

From Thatcher to Warnock: Dyslexia, Its Discontents, and Continued Frustration (1970-87)

Margaret Thatcher entered the Department of Education and Science in 1970 with a commitment to overturning many of the key educational policies of the Wilson government. These included (most notably) compulsory comprehensive education and (most notoriously) free milk for schoolchildren aged seven to eleven. In May 1971, Thatcher appointed Jack Tizard, a psychologist, to lead an advisory committee on handicapped children. In part, Tizard was to look at what the government should be doing (if anything) about dyslexia, given its reference in the Chronically Sick and Disabled Persons Act. Superficially, Thatcher's concern stemmed from the repeated questioning of Labour MP Jack Ashley, an outspoken advocate for disability rights; but there is some suggestion that she may have held a personal interest in the topic. In February 1971, Ashley asked Thatcher for an estimate of the number of children with dyslexia in Britain, and for a description of what provision was available to them.[38] William van Straubenzee MP, a junior minister at the Department of Education and Science, replied on Thatcher's behalf, exemplifying the scepticism with which her department apparently viewed the term: 'The term "dyslexic" has come to be applied to a small minority amongst those children who are late in learning to read whose difficulties are severe and otherwise unexplained. But there is not general agreement about the cause of the condition and no proof that it is due to a single specific cause. As dyslexia cannot be satisfactorily defined it is impossible to provide reliable statistics of the number of children suffering from it, or of the numbers of such children receiving different sorts of special education.'[39]

Later in the year, Thatcher herself commented on the work of the advisory committee. Asked in a House of Commons debate about the committee's general progress, she flagged its work on dyslexia specifically: 'This year the Committee has submitted reports on research and on a question [Jack Ashley's] I referred to it concerning dyslexia. I have approved its recommended programme of research into various aspects of special education down to 1978, which will be financed by my Department at a total cost of £316,000. The Committee's report on dyslexia was submitted to me very recently, and I am considering it.'[40]

Asked whether *all* of the committee's work would be published, Thatcher again brought the question back to dyslexia: 'The report on dyslexia will be published. The Committee has let me know that it will have no objection to its being published'.[41]

The reason for Thatcher's eagerness to publish the committee's dyslexia report would later become clear. Tizard, the report's author, was a researcher on the Isle of Wight study of learning disorders, which began in 1964, and, despite its other benefits to the science of reading difficulties, queried the use of the term dyslexia. Indeed, this may have been one of the reasons for Tizard's appointment to the review by Thatcher. Tizard's report on dyslexia, tellingly, was entitled, *Children with Specific Reading Difficulties*, and declared that: 'We are highly sceptical of the view that a syndrome of developmental dyslexia with a specific underling cause and specific symptoms has been identified.'[42]

The refusal of Thatcher's Department of Education and Science to recognise dyslexia reached its apotheosis in 1974. In November 1973, Thatcher created a committee with the following objectives: 'To review educational provision in England, Scotland and Wales for children and young people handicapped by disabilities of body and mind, taking account of the medical aspects of their needs, together with arrangements to prepare them for entry into employment; to consider the most effective use of resources for these purposes; and to make recommendations.'[43]

The emphasis on economic productivity in the committee's remit fit with Thatcher's broader belief in neoliberal approaches to state policy, which were on the ascendancy in the 1970s and would characterise her later prime ministership (1979–90). The purpose of education, in such understandings, was to make Britain competitive in the global marketplace, rather than as an end in itself or to provide children with richer intellectual lives.[44] However, despite the increasing importance of literacy to becoming an economically productive worker – a context that one might assume would have made reading difficulties of especial concern – dyslexia remained taboo in the Department of Education and Science. Warnock recalls that

> by '74, when the Committee of Enquiry was set up, although the Department was perfectly aware that there were a comparatively large number of children with special needs that was when their complete hostility to the concept of dyslexia became clear to me. I knew well about Millfield and I knew well about their [Millfield's] target of sending these people [with dyslexia] to university and indeed we went to Hertford [College, Oxford] in '71 [when Warnock's husband was appointed principal] and there was a Millfield boy as an undergraduate and we perfectly recognised that this boy was going to be given extra time for his exams.[45]

However, as Warnock continues: 'The hostility in the Department to this concept was manifest by the instructions we were given when we were set up at the beginning of '74, when I was summoned by the person in the Department who was responsible [for the Committee of Enquiry]. He said, "you understand your terms of reference?", and I said, "yes, I do", and he said, "well, you must understand that you must not suggest that … there is a special category of learning difficulty called dyslexia."'[46]

Warnock contested this: 'I said, "but you can't say that dyslexia is not a learning difficulty", then I trotted out this boy at Hertford [College] and all the things I knew – anecdotal, but still. He didn't answer the question that even Oxford University recognised dyslexia as requiring various exemptions from this and that. He simply said, "well I expect he is a middle-class boy". Of course, he was, and that was the very end of the conversation.'[47]

The origin of the pressure on Warnock is unclear. Certainly, it was of a piece with the earlier dismissal of the term 'dyslexia' in the Tizard report, about which Thatcher was enthusiastic. In another recollection, Warnock cites pressure from Thatcher specifically, but does not elaborate.[48] The civil servants appointed to oversee Warnock's review were involved substantially in the committee's work; it was never granted full independence. Warnock attempted to place two persons on the committee whom she respected: the head of social services for Oxford County Council, and a paediatrician of her acquaintance. As Warnock recalls, 'My two attempts were frustrated. I didn't know any of the people who were there [on the committee] nor why they had been selected.'[49] At least one member of the committee later expressed dissatisfaction with the concept of dyslexia.[50] The final report of 1978 highlighted the importance of voluntary organisations in achieving political recognition for special educational needs, but mentioned dyslexia just twice, despite receiving evidence from the British Dyslexia Association (of which Warnock later became president), the Dyslexia Institute, the Bangor Dyslexia Unit, Bevé Hornsby, and various local associations.[51] When it came to dyslexia, Warnock ultimately deferred to the recommendations of the Tizard report: 'We have received much evidence from dyslexia associations about the needs of children with specific learning difficulties in reading, writing and spelling. The Secretary of State's Advisory Committee's Pamphlet *Children with Specific Reading Difficulties* [the Tizard report] published in 1972 discusses the issues and we generally concur with its conclusions. There are many reasons for perceptual and learning difficulties in reading, writing and spelling, and careful assessment is required.'[52] The influence of a guiding hand seems clear in this paragraph; the term 'specific learning difficulties' was, Warnock recalls, 'our way of referring to dyslexia without using that wicked word'.[53]

Nevertheless, the Warnock report made progress for those with dyslexia in other ways. Although the term 'specific learning difficulties' did not capture the linguistic dimension of dyslexia, it clearly differentiated dyslexia from general learning difficulties. As we have seen, dyslexia in the 1970s was often conflated by teachers and educational psychologists with low intelligence; Warnock's term made clear the limits of the condition. In this way, it mirrored the discrepancy diagnostic model, which was then finding consensus in dyslexia's science. The report also brought responsibility for specific learning difficulties firmly under the purview of education, rather than medicine, as the field best able to ameliorate dyslexic difficulties.[54]

In addition, Warnock recommended the implementation of a more sophisticated system for assessing the needs of individual learners, including statementing, which would go on to have a beneficial effect on how children with dyslexia, and with other learning difficulties and disabilities, were supported: 'Our proposed system of recording children as in need of special educational provision will differ from the present system of categorisation in several important ways. First, it will lay an obligation on a local education authority to make special educational provision for any child judged to be in need of such provision on the basis of a profile of his needs prepared by a multiprofessional team, whatever his particular disability. Secondly, it will not impose a single label of handicap on any child. Thirdly, it will embody a positive statement of the type of special provision required.'[55]

This proposal – later legislated in the 1981 Education Act, which came into force in 1983 – created a clear mechanism for how children with special educational needs were to be assisted, which was welcomed by the dyslexia community.[56] Statementing, in particular, created a written record of the obligations of schools and local authorities to children with diverse learning needs. While the statementing process was cumbersome, and often effective only when parents had the financial resources to ensure its enforcement (by way of legal fees), dyslexia assistance was now available by law in state education.

However, the Warnock report, because of its ambivalence about dyslexia, continued to frustrate efforts at explicit government recognition of the same. Moreover, it unintentionally provided the government – now led by Margaret Thatcher after her election as prime minister in 1979 – with an excuse not to engage when asked about the condition. The 1981 Education Act, at the report's recommendation, replaced the single statutory categorisation of 'handicapped' pupils with the concept of a 'continuum of need'.[57] This was a progressive step, hindering the long-standing bias against non-traditional learners in state schooling (and prefiguring the 'neurodiversity' paradigm, as we will see). However, the government used the concept of a spectrum of need to avoid acknowledgement of dyslexia throughout the mid-1980s. When asked what criteria local education authorities should use to diagnose dyslexia, the government typically replied that 'the duty of local education authorities under the Education Act of 1981 is not to categorise children, but to assess their individual special educational needs'.[58] In this way, the government could dodge questions regarding dyslexia's existence.

It appears that civil servants in the Department of Education and Science remained sceptical of the term, too. In the mid-1980s, Conservative MP Peter Walker met with the Conservative secretary of Education and Science, Keith Joseph, to discuss dyslexia. A centrist and founder of the progressive Tory Reform Group, Walker recalls that he

> outlined the details of the problem [to Joseph], the failure of the whole education system to recognise it [dyslexia], and the failure of the education authorities either to identity the problem or to provide the appropriate education. Being the kind and compassionate person that he was, Sir Keith listened with immense interest. I must confess that the observations of the officials who surrounded him rather frightened me. They suggested that many parents used dyslexia as an excuse for the bad performance of their children. There was a slight atmosphere of suspicion about whether the problem was of the order that I was suggesting and whether it was something that could be clearly identified and treated.[59]

However, the Thatcher government's views, at least superficially, were about to change.

From Thatcher to Blair: Neoliberalism, 'Dispelling a Myth', and the Pathway to Government Recognition (1987-97)

In 1987, Conservative MP David Amess opened a debate on dyslexia provision in the House of Commons with the following comments to the parliamentary under-secretary of state for education and science, Robert Dunn MP: 'Dyslexic or not dyslexic? That is the question. At least, it is a question that is posed by many parents who are desperately concerned about the progress that their offspring are making at school. I shall not waste time by discussing whether the Department of Education accepts that there is such a thing as dyslexia; I shall assume that it does.'[60]

Dyslexia Legislated (1962–2010)

In making the final point, of course, Amess was implying that the department still might *not* believe in the concept – a sensible precaution, given the department's history of pronouncements on the topic. Amess went on to pay tribute to the work of the BDA in assisting children with dyslexia, and highlighted the strengths and weaknesses of the statementing process, as recommended by the Warnock report:

> The Education Act 1981 requires local education authorities to provide for proper assessment of children. That procedure can take a long time ... After the assessment stage, the child must have a statement of his disability drawn up. From the time of the recognition of the problem to the final statement of disability, over two years may have passed. To alleviate some of the problems, an informal assessment can be made, but if the child shows signs of disability, he must go on to a formal assessment so that he can have a statement made. Even after that, it can often prove difficult to get adequate help for him.[61]

Amess concluded by requesting that 'those with learning disabilities be given the same consideration and opportunities as other children'.[62]

Dunn's response concurred with Amess that the 1981 Education Act remained the legislation that governed dyslexia provision in schools. However, in response to Amess's loaded observation about the department's belief in the concept, Dunn carefully omitted the scepticism that had characterised the department's previous dealings with dyslexia: 'I open my response to this short but important debate by trying to dispel a myth – that the Department of Education and Science and its Ministers do not recognise dyslexia as a problem. The Government recognise dyslexia and recognise the importance to the education progress of dyslexic children, their long-term welfare and successful-function [sic] in adult life, that they should have their needs identified at an early stage. Once the assessment has been made ... the appropriate treatment should be forthcoming.'[63]

With reference to how the statementing process and general provision might be improved, Dunn shifted responsibility to local education authorities. Indeed, he suggested that, if any part of government was sceptical about dyslexia, it was local government: 'I know that there are some local education authorities, which as a matter of policy, refuse to accept the word dyslexia. They argue that there are very few children who present a common pattern of dyslexic symptoms. Certainly there is no one characteristic which defines a child as dyslexic or not dyslexic. There is a range of criteria, and a child who shows a particular pattern of difficulties may be termed dyslexic. Whether or not the term is used, the important thing is to be sure that something is being done about the problem.'[64]

As to what this something might be, Dunn was noncommittal. Nevertheless, members of the dyslexia community interpreted Dunn's statement as a turningpoint in government recognition of dyslexia, providing them with a black-and-white acknowledgement of the condition, clearing the way for greater political progress in the 1990s.[65] To an extent, such optimism was justified. As we have seen, legislation like the 1970 Chronically Sick and Disabled Persons Act mentioned dyslexia, but there had been little follow-up. Certainly, follow-up was greater after Dunn's announcement, if still stop-start. In 1987, two debates, Dunn's and another in the House of Lords, considered dyslexia. These were followed by further debates in 1988, 1991, and 1993, covering various aspects of the condition – from provision in Wales, to the difficulties faced by people with dyslexia on training schemes, to exam arrangements for students with dyslexia.[66] In these debates, dyslexia was discussed as a matter of fact; government spokespersons no longer queried the condition's existence or its evidence base.

The vehicle for providing greater support remained the statementing process, and, of any political action, it is the expansion of this during the 1990s that probably benefited dyslexic pupils in Britain the most. Between 1991 and 2000, the number of pupils with statements in mainstream schools increased by over 95,000.[67] This followed a gradual increase over the 1980s after statementing was introduced in the 1981 Education Act. Of these statements, the majority for secondary school pupils were for specific learning difficulties, which referred primarily to dyslexia.[68] The 1993 Education Act, and the subsequent *Code of Practice* which referenced dyslexia specifically, placed further responsibility on schools to identify and support children with learning difficulties.[69] In 1995, the Disability Discrimination Act made it mandatory for local education authorities to provide equal access to the curriculum for pupils with disabilities; in 1996, a further Education Act spec-

Dyslexia Legislated (1962–2010)

ified procedures for identifying and supporting children with special educational needs, including dyslexia.[70]

There were several reasons for this progress. As we have seen, Thatcher entered the Department of Education and Science with a firm belief that education was the method through which children would obtain the skills necessary to thrive in the new, post-industrial economy. Through this, Britain as a whole would become more competitive in the global marketplace.[71] As prime minister, Thatcher was empowered to accelerate this neoliberal revolution across society. In education, the 1980s saw a 'moral panic' over standards in schools. The National Curriculum of 1988 centralised decisions about what pupils were taught, allowing for comparison between schools. Increasingly, children's performance in key areas like literacy was prescribed and assessed. Whether Thatcher herself, or her civil servants at the Department of Education and Science, were the main drivers of official scepticism toward dyslexia, it is impossible to answer with certainty. Either way, Thatcher no longer held direct control over dyslexia provision, and the department showed a greater willingness to engage with the concept.

Amess's reference to the work of the British Dyslexia Association was revealing, too. After the closure of the Word Blind Centre, the BDA and the Dyslexia Institute took the lead in building awareness of dyslexia – both publicly and politically. As mentioned, this included a media campaign that started in the early 1970s, represented by celebrities like the actress Susan Hampshire, which increased public awareness of dyslexia via television and radio programmes.[72] Throughout the 1980s, the BDA was cited frequently in parliamentary debates in the House of Commons and in the House of Lords.[73] In 1987, the year of Dunn's announcement, the European Dyslexia Association was formed, amalgamating organisations in Belgium, Denmark, France, Germany, Holland, Ireland, and Norway. The European Dyslexia Association's creation was championed by the BDA.[74]

The reticence of educational authorities to acknowledge dyslexia had long been predicated on the contention that the evidence base for the condition was slim, but, as we have seen, this increased significantly after experimental psychologists became involved in its study in the 1970s.[75] It is not clear that the expansion of this research directly influenced government opinion, however. Ironically, the only reference in Dunn's statement was to the 1968 definition of dyslexia by the World Federation of Neurology – in his paraphrase, 'a disorder in children who, despite conventional classroom experience fail to attain the language skills of reading, writing and spelling commensurate with their intellectual abilities' – a definition which by 1987 had been superseded by scientists working on dyslexia.[76] Nevertheless, it seems likely that the depth and range of dyslexia studies, coupled with the work of organisation like the BDA, who cited this work frequently, further eroded governments' historical position of scepticism.

By the late 1990s, a further shift in Britain's political landscape accelerated dyslexia support. In 1997, Tony Blair was elected the first Labour prime minister since James Callaghan. The first white paper (policy proposal) of Blair's 'New Labour' was *Excellence in Schools*. Building on Thatcher's legacy, this stated that, 'to compete in the global economy, to live in a civilised society and to develop the talents of each and every one of us, we will have to unlock the potential of every young person'.[77] New Labour's flagship National Literacy Strategy aimed, by 2002, to increase the proportion of eleven-year-olds who obtained the standard expected for their age in English from 60 per cent to 80 per cent, including children with specific reading difficulties like dyslexia.[78] Funding for children with special educational needs increased substantially – from £4 million in 1997–98 to £30 million in 2001, with further increases to follow.[79]

New Labour's emphasis on literacy, and on those with difficulties in literacy, was mirrored elsewhere in the world – in part, at least, because of the same adherence to neoliberal education policies. In America, with the unification of dyslexia science around the phonological deficit hypothesis and the support of the Orton Society, substantial government funds were awarded during the 1990s and early 2000s to researchers exploring reading disability.[80] In contexts as diverse as Sweden, Poland, and the Caribbean, hesitance by educational authorities to deal with the issue in the 1970s and 1980s was replaced by greater willingness to engage with national campaigns, often citing British legislation such as the Warnock report to justify support.[81] In 1997, the American Orton Society became the International Dyslexia Association, highlighting a global groundswell of support for the condition and those affected.

In addition to this policy context, dyslexia in Britain had a new and sympathetic ear. David Blunkett, the incoming education secretary, was perhaps

Dyslexia Legislated (1962–2010)

the first holder of that office to have direct experience of dyslexia (two of Blunkett's sons had dyslexia and possibly Blunkett himself).[82] A supporter of the term, one of Blunkett's first actions as secretary of Education and Employment (as the department had been renamed in 1995) funded two research projects – one at the Helen Arkell Dyslexia Centre and one at Manchester Metropolitan University. These projects examined how teachers without specialist training could be assisted in identifying and helping children with dyslexia.[83] Blunkett recalls that he encountered little criticism of his efforts at obtaining greater support for those with dyslexia in state education, 'because we [the incoming Labour government] were in a quite powerful position':

> We'd got a massive majority [winning 418 of 659 seats in the general election of 1997], the commitment of the Prime Minister, someone [Blunkett] who himself had been to a special school with at least two sons who'd experienced this particular specific educational need, a very understanding ministerial team, and we'd got Michael Barber heading the [School] Standards Unit. So it was quite formidable for people to take it [the government's stance on dyslexia support] head on. But they did. There were people both outside schools and inside schools still mumbling that: 'Oh god, this is another fetish. This is something coming down from government. They've got the idea that this is a good thing.' Then [some] people started to be very cynical about it: 'This is an electoral commitment, ticks the box', and all the rest of it. Whereas I saw it as part of trying to get to grips with both literacy and numeracy and related issues that were affecting a large number of children, who couldn't possibly just be slow learners.[84]

In this political climate of greater inclusion, influential bodies in the UK turned their attention to dyslexia. In 1999, the Division of Educational and Child Psychology of the British Psychological Society convened a working group to consider the role of the profession in the assessment of dyslexia. The group's resulting report recognised the 'plight of learners with difficulties of a dyslexic nature', and concluded that central to the definition of dyslexia and to its assessment was the concept of severity or persistence.[85] It stated three criteria for assessing dyslexia: (1) the fluency of word reading and spelling; (2) the accessibility or otherwise of appropriate learning opportunities; and (3) the progress made by the student given specialist instruction.[86] The report was influential and served as a starting point for policy decisions within UK legislation at the local authority level. Like the more progressive education reviews before it, including those of Plowden and Warnock, the report recommended that educational psychologists help teachers and parents to 'notice' individual children's needs and to adjust responses accordingly. What happened if educational psychologists and teachers failed to notice dyslexia would be at the heart of a landmark legal case.

Dyslexia and the Law: Dyslexia, Legal Provision, and Disability Rights to the Equality Act (2010)

A combination of sympathetic personalities, changing economic priorities, and an evolving educational landscape in which all children were to receive adequate education regardless of specific need, led to greater support for those with dyslexia in Britain during the 1990s. Since the Education Act of 1981, efforts to achieve this support were built on statementing, which for the first time provided a legal guarantee of assistance for children with dyslexia, albeit under the descriptor 'specific learning difficulties'. Through this procedure, parents were able to hold local authorities accountable for providing specialist support to their children – in theory, if not always in practice. With the explicit political acknowledgement of dyslexia in the 1990s, the legal recognition of, and protections for, people with dyslexia expanded – in schools, but also in the workplace and in later life. In 1997, a legal case crystallised the new legal responsibilities of the state toward the individual with dyslexia: *Phelps vs London Borough of Hillingdon*.

Born in 1973, Pamela Phelps attended Hayes Park Infants School in Hillingdon from 1978. In 1980, she was assessed by a state-appointed educational psychologist because of a lack of academic progress. The psychologist determined that Phelps was of normal intelligence, but recommended that she attend a child guidance clinic. At secondary school, Phelps's progress stalled further, with her reading of particular concern to her teachers. The child guidance clinic attributed responsibility for her problems to emotional causes, and to Phelps's relationship with her parents. Subsequently (and perhaps unsurprisingly) the relations between her parents and the child guidance clinic deteriorated. At Mellow Lane School in Hillingdon, Phelps was assessed by another educational psychologist, who found her reading age significantly below average, but did not diagnose dyslexia. According to Phelps, the term was not used by any of the teachers or the remedial specialists at her schools.[87]

In 1990, shortly before she left state education, Phelps's parents arranged a private dyslexia assessment at the Dyslexia Institute. This assessment did diagnose dyslexia. At the age of seventeen, when the assessment was conducted, Phelps's reading age was estimated to be below that of an average eight-year-old. After leaving school, where she had increasingly played truant, Phelps struggled to maintain employment, ostensibly because of her literacy difficulties. She received some specialist dyslexia tuition, but, by the time her case was heard by the High Court in 1997, she had found no further permanent employment. In the writ Phelps issued against Hillingdon Council, she alleged that the council had failed in its obligations under the Education Acts of 1944 and 1981 to afford all pupils the opportunity for education.[88] This, Phelps said, had consigned her to a life of 'temporary menial' employment, given the requirement for literacy in the majority of better-paying professions.[89]

The High Court found in Phelps's favour, the judge ruling that the educational psychologist who had initially missed Phelps's dyslexia had demonstrated professional incompetence. This made Hillingdon Council liable, and they were duly ordered to pay Phelps a little under £46,000 in compensation for lost earnings and general damages. In response, David Hart, general secretary of the National Association of Head Teachers, warned that the ruling would have dire consequences for schools: 'It implies that schools are going to be at much greater risk of claims for damages'.[90]

Building on arguments such as Hart's, the UK Appeals Court overturned the High Court's judgement in 1998, highlighting the 'serious risk that vexatious claims may be brought against many teachers or educational psychologists many years after the relevant decisions were taken'. However, a further and final appeal by Phelps, to the House of Lords in 2000, was successful, and Phelps's damages, which had been rescinded after the Appeals Court's verdict, were reinstated.[91]

The case was controversial at the time, and remains so today. For proponents of dyslexia, it represented the ultimate official validation of the condition's existence, and of the responsibility of educational authorities to deal with the difficulties it posed to the individual. For opponents of dyslexia – and even for some who supported the term – the judgement was excessive, making local authorities, schools, and even individual teachers legally responsible for all children who struggled in later life for educational reasons.[92]

The case, then, illustrates three points. First, and most obviously, it shows how far political recognition of dyslexia had come by the end of the twentieth century in Britain. While the flood of lawsuits against local authorities never materialised – in part because it took several years for the case to be resolved, by which time the media and the public appear to have lost interest – *Phelps vs Hillingdon* represented a watershed moment in the campaign for dyslexia rights, which was cited frequently by the dyslexia movement in later years.[93] For their part, the government made no comment on the ruling, maintaining their constitutional distance from judicial decisions. Asked what impact the judgement would have on the budgets of local authorities, Jacqui Smith, parliamentary under-secretary at the Department for Education and Employment, exercised discretion. However, in her brief remarks, Smith did suggest a further reason why a spate of lawsuits did not follow: 'the judgement recognised that "the professionalism, dedication and standards of those engaged in the provision of educational services are such that cases of negligence will be exceptional"'.[94]

Second, the Phelps case highlights the role that dyslexia research and advocacy had in influencing official opinion. In the original High Court decision it was concluded that, if Phelps had been administered a recognised dyslexia test, such as the 'Bangor' test, her condition would not have been missed: 'This was more than an error of judgement [by the educational psychologist at Phelps's primary school]: it was a failure to exercise the degree of care and skill to be expected of an ordinarily competent member of her profession.'[95] In all three judgements, Phelps's 1990 diagnosis by the psychologist at the Dyslexia Institute was taken as conclusive, suggesting that the organisation's reputation – and, by this point, the science of dyslexia – was beyond dispute. Again, this was a judicial decision, not a political one, but it shows how far the respectability of dyslexia organisations had come since the Word Blind Centre and its representatives were rebuffed by the

Ministry of Education in the early 1960s, and since the dyslexia organisations of the 1970s were excised from the Warnock report.

Third, the Phelps case demonstrates how, by the beginning of the twenty-first century, new understandings of disability and disability rights were emerging. The work of disability scholars and campaigners since the 1970s had stressed the role of society in framing, exacerbating, even producing disability.[96] In such understandings, people with dyslexia were impaired by biologically based reading difficulties, but disabled by the societal requirement for literacy and the inability of state education to address reading difficulties successfully in all cases. In the Phelps case, the influence of society on the experience of dyslexia was explicitly acknowledged. Indeed, this was one of the points debated during the various court and parliamentary proceedings. In overturning the original High Court decision, the Appeals Court contended: 'Even if dyslexia can be regarded as an impairment of the applicant's mental condition, it is not caused by the potential defendant [Hillingdon Council]. It is a congenital and constitutional condition. Failure to diagnose it does not exacerbate the condition.'[97] In response, the House of Lords judgement argued that, contrary to the reasoning of the Appeals Court, failure to diagnose dyslexia *did* exacerbate Phelps's difficulties, making Hillingdon Council liable for her later struggles in employment.

This increasing emphasis on the social in dyslexia's production marked official publications on dyslexia in the years to come. In 2008, Ed Balls MP, the secretary for Children, Schools and Families (as the Department for Education was renamed from 2007–10), announced that a review would be held of dyslexia provision – the first time that the UK government had requested an independent review of dyslexia, per se. The Rose review, like the ultimate judgement by the House of Lords in the Phelps case, emphasised that the difficulties faced by children with dyslexia stemmed from their treatment in literate society, as well as from an individual impairment. Thus, 'children and adults with dyslexia who responded to the call for evidence said that they often felt deeply humiliated when asked to read. They reported being ridiculed and bullied because of their reading difficulties. Further, because so much depends on being able to "read to learn" the overall educational progress of such children is often seriously hampered with worrying consequences for gaining qualifications and for their life chances.'[98]

In parliamentary debates following the Rose review, the role of the social in shaping life outcomes for dyslexic children was brought into focus, often linked to efforts at achieving greater social mobility. The Rose review drew attention to the preponderance of people with dyslexia in the prison population and from disadvantaged socio-economic groups; in the debates that followed, greater specialist support for children with dyslexia was viewed as an issue of 'social justice'. Thus, Kelvin Hopkins MP (Labour) stated that, 'if we are to have a society that is less divided, we must ensure that we provide education for those who do not have natural advantages'. Sarah Teather MP (Liberal Democrat) concurred: 'we must ensure that all children, regardless of their background, are given the same benefits of that sound education'. Sharon Hodgson MP (Labour), chairperson of the All-Party Parliamentary Group on Dyslexia and Specific Learning Difficulties, contended that even 'the additional 5% [of total marks in GCSE exams for spelling, punctuation and grammar] can make the difference between an A and an A* for a very bright, dyslexic pupil'.[99]

While the years since the Phelps case showed a willingness by some politicians to legislate to make up for the social factors that exacerbated dyslexia – most obviously by providing greater support in schools – dissenters remained. In the same parliamentary debate on the Rose review above, Graham Stringer MP (Labour) quoted from a report on literacy interventions by the Science and Technology Committee, of which he was a member: 'The Rose Report's definition of dyslexia is exceedingly broad and says that dyslexia is a continuum with no clear cut-off points. The definition is so broad and blurred at the edges that it is difficult to see how it could be useful in any diagnostic sense ... The Government's focus on dyslexia, from a policy perspective, was led by pressure from the dyslexia lobby rather than the evidence, which is clear that educational interventions are the same for all poor readers, whether they have been diagnosed with dyslexia or not'.[100] Stringer's reading of Rose's 'broad' definition arguably overlooked two specific points from the same definition, however: that dyslexia primarily affected 'the skills involved in accurate and fluent word reading and spelling', and that characteristic features of dyslexia were 'difficulties in phonological awareness, verbal memory and verbal processing speed'.[101]

The fact that voices such as Stringer's did not disappear after the Rose review, and after increased awareness of dyslexia in Parliament, suggests that

Dyslexia Legislated (1962–2010) 159

scepticism is best considered a perennial aspect of the dyslexia story (discussed further in the next chapter). Despite these criticisms, though, dyslexia endured – outside of the Rose report, dyslexia found support in various legislative measures from the turn of the twentieth century, including the 2010 Equality Act.[102] The term was now far more resistant to criticism than it had been when the Word Blind Centre first brought dyslexia to the attention of British policymakers in the early 1960s.

Chapter 6 – Key Points

- As dyslexia awareness spread in British civil society, so too did efforts at obtaining political recognition
- The first concerted lobbying in Britain was undertaken by the Word Blind Centre, then by the associations that followed in its wake
- Despite an expanding evidence base for dyslexia, efforts at obtaining political recognition met substantial resistance from policymakers, although policies such as 'statementing' offered a pathway to some support
- By the 1990s, substantial progress had been made, and dyslexia support started to become more widely available, with further protections under legislation such as the 2010 Equality Act

PART 4
Legacies

7

Dyslexia Today and Tomorrow: Discourses of Dyslexia in the Twenty-First Century

The scope of dyslexia at the start of the 2020s is vast. Different interpretations of the condition exist in science and education, in provision and politics, in the media and advocacy. While the processes of globalisation have unified some of these perspectives – especially in science, where researchers no longer need to sail across the Atlantic to discuss their findings as Samuel T. Orton once did – others remain at the dictate of changing priorities in state funding and of the 'fashionableness' of certain cognitive difficulties relative to others.[1] A person born with dyslexia in the West today will engage with a myriad of views on the condition during their lifetime, from teachers, educational psychologists, child psychiatrists, parents, employers, journalists, filmmakers, and others – those with dyslexia and those without. To capture this complexity, this chapter weaves together several contemporary narratives of dyslexia.

First, we consider the place of dyslexia in popular culture. In recent decades, diverse disciplines have recognised analyses of contemporary popular culture as a way of revealing, indeed reproducing, societal mores and understandings.[2] Having considered how dyslexia has been thought about by physicians and ophthalmologists, scientists and politicians, campaigners and those with dyslexia, we address here how popular books, television series, and films have represented dyslexia. While dyslexia has widespread name recognition in English-speaking societies today, the majority of knowledge about it in the public consciousness comes not from scientific books and articles but from popular media with its substantially greater audience. Here, a script repository, QUODB, linked to the Internet Movie Database (IMDb), the world's largest repository of film and television data, is used to survey dyslexia references in these productions, alongside references to dyslexia in other, bibliographic databases.[3] The focus is on British and American productions. We reflect on the positive and negative effects of this diverse range of representations, which has brought dyslexia to greater public attention, but also confused definitions of the condition.

Second, we discuss the latest iteration of the dyslexia myth. As we have shown, scepticism of dyslexia has marked the condition's history since the Victorian period. In Britain, such scepticism reached a zenith in the 1960s and 1970s, with the government claiming (in public) that no clear evidence for dyslexia existed and opining (in private) that it was a middle-class invention. Educational authorities around the world were similarly reticent to engage with dyslexia, many into the twenty-first century.[4] Not only educational leadership, but teachers, psychologists, and media commentators have expressed scepticism about dyslexia. In recent years, critiques have reached a wider audience through documentaries such as *The Dyslexia Myth* (2005) and books such as *The Dyslexia Debate* (2014), which have cast shade on the term and/or on aspects of the dyslexia 'construct'.[5]

Third, we consider how dyslexia fits with policy agendas and public discourses around 'neurodiversity', which have emerged over the first decades of the twenty-first century and represent the newest interpretation of the concept. Increasingly, governments, employers, and schools are treating cognitive difference as a universal. In such understandings, there is no single or 'normal' mode of functioning; there are a plurality of thinking styles, each with their own positive and negative qualities. Thus, for Steve Silberman, a historian of autism, 'one way to understand neurodiversity is to think in terms of *human operating systems* instead of diagnostic labels like *dyslexia* and *ADHD*. The brain is, above all, a marvellously adaptive organism, adept at maximizing its chances of success even in the face of daunting limitations.'[6] Here, neurodiversity is used to reflect on what dyslexia tells us about the normative role of literacy in modern society. We also reflect on how key elements of the neurodiversity paradigm were prefigured in earlier debates around dyslexia.

Dyslexia in Popular Culture: Dyslexia as Limitation, Gift, and Comedy (1980s-Present)

In the late Victorian period, dyslexia encountered its first attention in popular culture via a series of British newspaper reports. These articles, which frequently referred to the case studies of physicians like William Pringle Morgan and James Hinshelwood, presented 'word-blindness' as a medical curiosity. Terms used to describe the condition, in both tabloids and broadsheets, included 'extraordinary', 'strange', and 'curious'.[7] In this way, word-blindness was positioned alongside other 'anomalies' of the mind and body. Such understandings of dyslexia persisted into the later decades of the twentieth century, and, while dyslexia is well-known in society today, the majority of knowledge about the condition comes from popular culture that exhibits some of the same limitations as Victorian coverage: personal experiences of dyslexia are emphasized and anecdotal evidence is frequently highlighted.

In 1972, one of the first television programmes on dyslexia in Britain, part of the documentary series *Man Alive*, aired on the terrestrial station BBC Two. There, audiences were introduced to Robert Payne: 'normal in every way except that he can barely read and write ... He suffers from what some experts call dyslexia. Dyslexic children find it very difficult to learn what comes so naturally to most of us.' In more than seventy-five years since the Victorian newspaper reports of word-blindness, perceptions of dyslexia in popular culture as unexpected, and as a curiosity, had altered very little.

During the 1980s, political attention to dyslexia in high-income countries increased substantially, as we have seen, and the term became more commonly used by teachers and educationalists. In popular culture, dyslexia began to lose some of its mystique; increasingly, it was accepted as an authentic learning difficulty. The earliest depictions of dyslexia as a learning difficulty are captured in American films, especially those made directly for television. In these, a character with dyslexia is typically diagnosed in adulthood, with narratives frequently oriented around this character securing initial assistance for their difficulty, often through a sympathetic friend or teacher. Thus, in the romantic film *The Princess and the Cabbie* (1981), an educated taxi driver helps a chance fare lost in downtown Manhattan with navigational difficulties ascribed to dyslexia. In the dramas *Backwards: The Riddle of Dyslexia* (1984) and *Love, Mary* (1985), the helper role is fulfilled by a teacher and a social worker, respectively.[8] In each film, the exoticism of dyslexia is invoked to garner audience interest, but dyslexia is also posited as a legitimate difficulty, with a firm evidentiary basis, for which support is available.

Such depictions of dyslexia as a functional limitation remained common in Western popular culture throughout the 1990s. However, a further interpretation of dyslexia also emerged during this decade, perhaps partly as a reaction to these earlier representations: dyslexia as a gift. In 1994, Ron Davis published *The Gift of Dyslexia* for a general audience, which postulated an association between dyslexia and giftedness.[9] Davis's work followed in the wake of the *Rain Man* phenomenon – named after the 1988 film drama about autism, which spurred a public fascination with the possible benefits of alternative modes of thinking.[10] While there was no robust scientific evidence for these claims in the case of dyslexia, books, television shows, and films from the early 2000s increasingly engaged with the trope.[11] In some cases, they were intended as informal advocacy to support the self-esteem of learners with dyslexia, and so might be aligned with the broader history of campaigns to obtain political and public acceptance of dyslexia.

The foremost example of dyslexia 'boosterism' in popular culture is the work of the American author Rick Riordan. In 2005, Riordan published *Percy Jackson and the Lightning Thief*, the first title in his young adult fiction series, *Percy Jackson and the Olympians*.[12] The book sees the titular hero of the series, a twenty-first-century teenager from New York, discover that he possesses superhuman lineage – he is the son of the Greek god of the sea, Poseidon, his name an abbreviation of Perseus. The series details Percy's various adventures as he and his friends thwart a plot by the Titans to retake control of Mount Olympus (accessed, naturally, via the Empire State Building). The series weaves fantasy into the modern world in a manner akin to that of other young adult franchises of recent years, such as the *Harry Potter* saga. What makes *Percy Jackson* unusual is that Percy possesses dyslexia and ADHD. Indeed, these conditions, which cause him to struggle at school (but not in his adventures), are a product of his divine parentage. Early in the first book, his friend Annabeth explains to Percy: 'The letters float off the page when you read, right? That's because your mind is hardwired for Ancient Greek. And the ADHD – you're impulsive, can't sit still in the classroom. That's your battlefield reflexes.'[13] The series was a commercial success, and two further book series and two Hollywood adaptations followed, Percy Jackson and the Lightning Thief and Percy Jackson: Sea of Monsters, respectively.[14]

In the 2010s, books like The Gift of Dyslexia and productions like Percy Jackson were joined by popular science works that suggested, from a non-scientific perspective, the links between dyslexia and giftedness. These included the American journalist Malcolm Gladwell's David and Goliath (2013), which argued that dyslexia is associated with entrepreneurism. Gladwell cites examples such as Richard Branson, founder of the Virgin Company, and David Boies, the celebrated American lawyer.[15] Such works have supplemented literature published by dyslexia voluntary organisations, which have sought to 'claim' famous persons with dyslexia, including Leonardo da Vinci and Albert Einstein, and to highlight celebrities with a formal diagnosis, such as the actors Tom Cruise, Jim Carrey, and Keira Knightley, with whom we began this book.[16] These claims have paralleled earlier assertions, sometimes championed by dyslexia advocates, that dyslexia is associated with high performance in areas outside of literacy, such as general intelligence. Such discourses, though, have attracted substantial criticism from researchers in the science of reading, who note that, amongst other things, they can create unfair expectations of students with dyslexia.[17]

The third and final major way in which dyslexia has been portrayed in Western popular culture is as comedy – jokes that are sometimes, but not always, sympathetic to those with dyslexia. Here, we focus on jokes in television and film, but dyslexia is also a common subject for cartoonists. Like the association with giftedness, references to dyslexia as joke have increased as dyslexia has obtained widespread political and public acceptance, especially from the early 2000s. Broadly, jokes about dyslexia have been predicated on two types of humour: superiority (humour that stems from some kind of dominance over another), and incongruity (humour elicited by the shock of a sudden contrast).[18]

In the first type of joke, superiority, dyslexia has been contrasted to normal functioning in television and film for comedic effect. Thus, in the television comedy Call Me Fitz (2011), a character laughs off dyslexia as a relatively minor learning difficulty ('dyslexia's really not that serious'). In the drama Studio 60 on the Sunset Strip (2006), developed by the Oscar-winning scriptwriter Aaron Sorkin, an elderly character contends that although dyslexia may be a fashionable term in the twenty-first century, 'in my day, you were just stupid'. In the popular animated comedy *The Simpsons* (2007), created by Matt Groening, dyslexia is described in jest as a character's 'secret shame'. In each, the implication is that, if dyslexia qualifies as a learning difficulty at all, it is an inconsequential one, certainly relative to other difficulties.

In the second type of joke, incongruity, dyslexia has been aligned with other disabilities with markedly different characteristics, or used to explain an unrelated difficulty, making the reference to dyslexia unexpected. Thus, in the medical comedy *Scrubs* (2003), a character describes their stress-induced dyslexia; in the sit-com *The Mindy Project* (2014), the titular lead says that her dyslexia is exacerbated by drinking. Elsewhere, in an array of television shows, dyslexia is used to explain an unrelated condition. In the comedy *The Pest* (1997), a character describes their 'stuttering dyslexia'; in the television drama *Felicity* (2002), their 'dance dyslexia'; in the crime series *Bones* (2009), their 'chronological dyslexia'; and in the political comedy *The Thick of It* (2012), their 'directional dyslexia'.[19]

Dyslexia's representation in popular culture intersects with its broader social history in several ways. First, the increase in references to the term since the 1980s, and especially since the 1990s, reflects the greater recognition provided to dyslexia in educational and political circles during these decades. The timeline suggests that references to dyslexia in popular culture have emerged contemporaneously with these policy advances. Indeed, they may have helped to establish a public awareness of dyslexia that made the condition more difficult for policymakers to ignore, attesting to popular culture's 'mutually constitutive' relationship with political discourse.[20] It is also notable that, from the 2000s, dyslexia has been invoked in popular culture as a device to explain other, unrelated difficulties. This indicates that, by the start of the twenty-first century, dyslexia and its characteristics were considered such common knowledge by film and television producers that they could be used as a benchmark for explaining diverse cognitive difficulties to audiences.

Second, and relatedly, representations of dyslexia in popular culture are important for how they have captured a plurality of understandings of the condition. Definitions of dyslexia are far broader in popular culture than the medical, educational, and psychological understandings that monopolised dyslexia before the 1980s. Certainly, this has better captured how some of those with dyslexia, especially advocates for dyslexia rights, understand the condition (for example, as a possible strength). In interviews for the Oxford Dyslexia Archive, interviewees frequently cited the possible association of dyslexia with creativity and artistic talent, and the importance of humour in mitigating the effects of dyslexia.[21] In this way, representations of dyslexia in popular culture have arguably contributed to dyslexia's further integration into society.

However, there has been a downside to this proliferation of understandings, too. There are now many 'dyslexias'; the term has lost some of the coherence that it possessed when definitions were restricted to the professional domains of science and education. References to dyslexia in popular culture have radically expanded awareness of dyslexia, but they have simplified the concept in the process and have arguably opened the door to 'miracle cures'.[22] Until the 1980s, the history of dyslexia was marked by limits to knowledge and awareness of the condition. The infrastructure of specialist support was small; there were relatively few places where a layperson might encounter dyslexia, apart from directly or via friends and family. Today, there is a surfeit of information on the condition (a Google search in the summer of 2020, for example, returns over 32 million results for 'dyslexia', with over 150,000 results on Google's news service alone). This complexity has been seized upon by dyslexia's critics, allowing them to argue that if dyslexia means so many things, then it means nothing at all.

Dyslexia Debated (Again): The Return of the Dyslexia 'Myth' (2005–Present)

In October 2018, in a review of guidance around special educational needs, Warwickshire County Council in Britain commented that, despite scientific advances, the dyslexia research field 'lacked consensus'. 'The diagnosis of dyslexia', it continued, 'is scientifically questionable and can be misleading.'[23] After several years of government austerity policies and shrinking local authority budgets, dyslexia advocates were quick to reply that the council's policy was likely based on economic need, rather than genuine scientific scepticism.[24] In the House of Lords, Lord Invergowrie, a proponent of the term and of dyslexia rights, pondered whether the council 'has also advised their residents that the earth is actually flat and that there is no such thing as global warming'.[25] Nevertheless, following the council's announcement, a conference was held at University College London in early 2019 called 'Dyslexia Diagnosis, Scientific Understandings, and Belief in a Flat Earth', organised by a leading detractor of the term, Julian Elliott, and supporting the council's position.[26]

At the conference, Elliott reiterated the claims of his 2014 book, *The Dyslexia Debate*, co-authored with the psychologist Elena Grigorenko. There, it was contended that, 'while biologically based reading difficulties exist', 'there are very significant differences in the ways in which this label [dyslexia] is operationalised, even by leading scholars'.[27] The definition of dyslexia in the 2009 Rose review was 'highly general', the authors suggested, and there was no clear difference between definitions of dyslexia and of other reading difficulties. In dyslexia's stead, Elliott and Grigorenko proposed 'the construct *reading disability* ... This term dispenses with much of the conceptual and political baggage associated with dyslexia'.[28] As for whether their recommendations would be heeded, Elliott and Grigorenko were pessimistic: 'Although dyslexia is a term that is ... ready to be consigned to the history books, it offers a diagnostic label that is typically sought after rather than shunned, and its advocates will surely put up a fight to retain its use.'[29] As to why dyslexia advocates would put up this resistance, Elliott and Grigorenko suggested that 'the term continues to meet the psychological, social, political, and emotional needs of so many stakeholders'.[30]

As well as Warwickshire County Council, a number of other parties welcomed Elliott and Grigorenko's work. The journalist Rod Liddle stated in the British current affairs magazine the *Spectator* that 'for decades now dyslexia has been the crutch upon which middle-class parents support themselves when they discover that their children are actually dense ... contrary to their expectations'. The term itself, Liddle continued, 'should be consigned to the history books. It is utterly meaningless ... a pretentious word for "thick"'.[31] Peter Hitchens, writing in the *Daily Mail* after the publication of *The Dyslexia Debate*, claimed that 'dyslexia is not a disease. It is an excuse for bad teachers.'[32] Elsewhere, Tom Bennett, an educationalist who led the UK Conservative government's 2017 independent review of student behaviour in schools, described dyslexia as a 'crypto-pathology'.[33] *The Dyslexia*

Debate and its arguments received coverage, if not endorsement, in outlets around the world, including Australia, India, and the United States.[34] Elliott argued that its recommendations should lead to revised policy not just in Britain, but also abroad.[35]

From a scientific perspective, Elliott and Grigorenko's arguments have received both criticism and some support. Many dyslexia researchers agree that greater specificity is required around the criteria constituting dyslexia, including differentiation between core deficits and co-occurring features.[36] In addition, dyslexia scientists have called for greater dialogue with policy-makers about evidence-based approaches to the teaching of literacy, and about the characteristics of those who are at high risk of reading difficulties.[37] To do so, contemporary dyslexia researchers have argued that science must better bring together what is known about biological, environmental, and cognitive factors that place a child at risk of dyslexia, with what is known about evidence-based approaches to intervention.[38] Moreover, there have been concerted calls for dyslexia science to embrace the 'reproducibility agenda' to ensure that chance findings from small-scale studies no longer inform theoretical development.[39] Relatedly, meta-analyses have begun to assure reading researchers that various research findings are robust.[40]

From a historical perspective, however, what is most interesting about the arguments of *The Dyslexia Debate*, and its related coverage, is how they reiterate a series of arguments against the term – five, in particular – that have been made throughout dyslexia's history and that dyslexia advocates have never fully shaken off. These are that dyslexia is: (1) poorly defined in the scientific literature, and so impossible to differentiate from other reading difficulties; (2) an invention of worried parents, used primarily to explain away their children's difficulties; (3) a middle-class myth, more prevalent in children from wealthier backgrounds simply because their parent are better able to afford a diagnosis; (4) over-diagnosed, not least by private educational psychologists willing to offer a diagnosis to the aforementioned parents for a fee; and (5) frequently linked to high intelligence by advocates of the term, despite there being no scientific evidence for this connection.[41]

Current debates over dyslexia's definition might be compared to similar discussions in the Victorian era. In 1895, James Hinshelwood first laid out his ideas about reading disability, differentiating between 'word-blindness', '*cécité verbale*', '*Wortblindheit*', and 'dyslexia'.[42] In response, William Broadbent, with specific reference to word-blindness, stated that, 'in my judgement, the employment of this term has been misleading and unfortunate'; reading disability, he suggested, was 'part of a much larger deficit'.[43] In turn, Hinshelwood contended: 'I quite agree with Sir William Broadbent that the word has frequently been used by writers loosely with different meanings attached to it and therefore it has been frequently misleading'.[44] However, Hinshelwood continued, 'the fault ... lies not in the word, but in the fact that those who use it have not always had a clear conception of what [Adolph] Kussmaul meant by it'.[45] Over a century later, Elliott and Grigorenko, in similar language, lamented that 'there are very significant differences in the ways in which this label [dyslexia] is operationalized, even by leading scholars in the field [of reading science]'.[46]

Second, we might consider the invocation of worried parenthood in recent arguments against the condition, which have also recurred across dyslexia's history. In Rod Liddle's denunciation of the term, 'dyslexia has been the crutch upon which middle-class parents support themselves when they discover that their children are actually dense'.[47] For Elliott and Grigorenko, employing more nuanced language, 'some parents believe that [by being labelled with dyslexia] their child will be treated more sympathetically by teachers, and expectations of their intellectual and academic potential will be higher'.[48] As we have seen, the idea that dyslexia has been promoted by over-anxious parents seeking to justify their children's difficulties marked backroom political discussion of dyslexia in Britain from the 1960s well into the 1980s.

Third, we might consider how it has been *middle-class* parents, in particular, who have been charged historically with promoting the cause of dyslexia for their own ends. Liddle cites middle-class parents in his denunciation of the term; Elliott, discussing dyslexia at the University College London conference of 2018, relays the well-publicised story of the British dyslexic pupil, Alex Walker, in order to query the possible vested interests of parents in obtaining a dyslexia diagnosis: '(Mum) ... had paid around £2,000 on commissioning reports showing how bright and intelligent Alex was despite his condition'.[49] In other words, Walker's mother had the time and money to pursue a diagnosis of dyslexia, which perhaps other parents did not. As we have seen, during the consultation phase of the Warnock report in the mid-1970s, Baroness Warnock's example of a pupil with dyslexia was dismissed by a civil servant attached to the review as a 'middle-class boy'.

Fourth, Elliott's comment concerning a mother's efforts to secure a dyslexia diagnosis to prove 'how bright and intelligent' her son was mirrors long-standing suggestions that dyslexia diagnoses have been sought principally by parents to affirm that their children possess no broader learning disability. As we have seen, this was one of the main side-effects of the discrepancy diagnostic model of dyslexia, in that a diagnosis of dyslexia automatically suggested otherwise high ability. During the Victorian era, William Pringle Morgan's Percy was described as 'a bright and intelligent boy'; James Hinshelwood's unnamed patient was 'bright and in every respect an intelligent boy'.[50] In both cases, the children had been brought to the attention of physicians by their concerned parents.

Fifth, we might compare the arguments of contemporary dyslexia critics with those of educational psychologists in the 1940s. For Tom Bennett, writing in 2017, dyslexia is an 'over-diagnosed crypto-pathology', 'barely understood'.[51] In *The Dyslexia Debate*, dyslexia is described as 'a *meme*, a unit of cultural transmission, complementary to genetic transmission, in which ideas and behaviors are passed on from one person to another'.[52] 'The meme's ability to survive by other means of replication', Elliott and Grigorenko continue, 'does not depend on whether it is true, useful, or even potentially harmful. What is crucial is that it is "easy to understand, remember, and communicate to others".'[53] For Cyril Burt, writing in the mid-1940s, dyslexia was similarly over-diagnosed: 'nearly every educational psychologist', he lamented, 'has had cases referred to him in which this verdict has been pronounced'.[54]

The brief comparisons here are with episodes of dyslexia's history discussed in greater depth in earlier chapters and elsewhere.[55] What the comparisons demonstrate is that the latest iteration of the dyslexia debate is less a unique set of arguments against the condition, and more an ongoing series of criticisms of the term. Moreover, each argument references a social aspect of dyslexia's history, which makes a historical perspective instructive in their interpretation.[56]

Thus, the first argument, that dyslexia's definition remains ambiguous, overlooks the greater specificity that has been brought to the term since the Victorian era. Certainly, the science around dyslexia has been contested, as this book has shown, but it is not obvious that this contestation exceeds that expected of any field of scientific inquiry. In this respect, the history of dyslexia mirrors that of other 'invisible disabilities', such as depression, autism, and ADHD.[57] Histories of depression show that it has never possessed an uncontroversial definition nor widely accepted aetiology or treatment.[58] Medical research continues to debate, as with dyslexia, how best to define depression, how it differs from other, related issues, and how those with depression can be helped.[59] Nevertheless, depression is widely accepted as a useful diagnosis, even if it awaits further understanding.

The social and the scientific are blurred elsewhere in the latest iteration of the dyslexia debate. As we have seen, middle-class parents – usually, but not always, mothers – brought dyslexia to the attention of teachers and policymakers. However, this was not because it was their special invention, but because they were in a societal position to notice the condition and to pioneer support. This was the case during the Victorian era, during the resurgence of interest in dyslexia from the 1960s, and remains the case today.

Similarly, we have seen previously why initial scientific work on dyslexia associated the condition with high intelligence, and why this discrepancy diagnostic model was ultimately superseded. Because those with dyslexia were at a disadvantage in education, in the workplace, and in many other areas of societally prescribed functioning, campaigners used the discrepancy diagnostic model as a method of empowerment, and it is they, rather than scientists, who have been responsible for sustaining the model.[60] Likewise, accusations that dyslexia is over-diagnosed are less a criticism of the term itself than a product of the success of the campaign for political and public recognition of dyslexia, which has made it one of the best-known learning difficulties in the world.[61]

Dyslexia, the Social Model of Disability, and the Rise of the Neurodiversity Paradigm (1998–Present)

In *The Dyslexia Debate*, the idea that dyslexia is a 'social construct' is invoked frequently – principally to criticize the term. Elliott and Grigorenko pose themselves the question: 'perhaps we should accept that there are many types of dyslexia, social constructs that are created by, and reflect the values and agendas of, different groups'; they respond that 'to accept such a position must surely be to dispense with any suggestion of scientific rigor'.[62] But, finding more encompassing and flexible language has formed a core part of new understandings of cognitive differences like dyslexia, frequently bracketed under the term 'neurodiversity'.[63]

In 1998, Judy Singer, an Australian sociologist, laid out the agenda for a new 'neurodiversity' paradigm.[64] In the context of autism, she remarked that 'the key significance of the "Autistic Spectrum" lies in its call for and anticipation of a politics of Neurological Diversity, or "Neurodiversity". The "Neurologically Different" represents a new addition to the familiar political categories of class/gender/race and will augment the insights of the social model of disability'.[65] She continued that 'even our most taken-for-granted assumptions: that we all more or less see, feel, touch, hear, smell, and sort information, in more or less the same way, (unless visibly disabled) are being dissolved'.[66]

Of this new approach, Singer suggested: 'Perhaps as the voices of the "neurologically different" are heard more loudly, a more ecological view of society will emerge: one that is more relaxed about different styles of being, that will be content to let each individual find her/his own niche, based on the kinds of mutual recognition that can only arise through an ever-developing sociological, psychological, and now neurological, self-awareness'.[67] In other words, Singer argued that differences like autism were less disabilities, more natural variations in human characteristics that should be recognised as such.

Neurodiversity has emerged as part of a new wave of social justice efforts in the West since the start of the twenty-first century. In the main, these seek to further the rights of historically marginalised or unrecognised groups. As debates over the power to label make clear, the terrain of the discursive and the symbolic has been keenly contested as part of these efforts, especially in social media and online fora.[68] As we have seen, a key goal of the campaigns of learning disability advocates during the second half of the twentieth century was to attain public and political recognition for specific labels as a method of obtaining funding and support. The neurodiversity agenda has nuanced this objective, seeking to obtain recognition for those with alternative thinking styles not as a separate group, but as persons on a spectrum of human abilities.

Since Singer's intervention, neurodiversity has become the most prominent term for describing efforts in the West – social, political, educational, legal – that seek to embrace multiple styles of thinking, rather than bracketing certain types as better (or, at least, more desirable) than others. Neurodiversity seeks to destabilise what is considered 'normal' and 'abnormal' thinking. Given Singer's initial application of the term to the autistic community, it is there that most discussion of the term has occurred.[69] However, neurodiversity has also been embraced by other communities who possess, or support those with, thinking styles different from the 'norm', including the dyslexia community.

In the United States, the term has appeared in publications by the International Dyslexia Association.[70] In Britain, the British Dyslexia Association has endorsed the term, too: 'It helps to promote the view that neurological differences are to be recognised and respected as any other human variation. It is used to counter negative social connotations that currently exist and to make it easier for people of all neurotypes to contribute to the world as they are, rather than attempting to think or appear more "typically".'[71] For the BDA, it is also an approach to individual learning that has utility in education: 'All classrooms are neurodiverse and will include learners who learn differently ... It is essential that teaching meets the needs of all learners, using appropriate methods to support weaknesses while also recognising and developing strengths and abilities.'[72] In this way, neurodiversity has been employed by dyslexia campaigners to expand the range of understandings of dyslexia in public discourse.

From a historical perspective, what is interesting is how much of the neurodiversity agenda, like the dyslexia debate, has been prefigured in dyslexia's history. As the ideas of Victorian researchers on dyslexia show, for over a century there have been commentators who have recognised that dyslexia exists on a spectrum of abilities and disabilities, and that its individual manifestations vary. In 1910, as we have seen, the ophthalmologist Edward Treacher Collins noted that 'if the British system had been phonetic the defect would not be nearly so noticeable', highlighting the arbitrary role of language in disabling readers with dyslexia (and, indeed, how dyslexia manifests differently in different languages).[73] Such statements remain part of a medical discourse that neurodiversity disputes, but, in drawing attention to how learning difficulties are framed by societal requirements, their sentiments are otherwise similar.

The language of Singer's initial aim for the neurodiversity project – that 'a more ecological view of society will emerge: one that is more relaxed about different styles of being, that will be content to let each individual find her/his own niche' – also echoes the objectives of the more progressive education legislation of the twentieth century, including the 1967 Plowden report in Britain. While Plowden objected to the term 'dyslexia', her child-centred approach to tackling learning difficulties is similar to Singer's position. Compare, for example, Singer's 'ecological' statement above to this oft-quoted passage from the Plowden report: 'At the heart of the educational process lies the child. No advances in policy, no acquisitions of new equipment have their desired effect unless they are in harmony with the nature of the child, unless they are fundamentally acceptable to him. We know a little about what happens to the child who is deprived of the stimuli of pictures, books and spoken words; we know much less about what happens to a child who is exposed to stimuli which are perceptually, intellectually or emotionally inappropriate to his age, his stage of development, or the sort of individual he is.'[74]

In the 1978 Warnock report on special educational needs, too, the notion of a spectrum of cognitive differences was invoked, a key tenet of the neurodiversity paradigm. There, instead of 'spectrum', Warnock employed the synonym 'continuum'. For Warnock, the notion of a continuum was explicitly linked to the differing needs of individual children: 'We have been concerned [in the review], however, not only with the severely handicapped but with all those children who require special education in any form. The help needed may range from continuous support from specialist services, including an intensive educational programme in a special school for a child with severe and multiple disabilities, to part-time assistance from a specially trained teacher for a child with mild learning difficulties. It is perhaps useful to regard this range of special educational needs as a continuum, although that is a crude notion which conceals the complexities of individual needs.'[75]

The language used by Singer and Warnock is highly similar. Moreover, Warnock's prediction of the limitations of terms like 'continuum' – namely, that they would conflate differences that affect individuals to a greater or lesser extent – has prefigured criticisms of neurodiversity. For example, the autism researchers Pier Jaarsma and Stellan Welin have argued that neurodiversity problematically subsumes cognitive differences under a single label. This, in their words, ignores the fact that some cognitive differences (or certain gradations within cognitive differences) are more problematic than others. Similar criticisms have been made of the social model of disability, which underpins the concept of neurodiversity.[76]

Where does this leave dyslexia and the neurodiversity agenda? The dyslexia advocacy community has long argued that those with dyslexia should have the same opportunities as those who do not. However, to expedite this it has argued *for*, rather than *against*, the dyslexia label, and research with those with dyslexia suggests that the label is generally favoured.[77] It remains to be seen whether the discourse of neurodiversity, which casts dyslexia as a difference rather than a disability, can incorporate responses to the range of difficulties that the condition precipitates in a literate society and so the diverse needs of individuals with dyslexia.

Dyslexia Tomorrow: Identity, Self-determination, and the Future of Dyslexia

The multiple portrayals of dyslexia in popular culture, the ongoing 'dyslexia debate', and the complex relationship of dyslexia to ongoing social justice efforts like the neurodiversity agenda lead to an obvious conclusion: dyslexia today is in flux. Victorian understandings of dyslexia were often prescient, as we have seen, but they were also few – the term was little known outside of specialist scientific circles. With the advent of dyslexia voluntary organisations in the 1970s, and their broad memberships, recorded understandings and experiences of dyslexia multiplied. These coincided with expanding knowledge of dyslexia in science, which brought greater understanding of the language-based difficulties underpinning the condition, but also highlighted dyslexia's myriad manifestations and its connection to co-occurring conditions (or 'co-morbidities') such as dyspraxia, dyscalculia, and ADHD. In politics, sporadic recognition across the twentieth century has only been cemented with the dedicated support made available in recent decades. However, this support faces threats in the wake of diverse economic challenges to Western and other states, and retrenchment in provision for special educational needs.[78] As knowledge and awareness of dyslexia have expanded across the twentieth and into the twenty-first centuries, the gaps in public understanding and provision have been made clearer.

Given this, what might the future of dyslexia be? To start, we should acknowledge again that the 'problem' of dyslexia is one that is contingent on a society in which literacy is widespread and so such difficulties are visible and pressing. While we have been concerned primarily with the Western experience in this book, since 2015 and the adoption of the Sustainable Development Goals by the United Nations, over 400 million children in low-income countries have failed to gain (or to be taught) basic literacy skills by age ten.[79] In a context in which literacy cannot be guaranteed, the concept of dyslexia is obscure.

Where dyslexia is widely recognised, political acknowledgement of, and support for, dyslexia is still not a given; rather, it is predicated on the ongoing work of individuals and organisations. Whether their efforts achieve success is due, in significant part, to the sympathy of political authorities, most obviously in state education where dyslexia support is most widely, if not always readily, available. The rise of social media in advocacy campaigns, a hallmark of recent social justice campaigns in developed economies, may make such political pressure easier to apply. Certainly, dyslexia lobbying groups will need to adapt to a new advocacy landscape in which 'digital presence' is increasingly important. It is difficult to envisage a truly positive future for those with dyslexia that does not incorporate the continuing work of a strong advocacy movement.

Is it possible that, whatever the future of political recognition, changes in the nature of social life will benefit those with dyslexia? Dyslexia 'boosterism', which promotes dyslexia as an advantage, is more common than at any point in dyslexia's history. In the wake of what has been called the 'third industrial revolution' (the rise of the digital economy), the extreme form of this argument suggests that those with dyslexia may be better placed than the general learner to succeed.[80] For observers like Malcolm Gladwell, as we have seen, 'dyslexia – in the best of cases – forces you to develop skills that might otherwise have lain dormant. It also forces you to do things that you might otherwise never have considered'.[81] For the sociologist Christian Marazzi, 'what was considered a linguistic handicap and a pathology less than a generation ago is potentially a "competitive advantage" for digital capitalism', because, in Marazzi's opinion, those with dyslexia think in images rather than words.[82] Other, more quantifiable research, including that of Julie Logan at Cass Business School in London, records that high proportions of entrepreneurs possess dyslexia in the UK and the United States.[83]

The potential links between dyslexia and particular abilities, such as creativity and entrepreneurship, continue to be debated.[84] It is also unclear whether, if such a relationship exists, it will be causal or correlational, and so the scientific consensus is for the need for more longitudinal studies of representative populations. Do those with dyslexia possess innate advantages? Or do they enter the creative professions at higher rates because of other, external factors, such as the fact that it is more difficult for them to succeed elsewhere? The question of where literate society 'channels' those with dyslexia should also be approached holistically. While some with dyslexia find opportunities in professions like acting, business, and the arts, in which literacy skills are usually less crucial, dyslexia may channel others in less advantageous directions.

Most concerningly, those with dyslexia continue to be overrepresented in prisoner and young offender populations. The reasons behind this are unclear, but the most sustained research on the subject suggests that those with literacy difficulties, especially from poorer backgrounds, struggle in conventional employment.[85] In younger populations, dyslexia can lead to difficulties in school, which, in turn, can precipitate educational disengagement.[86] In higher education, to cite one professional example, researchers with dyslexia have noted how the dictates of academic life, especially the publication process, can be particularly difficult to navigate.[87] This means that the majority of texts on dyslexia (including the one that you are reading) are written by those who do not have dyslexia. The recent global pandemic has led to concerns that pupils with dyslexia may be more adversely affected than other learners by changes to learning practices, including greater online teaching.[88] Clearly, those with dyslexia continue to face more disadvantages than advantages in education, in the workplace, and elsewhere in society.

In molecular genetics, the search for the 'dyslexia gene' – or, more accurately, the combination of genes that cause dyslexia – goes on. The repercussions of such a finding, though, would not be straightforward. Certainly, it would likely put an end to extreme arguments against dyslexia – namely, that it does not exist at all. However, genes act through the environment, and so such a discovery would not provide an unambiguous definition of dyslexia that satisfies all who are ambivalent about the term. Dyslexic difficulties, as we have seen, exist on a spectrum, and dyslexia is commonly associated with other issues. It is unlikely that genetic testing could provide an either/or diagnosis; rather, it is likely to provide a further arena for debates over what does and does not constitute dyslexia. Moreover, a genetic basis for dyslexia would further enshrine a medical model of dyslexia, the consequences of which are uncertain. If state support for individuals with dyslexia was aligned to their genetic profile, what might this mean for children with dyslexia or for their education? Who would have the power to draw the genetic line between dyslexia and non-dyslexia? How would such research intersect with the social movements discussed above, in which self-identification is considered more important than objective tests?[89]

This last question bears further reflection. In recent years, legislation in a series of Western states has increasingly enabled individuals to label (or not) their own characteristics, most notably gender.[90] For a longer time, categories like ethnicity and sexuality have been viewed as a matter of personal discretion, with certain exceptions. Increasingly, 'objective' tests for such characteristics are considered objectionable. Will 'disabilities' like dyslexia follow suit? As with debates over neurodiversity, for those with dyslexia there are potential advantages and disadvantages in who has the authority to label. Enabling those with reading and writing difficulties to adopt identifiers like dyslexia (or not) would rebalance the power differential between namer and named. At the same time, as we have seen, educational funding has been directed toward those with dyslexia only because of expert external assessments. Without such assessments, it is difficult to see how support for those with dyslexia could continue; self-identification would not necessarily locate all of those who required assistance.

With respect to remediation, more is known about how to help those with dyslexia than ever before, and this is cause for substantial optimism.[91] However, those with dyslexia continue to be subject to unproven interventions. Often, these are commercial enterprises, seeking to monetise parents' hopes for successful assistance.[92] The sheer size of what Sally Tomlinson has called the 'SEN [special educational needs] industry' shows that there continues to be a thriving market for the 'treatment' of learning difficulties like dyslexia, or at least the hope of remediation.[93] The retrenchment of state funding for special educational needs suggests that this SEN industry may expand, rather than contract, in the coming years. Given that dyslexia support is already more easily accessed by children from wealthier socioeconomic backgrounds, the possibility that poorer pupils with dyslexia will fall by the wayside is a serious one. If this were to happen, we might see a return of the extreme social gradient in dyslexia provision characteristic of earlier decades.

The immediate priority for dyslexia advocacy communities around the world, then, would seem clear: to safeguard state funding for specific learning difficulties, such as dyslexia, as education budgets are re-evaluated in the wake of diverse economic challenges, including the COVID-19 pandemic. This is especially important in that the shift to online learning and studying from home, which the pandemic has compelled on a generation of learners, may affect those with dyslexia more adversely than others.[94]

Also important to address is the teaching of reading in mainstream schools and the support of reading in the home. It is a truism that there is not a level playing field at school entry, but the science of reading is unanimous about what to do to correct this and to set more children on a stable pathway to literacy. Ongoing criticisms of the dyslexia label, such as the imprecision of its definition and the lack of a single universal test, have been used by political authorities to cast shade on dyslexia and to justify funding retrenchment. In the years ahead, it would seem crucial for those with dyslexia, and for their advocates, to ensure that policymakers recognise these as debates over aspects of dyslexia, rather than debates over the existence of biologically based differences in reading ability.

Chapter 7 - Key Points
- Dyslexia's representation in popular culture has expanded societal knowledge of the condition, but not always accurately or uniformly
- The present iteration of the 'dyslexia debate' rehearses many previous discussions of the condition
- Dyslexia's inclusion in new paradigms such as neurodiversity possesses both promise and limitations
- Dyslexia's possible futures are plural, but it seems certain that continued lobbying will be necessary for support to remain available

Conclusion

In a little under a century and a half, dyslexia has gone from a poorly understood problem, the scope and scale of which was unknown, to one of the most widely recognised learning difficulties in the world. This book has traced key episodes in this history – from dyslexia's Victorian origins, through its global expansion across the twentieth century, up to the present day. It has focused on the British experience, but highlighted it as part of a broader global dyslexia story. In telling this story, this book has had two aims.

First, it has sought to bring academic attention to a neglected area, adding dyslexia to historical accounts of other learning difficulties, including autism and ADHD. In so doing, it has offered a critical account of dyslexia's history, but one that also stands as a testament to the accomplishments of those with dyslexia, and of their advocates, in obtaining political and societal recognition for the condition. In this way, it contributes to ongoing debates around the term, which have arguably generated more heat than light. Dyslexia, as a scientific topic, will naturally be subject to critique; it is notable, though, that recent criticism of dyslexia has often been less about its scientific foundations than about aspects of its social history. A better appreciation of dyslexia's past, therefore, offers the potential to enrich, if not bring to a close, the ongoing dyslexia debate.

Second, it has offered a counterpoint to existing historical approaches to learning difficulties via a reconsideration of how social change is accomplished. It suggests that the emphasis on structural factors in previous accounts has sometimes conflated the contexts of dyslexia's emergence with its drivers, and has consequently downplayed the role of particular persons at particular times in fostering greater dyslexia recognition. As such, this book restates the importance of individual agency, often in the face of institutional intransigence, to effecting social change. It suggests that structural approaches, which posit dyslexia's emergence as part of a political project to problematise the dyslexic learner, overlook the historical reticence of political authorities to acknowledge the condition. It was social rather than political efforts which brought dyslexia to public attention.

In closing, we return to a question with which our book opened: how, given the history presented, is dyslexia to be defined? The science of dyslexia demonstrates with certainty that there is a biological basis for dyslexia, and more about its neurobiological bases is learnt every day. At the same time, dyslexia's broader history shows that these biological differences are only meaningful when framed as a problem via social norms and beliefs, the most obvious of which is the widespread requirement for skills in reading and spelling in most societies. That the uses of language can be more or less disabling to the individual, though, is not an original thought. It was well known to David Copperfield, with whom we began this book. He reminds us that, if a post-literate society is still some way off, society might at least think again about making language as accessible as possible:

> Mr. Micawber had a relish in this formal piling up of words, which, however ludicrously displayed in his case, was, I must say, not at all peculiar to him. I have observed it, in the course of my life, in numbers of men. It seems to me to be a general rule. In the taking of legal oaths, for instance, deponents seem to enjoy themselves mightily when they come to several good words in succession, for the expression of one idea ... We talk about the tyranny of words, but we like to tyrannize over them too; we are fond of having a large superfluous establishment of words to wait upon us on great occasions; we think it looks important.

Whether we are speaking of *Wortblindheit*, strephosymbolia, or specific learning difficulties, possessing 'difficulty with words' is an experience that tells us much about literate society's conventions, and about literate society's demands.

Timeline: Fifty Key Dates

1877 Adolph Kussmaul, a German physician, coins the term 'word-blindness' (*Wortblindheit*) in the volume *Cyclopaedia of the Practice of Medicine*

1883 Rudolf Berlin, a German ophthalmologist, coins the term dyslexia (*Dyslexie*) in the paper 'Über Dyslexie'

1887 Berlin publishes *Eine Besondere Art der Wortblindheit (Dyslexie)*, the first book-length discussion of dyslexia

1895 James Hinshelwood, a Scottish ophthalmologist, publishes the paper 'Word-Blindness and Visual Memory'

1896 James Kerr, a medical officer to the City of Bradford, publishes the paper 'School Hygiene, in Its Mental, Moral and Physical Aspects'

1896 William Pringle Morgan, a British doctor, publishes the paper 'A Case of Congenital Word Blindness', introducing the world to the schoolboy Percy F.

1900 The London *Globe* publishes what is perhaps the first dyslexia joke, mocking the confusion of some schoolboys between 'bear' (to display) and 'bear' (the animal)

1910 Edward Treacher Collins, a British ophthalmologist, discusses differences in the manifestation of word-blindness in German and English

1917 James Hinshelwood publishes his most comprehensive (and final) work on word-blindness, *Congenital Word Blindness*

1925 Samuel T. Orton, an American physician, publishes the paper '"Word-Blindness" in School Children'

1939 The Ordblinde Instituttet is founded in Copenhagen, Denmark, led by the Danish dyslexia pioneer Edith Norrie
1942 Martin Attlee, who is word-blind, joins Millfield School, which becomes one of the first schools to assist a student with word-blindness by that name
1946 Anna Gillingham and Bessie Stillman publish the book *Remedial Training for Children with Specific Disability in Reading, Spelling, and Penmanship*
1949 Formation of the American Orton Society, principally led by Samuel T. Orton's widow, June
1956 The Orton Society publishes the first issue of its journal, *Bulletin of the Orton Society*, to disseminate information about dyslexia
1962 Formation of the Word Blind Centre for Dyslexic Children in London, led initially by the British paediatrician Alfred White Franklin
1962 White Franklin publishes the proceedings of the first Word-Blindness Conference, featuring contributions from American, British, Danish, and French researchers
1962 First reference to 'dyslexia' in UK Parliament in a question by the Scottish Unionist MP Henry Brewis
1964 Beginning of the Isle of Wight population study of children's learning difficulties, led by the psychiatrist Michael Rutter and the psychologist William Yule
1966 Cyril Burt, the British educational psychologist, publishes the paper 'Counterblast to Dyslexia'
1967 The UK Plowden report, *Children and Their Primary Schools*, is published
1968 The World Federation of Neurology publish their influential definition of dyslexia, based on the discrepancy diagnostic model
1970 Macdonald Critchley, a physician at the National Hospital for Nervous Diseases, London, publishes the book *The Dyslexic Child*
1971 The Helen Arkell Centre is formed in London by Helen Arkell, a teacher and campaigner with dyslexia
1971 Bevé Hornsby, a speech and language therapist, sets up the Dyslexia Clinic at Barts Hospital, London, building on the work of her predecessor, Maisie Holt

Timeline: Fifty Key Dates

1972 The BBC broadcasts a two-part television special on dyslexia as part of the documentary series *Man Alive*

1972 Formation of the UK Dyslexia Institute, principally led by Kathleen Hickey and Wendy Fisher

1972 Formation of the British Dyslexia Association, an amalgamation of eight local associations, principally led by Marion Welchman

1972 Sandhya Naidoo, director of the Word Blind Centre, publishes the book *Specific Dyslexia*, based on her research at the centre

1972 The UK Tizard committee's report, *Children with Specific Reading Difficulties*, is published

1973 Margaret Newton, a psychologist, sets up the Language Development Unit at Aston University, Birmingham, UK

1977 The Bangor Dyslexia Unit is founded at Bangor University, Wales (then the University College of North Wales), led by Tim Miles and Elaine Miles

1978 The UK Warnock report, *Special Educational Needs*, is published, although discussion of dyslexia is largely omitted for political reasons

1979 Frank Vellutino, an American psychologist, publishes the book *Dyslexia: Theory and Research*

1982 The Orton Society becomes the Orton Dyslexia Society, highlighting increasing societal recognition of the term

1987 'Dyslexia' is formally recognised in the UK Parliament by the parliamentary under-secretary of state for education and science, Robert Dunn MP

1987 The European Dyslexia Association is formed, an amalgamation of organisations in Belgium, Denmark, Germany, Holland, Ireland, and Norway

1987 Maggie Snowling publishes the book *Dyslexia: A Cognitive-Developmental Perspective*, describing the evidence for the emerging 'phonological deficit hypothesis'

1991 Keith Stanovich publishes his influential paper, 'Discrepancy Definitions of Reading Disability: Has Intelligence Led Us Astray?'

1993 The US Society for the Scientific Study of Reading is formed to promote the science of reading

1994 Publication of the first British controlled trial of reading intervention for children with poor reading skills ('Sound Linkage'), taking research evidence through to practice

1995 Rick Riordan publishes *Percy Jackson and the Lightning Thief*, the first book in the popular young adult series featuring a hero with dyslexia

1997 The Orton Dyslexia Society becomes the International Dyslexia Association

1997 First hearings of the UK court case *Phelps vs London Borough of Hillingdon*, which considers the legal responsibility for reading difficulties

1998 First reference to 'neurodiversity' by the autism researcher Judy Singer

2005 The Dyslexia Institute and the Hornsby International Dyslexia Centre merge to form Dyslexia Action

2009 The UK Rose review's report, *Identifying and Teaching Children and Young People with Dyslexia and Literacy Difficulties*, is published

2010 The UK Equality Act is enacted, which legally protects people, including those with specific learning difficulties, from discrimination in the workplace and society

2014 Joe Elliott and Elena Grigorenko publish the book *The Dyslexia Debate*, continuing a series of dyslexia critiques that have appeared cyclically across its history

2020 A Google search for 'dyslexia' returns over 32 million results, nearly 140 years after Rudolf Berlin's first reference to the term

Notes

Introduction
1. Derbyshire, 'Virtual Teaching for Children with Dyslexia'; Prince, 'In for a Penny'; Addo, '"This Was the First Time I've Read Out Loud without Hesitation"', respectively.
2. Snowling, *Dyslexia* (Blackwell).
3. Ibid.
4. Rose, *Identifying and Teaching Children and Young People with Dyslexia*, 10.
5. Kussmaul, 'Chapter XXVII'.
6. Berlin, 'Über Dyslexie'; Berlin, *Eine Besondere Art der Wortblindheit*.
7. Hinshelwood, 'A Case of Dyslexia'; Pringle Morgan, 'A Case of Congenital Word Blindness'; Kerr, 'School Hygiene'.
8. For more on the relationship between the Orton Society and the BDA, see Chinn, 'A Brief History of Dyslexia'.
9. High-income countries, especially the UK and the US, are the focus of this book, because of their prominent role in historical understanding of dyslexia. This is, though, only one story of the condition, and future work is required to better understand dyslexia in other contexts.
10. The two entries refer to Jean Augur and Macdonald Critchley, who are discussed later in this book. This is changing, with a collection of biographies of dyslexia pioneers published in the ODNB in 2021, as part of the project behind this book.
11. Miles and Miles, *Dyslexia: A Hundred Years*; Tim Miles, *Fifty Years in Dyslexia Research*; Critchley, *The Dyslexic Child*.

12 For examples, see Campbell, 'From Aphasia to Dyslexia'; Campbell, *Dyslexia*; Guardiola, 'The Evolution of Research on Dyslexia'; Montgomery, *Dyslexia and Gender Bias*.
13 For one of the more comprehensive efforts to date, see Kirby et al., 'The Problem of Dyslexia' and further articles in this collection. For an excellent popular history of the topic, which is especially strong on the history of the Word Blind Centre, see Beard, *From Percy to Peter*. For a shorter popular history, see Kirby, 'What's in a Name?'
14 Evans, *The Metamorphosis of Autism*; Feinstein, *A History of Autism*; Nadesan, *Constructing Autism*; Waltz, *Autism*; Smith, *Hyperactive: The Controversial History of ADHD*.
15 Campbell, *Dyslexia*, 1.
16 Gallagher, Connor, and Ferri, 'Beyond the Far Too Incessant Schism', 1125.
17 Kudlick, 'Comment: On the Borderland of Medical and Disability History'.
18 Gallagher, Connor, and Ferri, 'Beyond the Far Too Incessant Schism'.
19 Macdonald, 'Windows of Reflection'.
20 Collinson, 'Dyslexics in Time Machines', 69.
21 Lopes, 'Biologising Reading Problems'; Paradice, 'An Investigation into the Social Construction'; Campbell, 'From Aphasia to Dyslexia'; Campbell, *Dyslexia*.
22 For more on understandings of dyslexia beyond social and medical models of disability, see Solvang, 'Developing an Ambivalence Perspective'; Macdonald, 'Towards a Social Reality of Dyslexia'; Macdonald, 'Windows of Reflection'. For further reflection on the possibility of moving beyond the binary of social/medical models in disability studies, see Hughes and Paterson, 'The Social Model of Disability'; Shakespeare and Watson, 'The Social Model of Disability'; Shakespeare, 'The Social Model of Disability'.
23 Solvang, 'Developing an Ambivalence Perspective'.
24 Hampshire, interview.
25 Saunders, interview.
26 Shawsun, interview.
27 Kirby, 'Gift from the Gods?', 1584. For further, autobiographical reflections by those with dyslexia, see Hampshire, *Every Letter Counts*; Hampshire, *Susan's Story*; Quinnell, *The Hardest Test*; Heseltine, *Misunderstood*; Strange, *War Baby*.

Chapter One

1. Caravalos, 'The Nature and Causes of Dyslexia'.
2. For further reflection on the difficulties of diagnosing persons in the past via modern medical definitions, see Millard, 'Concepts, Diagnosis and the History of Medicine'.
3. Critchley, *The Dyslexic Child*.
4. Ibid.
5. Ibid.
6. Cameron, 'Bodies', 17. For an excellent discussion of the body and the Enlightenment, see Muri, *The Enlightenment Cyborg*.
7. Fischer, *A History of Reading*.
8. Riddick, 'Dyslexia and Inclusion'.
9. Stone, 'Literacy and Education in England'. This is a rudimentary measure of literacy: the ability of persons to sign their own name.
10. Graff, *Literacy and Social Development*.
11. Pritchard, *Education and the Handicapped*, 9.
12. See Pickstone, 'Ways of Knowing'.
13. Campbell, *Dyslexia*.
14. Campbell, 'From Aphasia to Dyslexia', 450.
15. For more on Foucault's ideas of biopower, see, in particular, Foucault, *The History of Sexuality*.
16. Kerr, 'Beheading the King'.
17. Hinshelwood, 'Congenital Word-Blindness', 1508.
18. Ibid. Hinshelwood's publications on the topic were prolific. From 1895–1917, they include, in chronological order: Hinshelwood, 'Word-Blindness and Visual Memory'; 'Word-Blindness and Visual Memory [Letter]'; 'A Case of Dyslexia'; 'A Case of "Word" without "Letter" Blindness'; '"Letter" without "Word" Blindness'; *Letter-, Word- and Mind-Blindness*; 'Congenital Word-Blindness'; 'Four Cases of Word Blindness'; *Congenital Word-Blindness*; 'Congenital Word-Blindness [Letter]'.
19. McDonagh, *Idiocy*.
20. Ibid.
21. UK Parliament, 'The 1870 Education Act'.
22. Ibid.
23. Ibid.
24. Ibid. While the British 1870 Education Act is frequently seen as a landmark in education legislation worldwide, it was not the first mandate for

compulsory education. In Scotland, the 1616 School Establishment Act required every parish to establish a school, although it provided no means for the realisation of this mandate; in Prussia, a compulsory education system was implemented in 1763 (Rothbard, *Education*).

25 Similar provisions were made for Scotland in 1872 (UK Government, *Education Act of 1872*).
26 Specifically, the act defined the geography of the school boards as 'the Metropolis within the jurisdiction of the Metropolitan Board of Works; municipal boroughs; the district of the Oxford Local Board of Health; and elsewhere, in all parishes in England and Wales' (UK Government, *Elementary Education Act of 1870*, b2).
27 Ibid., b2, iii.
28 UK Parliament, 'The 1870 Education Act'.
29 Armstrong, 'Disability, Education and Social Change'. For the specific acts, see UK Government, *Elementary Education (Blind and Deaf Children) Act of 1893*; UK Government, *Elementary Education (Defective and Epileptic Children) Act of 1899*. The first of these acts followed the report of the 1889 Royal Commission on the Blind, Deaf and Dumb (*Report of the Royal Commission*).
30 Pritchard, *Education and the Handicapped*; Warnock, *Special Educational Needs*.
31 McDonagh, *Idiocy*. The Charity Organisation Society had a longer history of campaigning for the educational rights of children who fell outside of 'normal' functioning, especially blind pupils, with the first schools for blind pupils opening in the late eighteenth century (Warnock, *Special Educational Needs*, 8).
32 Charity Organisation Society, *The Feeble-Minded Child*. For further reflection on this report, see McDonagh, *Idiocy*.
33 Charity Organisation Society, *The Feeble-Minded Child*, 1.
34 Warnock, *Special Educational Needs*.
35 McDonagh, *Idiocy*, 306.
36 Warnock, *Special Educational Needs*, 10.
37 Ibid.
38 For examples, see Copeland, 'The Establishment of Models'; Jones and Williamson, 'The Birth of the Schoolroom'.
39 McDonagh, *Idiocy*.

40 Galton, *Inquiries into Human Faculty*.
41 Rehnberg and Walters, 'The Life and Work of Adolph Kussmaul'.
42 For example, Broca, 'Remarks on the Seat of the Faculty of Articulated Language'. The history of aphasia has been addressed in depth elsewhere, for example Penfield and Roberts, *Speech and Brain-Mechanisms*. For an account of the pioneering English neurologist John Hughlings Jackson and of his work on aphasia, see Perlman Lorch, 'The Unknown Source'.
43 Anderson and Meier-Hedde, 'Early Case Reports of Dyslexia', 10.
44 Kussmaul, 'Chapter XXVII', 770.
45 Berlin, 'Über Dyslexie'.
46 The latter is commonly, but erroneously, cited as the first reference to dyslexia; see the excellent untangling of the term's lineage by Howell, 'Dyslexia'.
47 Berlin, *Eine Besondere Art der Wortblindheit*, 1. The neologism 'dyslexia' is somewhat ambiguous. The Oxford English Dictionary ('Dyslexia') notes the following: 'Late 19th century: coined in German from dys- "difficult" + Greek lexis "speech" (apparently by confusion of Greek legein "to speak" and Latin legere "to read").' Alexia and paralexia both refer to acquired, rather than congenital, language difficulties; neither remains in common usage. Berlin himself seems to have recognised the etymological difficulties of terminology in the area, noting that alexia and paralexia 'have their somewhat questionable etymological side' (Berlin, *Eine Besondere Art der Wortblindheit*, 1). The translation here is courtesy of Lea-Sophie Steingrüber.
48 Wagner, 'Rudolf Berlin', 57.
49 Kerr, 'School Hygiene'.
50 Ibid., 659.
51 Pringle Morgan, 'A Case of Congenital Word Blindness'.
52 For example, Beard, *From Percy to Peter*. For excellent accounts of this period, see Anderson and Meier-Hedde, 'Early Case Reports of Dyslexia'; Behan, 'James Hinshelwood'. This was Pringle Morgan's only contribution to dyslexia research, but his legacy is preserved at the Seaford Museum, and (curiously) at the Instituto Pringle Morgan, a dyslexia organization based in Buenos Aires, Argentina (see *Sussex Express*, 'Why Argentina Remembers an Unsung Sussex Hero').
53 Pringle Morgan, 'A Case of Congenital Word Blindness', 1378.
54 Critchley, *The Dyslexic Child*, 7.
55 Hinshelwood, 'A Case of Dyslexia', 1452.

56 Pringle Morgan, 'A Case of Congenital Word Blindness', 1378.
57 Hinshelwood, 'Congenital Word-Blindness', 1507.
58 Hinshelwood, 'Word-Blindness and Visual Memory', 1564.
59 Ibid., 1565. The term 'cécité verbale' (word-blindness) is associated with the French neurologist Joseph Jules Dejerine (see Dejerine, 'Sur un Cas de Cécité Verbale').
60 Hinshelwood, 'A Case of Dyslexia', 1453.
61 On research on aphasia in Britain during this period, see Ball, 'A Contribution'; Bastian, 'On Some Problems'; Bramwell, 'Illustrative Cases'; Mantle, 'Motor and Sensory Aphasia'.
62 Berkhan, 'Über die Wortblindheit'. For discussion of these debates, and of Berkhan's view on the same, see Anderson and Meier-Hedde, 'Early Case Reports of Dyslexia', 16.
63 For example, in 1897, Byrom Bramwell, an eminent British surgeon, recorded several cases of aphasia, describing the features of one as including 'word-blindness' (Bramwell, 'Illustrative Cases'). Again, Bramwell's patient was almost certainly the victim of a stroke, and his use of 'word-blindness' was not synonymous with others' employment of the term at the time, including James Hinshelwood's. For further discussion, see van Gijn, 'The Pathology of Sensory Aphasia'.
64 Elsewhere, Anderson and Meier-Hedde ('Early Case Reports of Dyslexia', 12) suggest that the three most important qualities of early British work on congenital word blindness are its 'clarity and organization', 'attention to the plight of children', and 'accumulation of information about this enigma'.
65 Broadbent, 'Note on Dr Hinshelwood's Communication', 18.
66 Ibid.
67 Hinshelwood, 'A Case of Dyslexia', 1452.
68 Ibid.; Elliott, 'Dyslexia: Beyond the Debate', 76, 116.
69 Google Scholar (accessed 19 February 2020). The majority of these occurred from the 1970s onward, when Pringle Morgan's work was rediscovered by British researchers and others (Miles, *Fifty Years in Dyslexia Research*).
70 Pringle Morgan, 'A Case of Congenital Word Blindness', 1378; Hinshelwood, 'Congenital Word-Blindness', 1507.
71 For further reflection on speculation during the early twentieth century that dyslexia was hereditary, see DeFries, Alarcon, and Olson, 'Genetics and

Dyslexia'. For further references of the period to word-blindness running in families, see Lancet, 'Opthalmological Society'; Wood, 'Congenital Word-Blindness'.

72 Hinshelwood, '"Letter" without "Word" Blindness', 85.
73 For further contemporary reflection on the role of phonics-based instruction in the remediation of congenital word-blindness, and its efficacy in comparison to 'look and see' approaches, see Lancet, 'Ophthalmological Society'; and on the role of education, rather than medicine, in alleviating the symptoms of word-blindness, see Lancet, 'Congenital Word Blindness'.
74 Lancet, 'Ophthalmological Society', 1348. Treacher Collins is chiefly remembered today for his initial descriptions of what would come to be called Treacher Collins syndrome.
75 Ibid.
76 Ibid. For more on the manifestation of dyslexia in different languages, including German, see Goswami, 'Phonology'; Landerl, Wimmer, and Frith, 'The Impact of Orthographic Consistency'.
77 Critchley, The Dyslexic Child.
78 For example, Ranschburg, Die Leseschwäche (Legasthenie). For further reflection on the history of dyslexia provision in Hungary, see Gyarmathy and Vassné Kovács, 'Dyslexia in Hungary'.
79 Foerster, 'Beiträge zur Pathologie'; Peters, 'Über Kongenitale Wortblindheit'.
80 Humphries, 'Edward Humphries', 210.
81 For further reflection, and the first account to draw attention to this case in the context of reading difficulties, see Writing Lives, 'Edward S. Humphries'.
82 Irish News and Belfast Morning News, 'Word Blindness', 7; Dover Express, 'Science Notes', no pagination; Evening Telegraph, 'A Strange Case', no pagination; Scotsman, 'Science and Nature', 11.
83 Hampshire Telegraph, 'All Very Curious', 12; Dover Express, 'Science Notes', no pagination; Illustrated London News, 'Science Jottings', 358.
84 Globe, 6. There is an implicit reference here to the notion that word-blindness is over-diagnosed, i.e., an 'excuse' for schoolchildren unwilling to engage with their classes. Such accusations became more explicit in the decades to follow.
85 South London Press, 'South London Police Courts', 4.
86 For example, Campbell, Dyslexia; Anderson and Meier-Hedde, 'Early Case Reports of Dyslexia'.

87 *St James' Gazette*, 'Children', 10.
88 For example, *Cornubian and Redruth Times*, 'Word Blindness', 5; *Evening Telegraph*, 'A Strange Case', no pagination; *Preston Herald*, 'Education of the Brain', 11.
89 Hinshelwood, *Congenital Word-Blindness*.
90 *Scotsman*, 'Science and Nature', 11.
91 *Scotsman*, 'Scottish News', 4. The full entry reads: 'Dr James Hinshelwood, a Glasgow graduate, whose death at the age of 60 has taken place at his villa at Mentone, was an authority on eye diseases, and for a period was surgeon to Glasgow Eye Infirmary. He was the author of a book on "Congenital Word-Blindness".' Hinshelwood's obituary did at least reference his work on word-blindness. There was no similar reference in William Pringle Morgan's 1934 obituary in the *British Medical Journal* ('William Pringle Morgan').
92 Critchley, *The Dyslexic Child*, 7.

Chapter Two

1 Heywood, *A History of Childhood*.
2 For example, see Rose, *The Psychological Complex*; Walsh, Teo, and Baydala, *A Critical History and Philosophy of Psychology*; Alexander and Shelton, *A History of Psychology*.
3 Walsh, Teo, and Baydala, *A Critical History and Philosophy of Psychology*, 5.
4 Rose, *The Psychological Complex*, 3.
5 Campbell, 'From Aphasia to Dyslexia'; Campbell, *Dyslexia*.
6 Campbell, *Dyslexia*, 145.
7 Ibid., 153.
8 Hook, *Foucault, Psychology and the Analytics of Power*; Reisman, *A History of Clinical Psychology*; Walsh, Teo, and Baydala, *A Critical History and Philosophy of Psychology*.
9 Walsh, Teo, and Baydala, *A Critical History and Philosophy of Psychology*, 539.
10 For further discussion of mental testing and English education between 1880 and 1940, see Sutherland, *Ability, Merit and Measurement*.
11 McDonagh, *Idiocy*, 303.
12 Thomson, *England in the Twentieth Century*, 281.
13 Bolton, *Education*.
14 Snyder, *120 Years*.

15 Thomson, *England in the Twentieth Century*, 64.
16 Ibid.
17 Schuyler, 'A Short History of Government Taxing'.
18 For a case study, see Thomson, *England in the Twentieth Century*, 63.
19 Orton, 'Word-Blindness'. For earlier work published in the United States, see Chance, 'Developmental Alexia'; Clemensha, 'Congenital Word Blindness'; Heitmuller, 'Cases of Developmental Alexia'; Jackson, 'Developmental Alexia'; Schmitt, 'Developmental Alexia' (Anderson and Meier-Hedde, 'Early Case Reports of Dyslexia'). This was largely a continuation of the work of the British physicians of the late nineteenth and early twentieth centuries.
20 See Geschwind, 'Why Orton Was Right'.
21 Huston, *The Iowa State Psychopathic Hospital*. Largely rural, Greene County, Iowa, where the hospital was based, was the birthplace in 1901 of George Horace Gallup, the pioneer of public opinion polling, whose work also testified to the greater statistical attention being brought to populations in the first half of the twentieth century.
22 In fact, the clinic requested referrals for three types of pupil: those who were 'unusually bright', 'present[ed] behavior problems', or were 'retarded or failing in their school work' (Orton, 'Word-Blindness', 582). Throughout his career, Orton was most interested in the latter.
23 Critchley, *The Dyslexic Child*.
24 Orton, 'Word-Blindness', 581. The first footnoted reference in Orton's article is also to Hinshelwood's 1917 book, *Congenital Word-Blindness*.
25 Ibid., 583
26 For further critical discussion of these terms in the American context, see Gelb, 'Social Deviance'.
27 Orton, 'Word-Blindness', 585.
28 Ibid., 582.
29 Ibid., 611.
30 Noddings, *Philosophy of Education*. For a notable statement of Dewey's progressive approach to education, see Dewey, *Democracy and Education*.
31 Orton, 'Word-Blindness', 613.
32 Ibid.
33 Certainly, not all of those with dyslexia required the verdict of a psychologist to convince them of their own self-worth. Orton's patient, M.P., 'was at all times cooperative and entered willingly into all the tests and training

experiments ... He had apparently made a complete adjustment to his situation and was content to accept himself, as others rated him, as different from other boys' (ibid., 612).
34 Ibid., 581.
35 Elliott and Grigorenko, *The Dyslexia Debate*. For more on dyslexia and comorbidities, including effects on motor function and coordination (dyspraxia), see Nicolson, 'Dyslexia and Dyspraxia'.
36 The latter proposition led him to make perhaps the first reference to Leonardo da Vinci in the context of dyslexia; a figure who later dyslexia rights campaigners would be keen to claim as having dyslexia (e.g., Wolf, 'Dyslexia and the Brain').
37 Orton, 'Word-Blindness', 610.
38 Vellutino, *Dyslexia*; Snowling, *Dyslexia* (Blackwell).
39 Orton, 'Word-Blindness', 614.
40 Lemann, 'The Reading Wars'; Castles, Rastle, and Nation, 'Ending the Reading Wars'.
41 Lawrence, *Understanding Dyslexia*.
42 McClelland, 'Gillingham'.
43 Ibid., 37.
44 Ibid.
45 Ibid., 38.
46 Gillingham and Stillman, *Remedial Training*.
47 McClelland, 'Gillingham'.
48 Orton, 'Word-Blindness', 615.
49 McClelland, 'Gillingham', 38.
50 Fildes, 'A Psychological Inquiry'. For more on Fildes's life, see Valentine, '"A Lady of Unusual Ability"'.
51 Danforth, *The Incomplete Child*, 152.
52 Altenbaugh, *The Teacher's Voice*.
53 Bruland, 'Edith Norrie'.
54 Critchley, *The Dyslexic Child*.
55 For more on Norrie's views on word-blindness, including her knowledge of the work of James Kerr and William Pringle Morgan, see Hermann and Norrie, 'Is Congenital Word-Blindness a Hereditary Type of Gerstmann's Syndrome?'
56 Thomson, *Psychological Subjects*.

57 Walsh, Teo, and Baydala, *A Critical History and Philosophy of Psychology*, 258, after Bohan, 'Contextual History'.
58 Ibid., after Scarborough, 'Mrs. Ricord'.
59 Ibid., after Capshew, *Psychologists*.
60 Macdonald Critchley, for example, who would later become prominent in the dyslexia world, suspended his work on aphasia during World War II to provide psychiatric services to the Royal Navy; see Beard, *From Percy to Peter*, 57.
61 Mazumdar, 'Burt'.
62 Burt, 'Experimental Tests'.
63 For further discussion, see Mackintosh, *Cyril Burt*.
64 Mazumdar, 'Burt'.
65 Tucker, 'Burt's Separated Twins'.
66 Lloyd and Burt, *Report of an Investigation*.
67 Walsh, Teo, and Baydala, *A Critical History and Philosophy of Psychology*, 374.
68 Burt, 'The Definition and Diagnosis', 52.
69 Burt, *The Causes and Treatment*.
70 Burt and Lewis, 'Teaching Backward Readers', 117.
71 Ibid., 129.
72 Naidoo, *Specific Dyslexia*; Vellutino, *Dyslexia*; Bradley and Bryant, 'Categorizing Sounds'; Hatcher, 'Sound Links in Reading and Spelling with Discrepancy'.
73 Burt and Lewis, 'Teaching Backward Readers', 117.
74 Burt, 'Counterblast to Dyslexia'.
75 Evans, *The Metamorphosis of Autism*, 37.
76 See Burt and Banks, 'A Factor Analysis'; Burt, 'The Inheritance'.
77 Burt, 'The Inheritance', 180–2.
78 Thomson, *Psychological Subjects*, 110.
79 Stewart, *Child Guidance*.
80 Pritchard, *Education and the Handicapped*, 193.
81 Waltz, *Autism*, 79.
82 Ibid., 84. For further reflection on the gendering of scientific medicine during this period, see Pickstone, 'Ways of Knowing'.
83 Hall, 'Word Blindness', 468.
84 Ibid., 469.

85 Ibid., 470.
86 *Lancet*, 'Word-Blindness'.
87 Arkell, interview.
88 Ibid.
89 Ibid.
90 Millfield, 'Our History'. Famous alumni with dyslexia include the Olympic gold medallist swimmer Duncan Goodhew.
91 Personal records of the author (P.K.).
92 Armstrong, 'Disability, Education and Social Change'.
93 Shaw, 'History of Education', 6.
94 Thomson, *England in the Twentieth Century*, 221.

Chapter Three

1 Orton Society, 'Facts about the Orton Society'.
2 Welchman, 'A Personal Reflection'.
3 International Dyslexia Association, 'History of IDA'.
4 Geschwind, 'Why Orton Was Right'.
5 Whyte, 'Class and Classification'.
6 Ibid., 425–6.
7 For further reflection on the role of middle-class organisations in the disability rights movement in Britain, see Campbell and Oliver, *Disability Politics*.
8 Armstrong, 'Disability, Education and Social Change'.
9 Miles, *Fifty Years in Dyslexia Research*, 28. For more on White Franklin's life and work, see Kirby, 'White Franklin'.
10 White Franklin, *Word-Blindness*.
11 Ibid., I.
12 Whyte, 'Class and Classification'; McLeod, 'Prediction', 14.
13 White Franklin, *Word-Blindness*, ii.
14 Whyte, 'Class and Classification', 418; quotations in second sentence from Stewart, *Child Guidance*, 149–50; quotation in third sentence from Thom, 'Wishes, Anxieties, Play and Gestures', 202.
15 Whyte, 'Class and Classification', 419–20; quotations in fourth sentence from Wooldridge, *Measuring the Mind*, 153, 216.
16 For excellent accounts of Tim Miles and his life, see Evans, 'A Pioneer in Context'; Evans, 'Miles'.
17 Miles, *Fifty Years in Dyslexia Research*, 28.

Notes to pages 70–6

18 Burt and Lewis, 'Teaching Backward Readers'.
19 Naidoo, *Specific Dyslexia*, 20.
20 This official cannot have been the Ministry of Education's medical officer responsible for specific reading disability, J.N. Horne, who was visiting Edith Norrie's Ordblinde Instituttet at the time.
21 Whyte, 'Class and Classification'.
22 Ibid.
23 Ibid., 417.
24 Ibid.
25 White Franklin, *Word-Blindness*.
26 Naidoo, interview.
27 Miles, *Fifty Years in Dyslexia Research*; Naidoo, interview.
28 Miles, *Fifty Years in Dyslexia Research*.
29 Staff at the Word Blind Centre seem to have reached no consensus on whether to hyphenate 'word-blind' or not. The name of the centre itself was unhyphenated, but publications relating to the centre and the conference that preceded it (e.g., White Franklin, *Word-Blindness*) do use hyphenation.
30 Whyte, 'Class and Classification'.
31 Bannatyne, 'The Aetiology of Dyslexia', 20.
32 Nation, 'Naidoo'.
33 Ibid.
34 Beard, *From Percy to Peter*, 80.
35 Naidoo, interview.
36 Kellmer Pringle and Naidoo, *Early Child Care*. For further discussion of this episode, see Kirby, 'Worried Mothers?'
37 Naidoo, interview. Ultimately, the centre charged for teaching, but not assessment. The majority of this tuition was funded by local education authorities, while some was paid for by pupils' parents.
38 Nation, 'Naidoo'.
39 Ibid.
40 Beard, *From Percy to Peter*.
41 Ibid.
42 Ibid.
43 Nation, 'Naidoo'.
44 Ibid. Severe language difficulties would later become known as developmental language disorder.
45 Ibid.

46 Naidoo, *Specific Dyslexia*. Children also had to possess a verbal IQ of at least 86 on the Wechsler Intelligence Scale.
47 This system was superseded in 1990 by the National Statistics Socio-Economic Classification.
48 UK Office for National Statistics, 'Long-Term Trends'.
49 Naidoo, *Specific Dyslexia*, 5.
50 Whyte, 'Class and Classification'.
51 Naidoo, *Specific Dyslexia*.
52 Ibid., 6.
53 Ibid.
54 Beard, *From Percy to Peter*.
55 Oxford Dyslexia Archive, uncatalogued.
56 Hargrave-Wright, interview.
57 Whyte, 'Class and Classification', 424; quotation in second sentence from Yule and Rutter, 'Neurological Aspects', 58; statement in fourth sentence after Douglas, *The Home and the School*; quotation in fifth sentence from Naidoo, *Specific Dyslexia*, 28.
58 Naidoo, *Specific Dyslexia*, 28.
59 Ibid., 20.
60 *Times*, 'Obituary: Dr Alfred White Franklin'; Whyte, 'Class and Classification'.
61 Gregory, 'Zangwill'.
62 Tizard, 'Sheldon'.
63 Beard, *From Percy to Peter*.
64 Naidoo, *Specific Dyslexia*, xv.
65 Beard, *From Percy to Peter*.
66 Ibid.
67 Ibid.
68 Ibid.
69 White Franklin and Naidoo, *Assessment and Teaching*.
70 Draper, 'Assessment and Teaching', 206.
71 Critchley, *The Dyslexic Child*; *Developmental Dyslexia*.
72 Critchley, *The Dyslexic Child*, x.
73 Tizard, *Children with Specific Reading Difficulties*.
74 Beard, *From Percy to Peter*, 174–5.
75 *Man Alive*: 'Could Do Better: 1'.
76 Closer, 'Television Ownership'.
77 Miles, *Fifty Years in Dyslexia Research*, 30.

Chapter Four

1. This is not a straightforward bifurcation: causes operate at different levels, including the biological, cognitive, and environmental, and there have been attempts over time, in the area of dyslexia and elsewhere, to incorporate these different levels of causality into models of neurodevelopmental disorders. For further reflection, see Morton and Frith, 'Causal Modelling'.
2. Orton, *Reading, Writing and Speech Problems*. Orton had tried to make sense of these in his theory of strephosymbolia, described previously.
3. Fischer, Liberman, and Shankweiler, 'Reading Reversals'.
4. Blank and Bridger, 'Deficiencies in Verbal Labeling'; for responses, see Bryant, 'Comments on the Design'; Bryant, 'Cross-Modal Development and Reading'.
5. Johnson and Myklebust, *Learning Disabilities*.
6. Warrington, interview.
7. Ibid.
8. Kinsbourne and Warrington, 'The Developmental Gerstmann Syndrome'; Nelson and Warrington, 'Developmental Spelling Retardation'; Nelson and Warrington, 'An Investigation of Memory Functions'. The possible relationship between dyslexia and Gerstmann Syndrome had also been explored by Edith Norrie and her colleague, Knud Hermann, in the late 1950s; see Hermann and Norrie, 'Is Congenital Word-Blindness a Hereditary Type of Gerstmann's Syndrome?'
9. Naidoo, *Specific Dyslexia*; Newton and Thomson, *Aston Index*; Miles, *The Bangor Dyslexia Test*.
10. Franklin and Naidoo, *Assessment and Teaching*.
11. Backman, Mamen, and Ferguson, 'Reading Level Design'.
12. Rutter et al., 'Isle of Wight Studies'. For an account of the study on reading, see Rutter and Yule, 'The Concept of Specific Reading Retardation'.
13. Critchley, *The Dyslexic Child*, 11.
14. Rutter and Yule, 'The Concept of Specific Reading Retardation'.
15. Yule, interview.
16. Malmquist, 'A Decade of Reading Research in Europe'.
17. Yule, 'Differential Prognosis of Reading Backwardness'.
18. Berger, Yule, and Rutter, 'Attainment and Adjustment'.
19. Vellutino, *Dyslexia*.
20. Vellutino et al., 'Immediate Visual Recall'.

21 Influential background research on the speech code was reported by Liberman et al., 'Perception of the Speech Code'.
22 Liberman et al., 'Explicit Syllable and Phoneme Segmentation'. Shankweiler attended the Word-Blindness Conference in London of 1962.
23 Byrne, 'The Learnability of the Alphabetic Principle'.
24 Bryant and Goswami, 'Strengths and Weaknesses'.
25 Hulme, *Reading Retardation*; Snowling, 'The Development of Grapheme-Phoneme Correspondence'.
26 Brady, Shankweiler, and Mann, 'Speech Perception'; Brady, 'The Role of Working Memory'; Hulme, 'The Effects of Manual Tracing'.
27 Wolf, 'Rapid Alternating Stimulus Naming'; Wolf, 'Naming, Reading, and the Dyslexias'; Snowling, 'Phonemic Deficits'; Snowling et al., 'Segmentation and Speech Perception'.
28 Frith, *Cognitive Processes in Spelling*.
29 Marshall and Newcombe, 'Patterns of Paralexia'.
30 Coltheart, 'Acquired Dyslexias'; Coltheart, 'In Defence of Dual-Route Models'. The latter is part of a set of opinion pieces regarding the classic two-route model.
31 Temple and Marshall, 'A Case Study'.
32 Coltheart et al., 'Surface Dyslexia'.
33 Frith, 'Beneath the Surface of Developmental Dyslexia'.
34 Snowling, 'The Comparison of Acquired and Developmental Disorders'; Snowling, Bryant, and Hulme, 'Theoretical and Methodological Pitfalls'.
35 Snowling and Hulme, 'A Longitudinal Case Study'; Hulme and Snowling, 'Deficits in Output Phonology'; Funnell and Davison, 'Lexical Capture'; Campbell and Butterworth, 'Phonological Dyslexia and Dysgraphia'.
36 Stanovich, 'Explaining the Differences'.
37 Stanovich, 'The Right and Wrong Places'.
38 Shaywitz et al., 'A Matthew Effect for IQ'; Stanovich, 'Annotation: Does Dyslexia Exist?'
39 Pringle Morgan, 'A Case of Congenital Word Blindness'.
40 For example, Hallgren, 'Specific Dyslexia'.
41 LaBuda and DeFries, 'Genetic and Environmental Etiologies'.
42 DeFries, Fulker, and LaBuda, 'Evidence For a Genetic Aetiology'; and see Fisher and DeFries, 'Developmental Dyslexia'.
43 Pennington, 'Using Genetics to Understand Dyslexia'.
44 Olson, Wise, and Rack, 'Dyslexia'.

45 Keenan, Betjemann, and DeFries, 'Genetic and Environmental Influences'.
46 Olson, Byrne, and Samuelsson, 'Reconciling Strong Genetic and Strong Environmental Influences'; McGowan et al., 'Differential Influences of Genes and Environment'.
47 Olson et al., 'Specific Deficits'.
48 Smith et al., 'Specific Reading Disability'; Lubs et al., 'Familial Dyslexia'. For a review of the earlier studies, see Pennington, 'The Genetics of Dyslexia'.
49 Castles et al., 'Varieties of Developmental Reading Disorder'.
50 Ibid.
51 See Hulme and Snowling, *Developmental Disorders*; Hulme, 'Mind the (Inferential) Gap'.
52 Scarborough, 'Very Early Language Deficits'; Lefly and Pennington, 'Longitudinal Study of Children'; Gallagher, Frith, and Snowling, 'Precursors of Literacy Delay'.
53 For a review, see Snowling and Melby-Lervåg, 'Oral Language Deficits'.
54 Scarborough, 'Very Early Language Deficits'.
55 Snowling and Melby-Lervåg, 'Oral Language Deficits'.
56 Lyytinen et al., 'Developmental Pathways'.
57 For the British study, see Gallagher, Frith, and Snowling, 'Precursors of Literacy Delay'.
58 Lervåg, 'Correlation and Causation'. For an example, see Hulme et al., 'The Causal Role of Phoneme Awareness'.
59 Bradley and Bryant, 'Categorizing Sounds'.
60 Hatcher, Hulme, and Ellis, 'Ameliorating Early Reading Failure'.
61 For more on Clay's method, see Clay, *The Early Detection of Reading Difficulties*.
62 Hatcher, 'Reading Intervention'.
63 Hulme et al., 'The Causal Role of Phoneme Awareness'.
64 Galaburda and Kemper, 'Cytoarchitectonic Abnormalities'; Galaburda et al., 'Developmental Dyslexia'.
65 Turner et al., 'Functional Magnetic Resonance Imaging'.
66 Paulesu et al., 'Is Developmental Dyslexia a Disconnection Syndrome?'
67 Brunswick et al., 'Explicit and Implicit Processing'.
68 Morton and Frith, 'Causal Modelling'; Hulme and Snowling, *Dyslexia*. For a discussion using autism as an example, see Frith, Morton, and Leslie, 'The Cognitive Basis'.
69 Ramus, 'Neurobiology of Dyslexia'.

70 Swan and Goswami, 'Phonological Awareness Deficits'.
71 Stein and Walsh, 'To See but Not to Read'.
72 Nicolson and Fawcett, 'Automaticity'.
73 Ramus, White, and Frith, 'Weighing the Evidence'.
74 Snowling and Hulme, *The Science of Reading*.
75 Perfetti, 'Reading Ability'.
76 Perfetti, 'The Universal Grammar'; Vellutino et al., 'Specific Reading Disability'.
77 Wimmer, 'Characteristics of Developmental Dyslexia'; Goswami, 'Phonological Representations'; Seymour, Aro, and Erskine, 'Foundation Literacy Acquisition'.
78 Landerl, Wimmer, and Frith, 'The Impact of Orthographic Consistency'; Paulesu et al., 'Dyslexia'. For earlier research on dyslexia in German, employing the cognitive approach, see Valtin, *Legasthenie*.
79 Goulandris, *Dyslexia in Different Languages*; Caravolas, 'The Nature and Causes of Dyslexia'.
80 Shu et al., 'Properties of School Chinese'.
81 Ziegler and Goswami, 'Reading Acquisition'; Ziegler and Goswami, 'Becoming Literate in Different Languages'; Landerl et al., 'Predictors of Developmental Dyslexia'.
82 Nag and Snowling, 'Reading in an Alphasyllabary'.
83 Ziegler et al., 'Developmental Dyslexia in Different Languages'; Caravolas et al., 'Common Patterns of Prediction of Literacy Development'.
84 Bishop and Snowling, 'Developmental Dyslexia'; Pennington and Bishop, 'Relations among Speech, Language, and Reading Disorders'.
85 Snowling, Bishop, and Stothard, 'Is Preschool Language Impairment a Risk Factor'; Catts et al., 'Language Basis of Reading'; Catts et al., 'Are Specific Language Impairment and Dyslexia Distinct Disorders?'
86 Ramus, 'Developmental Dyslexia'; Talcott et al., 'Visual Motion Sensitivity in Dyslexia'; McAnally and Stein, 'Auditory Temporal Coding in Dyslexia'; Nicolson, Fawcett, and Dean, 'Developmental Dyslexia'.
87 Valdois et al., 'Phonological and Visual Processing Deficits'.
88 Ramus et al., 'Theories of Developmental Dyslexia'; White et al., 'The Role of Sensorimotor Impairments'; Saksida et al., 'Phonological Skills'.
89 Pennington, 'From Single to Multiple Deficit Models'.
90 Pennington, McGrath, and Peterson, *Diagnosing Learning Disorders*.
91 Pennington, 'From Single to Multiple Deficit Models'.

92 Moll, Snowling, and Hulme, 'Introduction'.
93 Frederickson and Reason, 'Discrepancy Definitions'; Savage et al., 'Relationships among Rapid Digit Naming'.
94 Rose, *Identifying and Teaching Children and Young People with Dyslexia*.
95 Ibid, 10.
96 Ibid.
97 Ibid, 30.
98 See Kirby, 'Dyslexia Debated'.

Chapter Five

1 R. Salter, interview; European Dyslexia Association, 'About EDA'.
2 Snowling, 'Reach for the Stars'; Smythe, Everatt, and Salter, *International Book of Dyslexia*.
3 Lawrence, *Understanding Dyslexia*.
4 For further reflection on Samuel T. Orton and the history of the Orton Society, see Geschwind, 'Why Orton Was Right'; Anderson and Meier-Hedde, 'Early Case Reports of Dyslexia'.
5 See, for example, in Sweden, Hallgren, 'Specific Dyslexia'; in Denmark, Hermann, *Reading Disability*. For an overview of dyslexia around the world, including brief reflections on individual countries' histories, see Smythe, Everatt, and Salter, *International Book of Dyslexia*.
6 Lowe, *The Welfare State*.
7 Clarke, *Hope and Glory*, 304.
8 Naidoo, *Specific Dyslexia*.
9 The Dyslexia Association of Ireland predated the BDA by one year. See Hughes, 'Dyslexia in Ireland'.
10 Matti, 'Marion Welchman'.
11 Ibid.
12 Other individuals, who followed a similar career trajectory, include the teachers/campaigners Helen Arkell, Gill Cotterell, and Violet Brand. Arkell is profiled below; Cotterell and Brand became influential figures in the dyslexia community through their work at the BDA and in developing specialist teaching materials. For further discussion of the lives of those in the British dyslexia movement, see the 2021 collection in the ODNB, including: Evans, 'Miles'; Fitzpatrick, 'Hinshelwood'; Kirby, 'White Franklin'; Nation, 'Naidoo'; Snowling, 'Hornsby'; Whyte, 'Welchman'.
13 Matti, 'Marion Welchman'.

14 Beard, *From Percy to Peter*; Matti, 'Marion Welchman'.
15 Welchman, 'A Personal Reflection', 7.
16 Ibid.
17 Smythe, Everatt, and Salter, *International Book of Dyslexia*.
18 Hargrave-Wright, 'Dyslexia Journey', 14.
19 These included the Dyslexia Teaching Centre founded by Sister Mary John in 1978 and the Arts Dyslexia Trust founded by Susan Parkinson in 1992.
20 For more on the Aston Index, a classroom test for identifying language difficulties, see Newton and Thomson, *Aston Index*.
21 For further reflection on the competition between organisations for ascendancy in the dyslexia movement, see Nicolson, 'Developmental Dyslexia'.
22 Arkell, interview.
23 These included Daphne Hamilton-Fairley, founder of the Fairley House specialist dyslexia school, who is profiled below.
24 Nation, 'Naidoo'.
25 Hamilton-Fairley, interview.
26 Chinn, interview.
27 Jenkins, *Women in the Labour Market*.
28 For an excellent discussion of women and social change in Britain in the twentieth century, see Zweiniger-Bargielowska, *Women in Twentieth-Century Britain*.
29 Oram, 'A Master Should Not Serve'. For further discussion, see Kirby, 'Literacy, Advocacy and Agency'.
30 Welchman, 'A Personal Reflection', 5.
31 Arkell, interview.
32 The Isle of Wight Council in 1942. For more on the biographies of these women, see: Tizard, 'Pringle, Mia Lilly Kellmer'; Wootton Bridge Historical, 'Miss Lucy May (Maisie) Holt'.
33 Naidoo, interview.
34 Snowling, 'Hornsby'.
35 Snowling, interview.
36 Beechey, 'Our Double Anniversary'; Snowling, 'Reach for the Stars'. The Hornsby International Dyslexia Centre merged with the Dyslexia Institute in 2005 to become Dyslexia Action.
37 Cooke, interview.

Notes to pages 122–7

38 Thomson, interview.
39 For examples, see Edwards, *The Scars of Dyslexia*.
40 Miles, *Fifty Years in Dyslexia Research*, 61.
41 Watkins, interview.
42 Edwards, *The Scars of Dyslexia*.
43 Cooke, interview.
44 Kirby, 'Worried Mothers'.
45 Wood, *Patient Power*.
46 Mold, *Making the Patient-Consumer*. For further discussion, see Kirby, 'Worried Mothers'.
47 Waltz, *Autism*; Silberman, *Neurotribes*; Murray, *Representing Autism*.
48 Waltz, *Autism*.
49 The same has been true more recently of ADHD. See Smith, *Hyperactive: The Controversial History of ADHD*.
50 See, for example, Bettelheim, *The Empty Fortress*.
51 Kirby, 'Worried Mothers?'
52 James, *The Middle Class*.
53 Pringle Morgan, 'A Case of Congenital Word Blindness'; Hinshelwood, 'Congenital Word-Blindness'.
54 Nadesan, *Constructing Autism*, 3. For more on changing conceptions of motherhood during the twentieth century, see Smith, *The Government of Childhood*.
55 Beard, *From Percy to Peter*, 101.
56 Edwards, *The Scars of Dyslexia*, 132.
57 Kirby, 'Worried Mothers'.
58 Ibid.
59 Hampshire, interview; Hampshire, *Susan's Story*, 138.
60 Hampshire, interview. For further discussion, see Kirby, 'Worried Mothers'.
61 Beard, *From Percy to Peter*, 159.
62 Hargrave-Wright, interview.
63 Bradley, interview.
64 Miles, interview.
65 Cooke, interview.
66 Miles, interview.
67 Kirby, 'Worried Mothers?'
68 Warnock, interview.

69 Warnock, *Special Educational Needs*.
70 The British general election of 1979, for example, returned 616 male MPS out of 635 in total. For her part, Warnock later became the president of the BDA.
71 Miles, *Fifty Years in Dyslexia Research*, 30.
72 J. Salter, interview.
73 Arkell, interview.
74 Start and Wells, *The Trend of Reading Standards*.
75 J. Salter, interview.
76 Williams, interview.
77 For example, Edwards, *The Scars of Dyslexia*; Hampshire, *Every Letter Counts*.
78 Hampshire, *Every Letter Counts*.
79 For examples, see Heseltine, *Misunderstood*; Quinnell, *The Hardest Test*; Strange, *War Baby*.
80 Hoyles and Hoyles, *Dyslexia from a Cultural Perspective*.
81 Ibid., 190.
82 For further discussion of race and dyslexia, see Hoyles and Hoyles, 'Race and Dyslexia'; Robinson, 'The Voice of a Gifted Black Male'.
83 Critchley, 'Reading Retardation'.
84 Snowling et al., 'Levels of Literacy among Juvenile Offenders'; Macdonald, *Crime and Dyslexia*.
85 See Brown, 'Foreword'; Hogenson, 'Reading Failure and Juvenile Delinquency'.
86 Rack, 'The Incidence of Hidden Disabilities'; Macdonald, 'Biographical Pathways', 430. For a recent study of criminality and dyslexia, see Hewitt-Main, *Dyslexia behind Bars*.
87 Thomson, interview.
88 Loucks, *No One Knows*; Hansard [HC], 553, col. 198WH, 21 November 2012.
89 Moss, 'Half of Britain's Prisoners'.
90 Sonday, 'The Road to Reading', 290.
91 Cameron, 'The Disabled People's Movement'.
92 Beard, *From Percy to Peter*, 108.
93 Ibid., 113.
94 Macdonald, *Towards a Sociology of Dyslexia*, 44.

Chapter Six

1. For example, Nadesan, *Constructing Autism*; Waltz, *Autism*; Smith, *Hyperactive: The Controversial History of ADHD*.
2. Some of Foucault's most famous works in this respect are *The Birth of the Clinic* and *Madness and Civilization*.
3. Smith, 'Hyperactive around the World?', 770.
4. Nadesan, *Constructing Autism*, 2. For further discussion of this position in the academic history of learning difficulties, see Kirby, 'Literacy, Advocacy and Agency'.
5. Campbell, *Dyslexia*, 5.
6. Ibid., 6.
7. Kale, 'The Battle over Dyslexia'.
8. For further discussion, see Kirby, 'Literacy, Advocacy and Agency'.
9. Ibid.
10. Campbell, *Dyslexia*, 37.
11. Kirby, 'Gift from the Gods?'
12. UK National Archives, Horne, *Reading Delay*.
13. UK National Archives, White Franklin, [Letter to Dr Henderson].
14. UK National Archives, Horne, [Letter to Dr White Franklin], 13 December 1962.
15. UK National Archives, White Franklin, [Letter to J.N. Horne].
16. UK National Archives, Horne, [Letter to Dr White Franklin], 19 December 1962. For further discussion of this episode, see Kirby, 'Literacy, Advocacy and Agency'.
17. UK National Archives, 'Dyslexia: Meeting with Professor Meredith'. Tim Miles of the Word Blind Centre later described Horne's final report as 'the work of a luckless amateur' (Beard, *From Percy to Peter*, 152).
18. For a recent iteration of this argument, see Elliott and Grigorenko, *The Dyslexia Debate*, 181. In his letter of 14 December 1962, White Franklin pressed Horne to 'let me know whose feelings have been deep', but apparently received no response.
19. For example, Elliott and Grigorenko, *The Dyslexia Debate*.
20. UK National Archives, Horne, *Report on a Visit to Copenhagen*, 8.
21. It might be argued that education officials highlighted (even exaggerated) dyslexia's undecided science specifically to avoid providing financial support. This is possible, of course, although the doubts around dyslexia

research expressed by education officials seem to have been more extensive than would have been necessary for this purpose alone.
22 UK National Archives, Horne, 'Meeting with Officers'.
23 Edwards, *The Scars of Dyslexia*, 20.
24 Hansard [HC], 654, cols. 63–4W, 22 February 1962.
25 If the latter, this suggests that dyslexia was not at this time of interest solely to those in the metropolitan sphere: Brewis was the MP for Galloway in Scotland, one of the most rural constituencies in the UK.
26 Hansard [HC], 654, cols. 63–4W, 22 February 1962.
27 Hansard [HC], 778, col. 307W, 26 February 1969; Hansard [HC], 763, col. 208W, 1 May 1968.
28 Hansard [HC], 724, col. 288, 17 February 1966.
29 UK National Archives, Meredith, *Dyslexia Research Project*.
30 Plowden, *Children and Their Primary Schools*.
31 Shaw, 'History of Education', 7.
32 Plowden, *Children and Their Primary Schools*, 214.
33 UK National Archives, Meredith, *Dyslexia Research Project*; Critchley, *The Dyslexic Child*; Naidoo, *Specific Dyslexia*.
34 For notable articles of 1970, see Sladen, 'Inheritance of Dyslexia'; White, 'Some General Outlines'.
35 Critchley, *The Dyslexic Child*, 96. Original in italics.
36 Armstrong, 'Disability, Education and Social Change'.
37 Heaton, 'Access', 1; UK Government, *Chronically Sick and Disabled Persons Act*, 13. Tim Miles writes that 'the word "acute" appears to have been poorly chosen, since this word is normally taken to mean "coming on suddenly". In this context, however, it should presumably be taken simply to mean "severe"' (Miles, *Fifty Years in Dyslexia Research*, 73). There was some debate over the term in the House of Lords, albeit none that explains why it was originally chosen (Hansard [HL], 310, cols. 865–6, 15 May 1970).
38 Hansard [HC], 811, col. 506, 17 February 1971.
39 Ibid.
40 Hansard [HC], 826, col. 618, 18 November 1971.
41 Ibid., col. 619.
42 Tizard, *Children with Specific Reading Difficulties*; ; quoted in Miles, *Fifty Years in Dyslexia Research*, 73.
43 Warnock, *Special Educational Needs*, 1.

44 Tomlinson, *Education*; Robertson, '"Remaking the World"'. This contrasted with the ultimate judgement of the Warnock report: 'Education in such cases [of learning difficulty] makes the difference between a proper and enjoyable life and something less than we believe life should be' (Warnock, *Special Educational Needs*, 6).
45 Warnock, interview.
46 Ibid.
47 Ibid. For further discussion of this episode, see Kirby, 'Literacy, Advocacy and Agency'.
48 UK House of Commons Education and Skills Committee, *Special Educational Needs*, 5.
49 Warnock, interview.
50 Miles, *Fifty Years in Dyslexia Research*, 74.
51 Warnock, *Special Educational Needs*, 311.
52 Ibid., 218.
53 Warnock, interview.
54 Lawrence, *Understanding Dyslexia*, 13.
55 Warnock, *Special Educational Needs*, 45.
56 UK Government, *Education Act of 1981*; Chasty, 'What Is Dyslexia?', 27.
57 Swain, French, and Cameron, *Controversial Issues*, 126.
58 Hansard [House of Commons], 71, col. 475W, 24 January 1985; 101, col. C50W, 7 July 1986.
59 Hansard [HC], 189, col. 545, 17 April 1991.
60 Hansard [HC], 119, col. 949, 13 July 1987.
61 Ibid., col. 950.
62 Ibid.
63 Hansard [HC], 119, col. 953, 13 July 1987.
64 Ibid.
65 Miles, *Fifty Years in Dyslexia Research*; Reid, *Dyslexia*.
66 Hansard [HC], 138, cols. 230–5, 25 July 1988; Hansard [HC], 186, cols. 1–2, 18 February 1991; Hansard [HC], 224, col. 644, 11 May 1993.
67 Blackburn, *Children's Services*.
68 UK Select Committee on Education and Skills, *Third Report*, Annex.
69 Nicolson, 'Developmental Dyslexia'; Lawrence, *Understanding Dyslexia*.
70 Dalton, *Dyslexia and Dyscalculia*, 2.
71 Exley and Ball, 'Neo-Liberalism and English Education'.

72 For more on the *Man Alive* programme, one of the first media productions to reference dyslexia in Britain, see Beard, *From Percy to Peter*, 175.
73 Hansard [HC], 69, cols. 487–8W, 12 December 1984; Hansard [HC], 482, cols. 125–7, 18 November 1986; Hansard [HC], 119, cols. 949–56, 13 July 1987; Hansard [HC], 1000, cols. 517–24, 5 March 1981.
74 R. Salter, interview.
75 Vellutino, *Dyslexia*.
76 Hansard [HC], 119, col. 953, 13 July 1987; Snowling, *Dyslexia* (Blackwell).
77 UK Department of Education and Employment, *Excellence in Schools*, 3.
78 Literacy Task Force, *Implementation of the National Literacy Strategy*. By 2001, 74 per cent of eleven-year-olds met the target (Pollard, *David Blunkett*, 231).
79 UK Department for Education and Skills, *Schools: Building on Success*, 12.
80 For further discussion, see Nicolson, 'Developmental Dyslexia'.
81 Andersson, 'Dyslexia in Sweden'; Bogdanowicz, 'Dyslexia in Poland'; Palmer, 'Dyslexia in the Caribbean'.
82 Blunkett, interview.
83 UK Department for Education and Employment, *Education for All*, 16.
84 Blunkett, interview.
85 Reason et al., 'Dyslexia, Literacy and Psychological Assessment', 8.
86 Ibid.
87 UK House of Lords, 'Judgments – Phelps'.
88 Ibid.
89 Ibid.
90 Streeter, 'People'.
91 UK House of Lords, 'Judgments – Phelps'.
92 Elliott and Grigorenko, *The Dyslexia Debate*, 123.
93 Streeter, 'People'; BBC News, 'Dyslexic Loses'.
94 Hansard [HC], 355, col. 194W, 26 October 2020. The government's position was made somewhat more awkward by the fact that, in the original proceedings, one of Phelps's lawyers was Cherie Booth QC, the wife of the prime minister, Tony Blair.
95 UK House of Lords, 'Judgments – Phelps'.
96 Barnes, Barton, and Oliver, *Disability Studies Today*.
97 UK House of Lords, 'Judgments – Phelps'.
98 Rose, *Identifying and Teaching Children and Young People with Dyslexia*, 10.
99 Hansard [HC], 537, col. 324WH, 14 December 2011. The final point here

shows how wedded educational achievement had become by this point to exam success. In a recent review of the English primary school curriculum, Mel Ainscow and colleagues have argued that this focus, along with a fragmentation of the school system, has taken attention away from a proper understanding of the diversity of special educational needs (Ainscow et al., *Primary Schools*).

100 Hansard [HC], 537, col. 306WH. The same statement is cited by the term's foremost academic critics; see Elliott and Grigorenko, *The Dyslexia Debate*, 8.
101 Rose, *Identifying and Teaching Children and Young People with Dyslexia*, 10.
102 UK Government, *Equality Act of 2010*.

Chapter Seven

1 Here, fashionableness refers to how policy interest in certain cognitive difficulties ebbs and flows. For further perspectives, see Haker, 'Asperger Syndrome'; Lowenstein, 'Dyslexia'.
2 Of an enormous interdisciplinary field, see Betts and Bly, *A History of Popular Culture*; Dittmer, *Popular Culture, Geopolitics, and Identity*; Mukerji and Schudson, *Rethinking Popular Culture*.
3 For further discussion, see Kirby, 'Gift from the Gods?'
4 Smythe, Everatt, and Salter, *International Book*.
5 *Dispatches*, 'The Myth of Dyslexia'; Elliott and Grigorenko, *The Dyslexia Debate*.
6 Silberman, *Neurotribes*, 471.
7 *Irish News and Belfast Morning News*, 'Word Blindness', 7; *Dover Express*, 'Science Notes', no pagination; *Hampshire Telegraph*, 'All Very Curious', 2.
8 More recently, the trope has been repeated in the World War II adventure *Pearl Harbor* (2001); the drama *A Mind of Her Own* (2006); and the independent short *bAd* (2007).
9 Davis, *The Gift of Dyslexia*.
10 Conn and Bhugra, 'The Portrayal of Autism'.
11 For example, see the independent film *Mean Creek* (2004), and the discussion of the *Percy Jackson* series below.
12 Riordan, *Percy Jackson*; *The Sea of Monsters*; *The Titan's Curse*; *The Battle of the Labyrinth*; *The Last Olympian*.
13 Riordan, *Percy Jackson*, 87–8. For a scholarly account of how dyslexia manifests in different languages, see Landerl, Wimmer, and Frith, 'The Impact of Orthographic Consistency'.

14 The book series are *The Heroes of Olympus* and *The Trials of Apollo*; the adaptations are *Lightning Thief* (2010) and *Sea of Monsters* (2013).
15 Gladwell, *David and Goliath*.
16 For example, Reading Well, 'Famous People'; Positive Dyslexia, 'What Is Dyslexia?'; Dyslexia Daily, 'Famous and Dyslexic'.
17 See, for example, Seidenberg, *Language at the Speed of Sight* (180), which criticizes Malcolm Gladwell's work in particular: 'Knowing that a celebrity is dyslexic may be motivating for a child who is struggling; no harm in that. But matters take a darker turn when it is asked if dyslexia could be a "desirable difficulty", as Malcolm Gladwell did in his 2013 book *David and Goliath*. Dyslexia is a serious condition that is challenging at best and often debilitating. Gladwell acknowledges this and then asks, "You wouldn't wish dyslexia on your child? Or would you?" My view is that his observations about dyslexia are so shallow they shouldn't merit serious attention. But this is an author whose books reach an enormous audience. This book is so well known it seems likely to create additional obstacles for dyslexics and their families.'
18 Dodds and Kirby, 'It's Not a Laughing Matter', 51.
19 For further discussion, see Kirby, 'Gift from the Gods?'
20 For example, Grayson, Davies, and Philpott, 'Pop Goes IR?', 158.
21 Hampshire, interview; Shawsun, interview; Saunders, interview.
22 For further discussion, see Goldacre, 'Dyslexia "Cure"'.
23 Henshaw, 'Council Attacked'.
24 Patoss, 'Dyslexia No Longer Being Diagnosed'.
25 Hansard, 30 October 2018, col. 1217.
26 For further discussion, see Kirby, 'Dyslexia Debated'.
27 Elliott and Grigorenko, *The Dyslexia Debate*, 4, 32.
28 Ibid., 178. Emphasis in original.
29 Ibid., 180. For further reflection on the dyslexia label and what it means to individuals, see Orton, 'Dyslexia in England'.
30 Elliott and Grigorenko, *The Dyslexia Debate*, 181. For further work by these authors on this theme, see Elliott, 'Dyslexia: Beyond the Debate'; Elliott and Grigorenko, 'The End of Dyslexia?'
31 Liddle, 'Dyslexia Is Meaningless'.
32 Hitchens, 'Dyslexia Is Not a Disease'.
33 Bennett, 'The Classroom Fad'.

34 Castles, Wheldall, and Nayton, 'Should We Do Away with "Dyslexia"'; Science Daily, 'US Dyslexia Policies'; *Indian Express*, 'The Early Years'.
35 Science Daily, 'US Dyslexia Policies'.
36 Willcutt et al., 'Understanding Comorbidity'; Moll, Snowling, and Hulme, 'Introduction'.
37 Rayner et al., 'How Psychological Science Informs'; Seidenberg, 'The Science of Reading'; Hulme et al., 'Children's Language Skills Can Be Improved'.
38 Tosto et al., 'The Genetic Architecture'; Andreola et al., 'The Heritability of Reading'; Little, Haughbrook, and Hart, 'Cross-Study Differences'; Snowling et al., 'Developmental Outcomes'; Galuschka et al., 'Effectiveness of Spelling Interventions'; Snowling, 'Early Identification and Interventions'.
39 Munafò et al., 'A Manifesto for Reproducible Science'.
40 On phonological processing, see Melby-Lervåg, Lyster, and Hulme, 'Phonological Skills'; on deficits beyond phonology, see Snowling and Melby-Lervåg, 'Oral Language Deficits'; on auditory and visual impairments, see Schulte-Körne and Bruder, 'Clinical Neurophysiology'; on brain imaging studies, see Taylor, Rastle, and Davis, 'Can Cognitive Models'; on effective and non-effective interventions, see Galuschka et al., 'Effectiveness of Treatment Approaches'.
41 For further discussion of this taxonomy, see Kirby, 'Dyslexia Debated'.
42 Hinshelwood, 'Word-Blindness and Visual Memory', 1564.
43 Broadbent, 'Notes on Dr. Hinshelwood's Communication', 18.
44 Hinshelwood, 'A Case of Dyslexia', 1452.
45 Ibid.
46 Elliott and Grigorenko, *The Dyslexia Debate*, 32.
47 Liddle, 'Dyslexia Is Meaningless'.
48 Elliott and Grigorenko, 'The End of Dyslexia?', 579.
49 YouTube, 'Dyslexia Diagnosis', after Oldham, 'Dyslexic Boy's Heartbreaking Diary'.
50 Pringle Morgan, 'A Case of Congenital Word Blindness', 1378; Hinshelwood, 'Congenital Word-Blindness', 1507.
51 Bennett, 'The Classroom Fads'.
52 Elliott and Grigorenko, *The Dyslexia Debate*, 182.
53 Ibid., after Kamhi, 'A Meme's Eye View'.
54 Burt and Lewis, 'Teaching Backward Readers', 117.

55 See Kirby, 'Dyslexia Debated'.
56 Ibid.
57 Smith, *Hyperactive: The Controversial History of* ADHD; Waltz, *Autism*; Lawlor, *From Melancholia to Prozac*.
58 Lawlor, *From Melancholia to Prozac*.
59 Beck and Alford, *Depression*.
60 For further reflection on parents' views of dyslexia and intelligence, as compared to educational professionals', see Paradice, 'An Investigation into the Social Construction'.
61 For further reflection on the 'myth of dyslexia', see Kirby and Snowling, 'Refuting the "Dyslexia Myth"'.
62 Elliott and Grigorenko, *The Dyslexia Debate*, 177.
63 Singer, '"Why Can't You Be Normal"'.
64 Ibid.
65 Ibid., 64.
66 Ibid.
67 Ibid., 67.
68 Indeed, the importance (and potential) of the internet in cultivating the term neurodiversity was cited in Singer's original publication on the topic ('"Why Can't You Be Normal"').
69 Silberman, *Neurotribes*.
70 E.g., Olivardia, 'Coping with Dyslexia, Dysgraphia and ADHD'; Chien, 'Graceful Advocacy'.
71 BDA, 'Neurodiversity and Co-Occurring Differences'.
72 BDA, 'Teaching for Neurodiversity'.
73 *Lancet*, 'Ophthalmological Society', 1348.
74 Plowden, *Children and Their Primary Schools*, 7.
75 Warnock, *Special Educational Needs*, 6.
76 Shakespeare, 'The Social Model of Disability', 220.
77 Macdonald, 'Towards a Social Reality'.
78 E.g. Havegal, 'Government Confirms Cuts'; London Councils, *Representation to Government*.
79 ONE, 'Lost Potential Tracker'.
80 Rifkin, *The Third Industrial Revolution*.
81 Gladwell, *David and Goliath*, 124.
82 Marazzi, 'Dyslexia and the Economy', 19.

83 Logan, 'Dyslexic Entrepreneurs'.
84 Snowling, *Dyslexia* (Oxford University Press).
85 Macdonald, *Crime and Dyslexia*.
86 Ibid.
87 Anonymous, 'I'm Dyslexic'.
88 Pons, 'Dyslexia Education'.
89 For further reflection on the role of neuropsychology in reframing understandings of autism in the twenty-first century, see Nadesan, *Constructing Autism*, 4.
90 For example, UK Government, *Gender Recognition Act of 2004*.
91 For an accessible review of the latest research on dyslexia remediation, see Snowling, *Dyslexia* (Oxford University Press), 92–119.
92 Wilsher, 'Is Medicinal Treatment'; Goldacre, "Dyslexia "Cure"".
93 Tomlinson, 'The Irresistible Rise'.
94 Reading in isolation, for example, rather than having information presented by a teacher in a structured form, has been found to disadvantage learners with dyslexia (Mortimore, *Dyslexia and Learning Style*).

Bibliography

Archive Sources
Oxford Dyslexia Archive.
  Uncatalogued. Files of the Word Blind Centre for Dyslexic Children.
  Arkell, Helen. Interview by M.J.S., Frensham, UK, 6 May 2015.
  Blunkett, David. Interview by P.K., London, UK, 25 November 2017.
  Bradley, Lynette. Interview by P.K., Oxford, UK, 22 December 2016.
  Chinn, Steven. Interview by P.K., Oxford, UK, 10 January 2017.
  Cooke, Ann. Interview by P.K., Oxford, UK, 24 January 2017.
  Hamilton-Fairley, Daphne. Interview by P.K., London, UK, 15 February 2017.
  Hampshire, Susan. Interview by P.K., London, UK, 15 May 2017.
  Hargrave-Wright, Joyce. Interview by Robert Evans, Bodmin, UK, 25 October 2017.
  Miles, Elaine. Interview by M.J.S., Bangor, Wales, 5 August 2013.
  Naidoo, Sandhya. Interview by M.J.S., Nottingham, UK, 27 August 2013.
  Salter, Jennifer. Interview by Kieran Fitzpatrick, Oxford, UK, 6 December 2017.
  Salter, Robin. Interview by P.K., Oxford, UK, 6 December 2017.
  Saunders, Kate. Interview by P.K., Bristol, UK, 4 January 2018.
  Shawsun, Rebekah. Interview by P.K., Oxford, UK, 12 July 2017.
  Snowling, Margaret J. Interview by P.K., Oxford, UK, 30 November 2016.
  Thomson, Patience. Interview by Denise Cripps, Oxford, UK, 5 July 2017.
  Warnock, Mary. Interview by M.J.S., London, UK, 8 August 2013.
  Warrington, Elizabeth. Interview by M.J.S., online, 9 January 2021.
  Watkins, Bill. Interview by Denise Cripps, Oxford, UK, 19 August 2015.
  Williams, Steve. Interview by P.K., Oxford, UK, 24 August 2017.

Yule, William (Bill). Interview by M.J.S., London, UK, 6 March 2018.
UK National Archives – E.D. 50-880. Survey on Dyslexia.
Horne, J.N. [Letter to Dr White Franklin]. 13 December 1962.
Horne, J.N. [Letter to Dr White Franklin]. 19 December 1962.
Horne, J.N. 'Dyslexia: Meeting with Professor Meredith of Leeds in London on 2nd August, 1963'. 15 August 1963.
Horne, J.N. 'Meeting with Officers of the Invalid Children's Aid Association (Word Blindness Group) on 20th December 1963 at the Ministry'. 6 January 1964.
Horne, J.N. *Reading Delay (Dyslexia): A Preliminary Report of a Survey by One of the Minister's Medical Officers*. 30 August 1962.
Horne, J.N. *Report on a Visit to Copenhagen, April, 1962*. 4 June 1962.
Meredith, P. *Dyslexia Research Project: First Annual Report*. 9 May 1966.
White Franklin, Alfred. [Letter to Dr Henderson]. 10 December 1962.
White Franklin, Alfred. [Letter to J.N. Horne]. 14 December 1962.

Published Works and Media

Addo, R. "'This Was the First Time I've Read Out Loud without Hesitation': Jessica Simpson Reveals She's Dyslexic as She Credits the Success of Her Audiobook for "Turning My Fears into Wisdom"'. 2 December 2020. *Daily Mail*. https://www.dailymail.co.uk/tvshowbiz/article-9010867/Jessica-Simpson-reveals-shes-dyslexic-celebrates-success-audiobook.html.
Ainscow, M., A. Dyson, L. Hopwood, and S. Thomson. *Primary Schools Responding to Diversity: Barriers and Possibilities*. York: Cambridge Primary Review Trust.
Alexander, B., and C. Shelton. *A History of Psychology in Western Civilization*. Cambridge: Cambridge University Press, 2014.
Altenbaugh, J., ed. *The Teacher's Voice: A Social History of Teaching in 20th Century America*. London: Falmer Press, 1992.
Anderson, P., and R. Meier-Hedde. 'Early Case Reports of Dyslexia in the United States and Europe'. *Journal of Learning Disabilities* 34, no. 1 (2001): 9–21.
Andersson, B. 'Dyslexia in Sweden'. In *The International Book of Dyslexia*, edited by I. Smythe, J. Everatt, and R. Salter, 215–21. Chichester, UK: John Wiley, 2004.
Andreola, C., S. Mascheretti, R. Belotti, A. Ogliari, C. Marino, et al. 'The Heritability of Reading and Reading-Related Neurocognitive Components: A Multi-Level Meta-Analysis'. *Neuroscience and Biobehavioral Reviews* 121 (2021): 175–200.

Bibliography

Anonymous. 'I'm Dyslexic and Academic Publishing Is Twice as Hard'. *Times Higher Education*. 4 July 2020. https://www.timeshighereducation.com/blog/im-dyslexic-and-academic-publishing-twice-hard.

Armstrong, F. 'Disability, Education and Social Change in England since 1960'. *History of Education* 36, nos. 4–5 (2007): 551–68.

Backman, J., M. Mamen, and H. Ferguson. 'Reading Level Design: Conceptual and Methodological Issues in Reading Research'. *Psychological Bulletin* 96, no. 3 (1984): 560–68.

Backwards: The Riddle of Dyslexia. Directed by Alexander Grasshoff. Aired 7 March 1984, ABC.

bAd. Directed by Vincenzo Giammanco. Chartwell School, 2007. DVD.

Ball, A. 'A Contribution to the Study of Aphasia, with Special Reference to 'Word-Deafness' and 'Word-Blindness''. *Archives of Medicine* 5 (1881): 136–61.

Bannatyne, A. 'The Aetiology of Dyslexia'. *The Slow Learning Child* 13, no. 1 (1966): 20–34.

Barnes, C., L. Barton, and M. Oliver, eds. *Disability Studies Today*. Cambridge: Polity, 2002.

Bastian, H. 'On Some Problems in Connexion with Aphasia and Other Speech Defects'. *The Lancet* 149, vol. 3841 (1897): 1005–17.

BBC News. 'Dyslexic Loses Claim against Council'. 4 November 1998. http://news.bbc.co.uk/1/hi/education/207865.stm.

Beard, J. *From Percy to Peter: A History of Dyslexia*. Hook, UK: Waterside Press, 2019.

Beck, A., and B. Alford. *Depression: Causes and Treatment*. Philadelphia, PA: University of Pennsylvania Press, 2009.

Beechey, J. 'Our Double Anniversary Year'. *Dyslexia Review* 29, no. 1 (2019): 6–8.

Behan, W. 'James Hinshelwood (1859–1919) and Developmental Dyslexia'. In *Twentieth Century Neurology: The British Contribution*, edited by F. Clifford Rose, 59–76. London: Imperial College Press, 2001.

Bennett, T. 'The Classroom Fads That Illustrate Education's Often Unhealthy Relationship with the Evidence'. TES. 12 May 2017. https://www.tes.com/news/classroom-fads-illustrate-educations-often-unhealthy-relationship-evidence.

Berger, M., W. Yule, and M. Rutter, 'Attainment and Adjustment in Two Geographical Areas II – The Prevalence of Specific Reading Retardation'. *British Journal of Psychiatry* 126, no. 6 (1975): 510–19.

Berkhan, O. 'Über die Wortblindheit, ein Stammeln im Sprechen und Schreiben, ein Fehl im Lesen'. *Neurologisches Centralblatt* 36 (1917): 914–27.

Berlin, R. *Eine Besondere Art der Wortblindheit (Dyslexie)*. Wiesbaden, Germany: J.F. Bergmann, 1887.

– 'Über Dyslexie'. *Medicinisches Correspondenz-Blatt des Wurttembergisohen Artzlichen Landesvereins* 53 (1883): 209–10.

Bettelheim, B. *The Empty Fortress: Infantile Autism and the Birth of the Self*. New York: Free Press, 1967.

Betts, R., and L. Bly, eds. *A History of Popular Culture: More of Everything, Faster and Brighter*. New York: Routledge, 2004.

Bishop, D., and M.J. Snowling. 'Developmental Dyslexia and Specific Language Impairment: Same or Different?' *Psychological Bulletin* 130, no. 6 (2004): 858–86.

Blackburn, P. *Children's Services*. London: Langbuisson, 2017.

Blank, M., and W. Bridger. 'Deficiencies in Verbal Labeling in Retarded Readers'. *American Journal of Orthopsychiatry* 36, no. 5 (1966): 840–7.

Bogdanowicz, M. 'Dyslexia in Poland'. In *The International Book of Dyslexia*, edited by I. Smythe, J. Everatt, and R. Salter, 190–6. Chichester, UK: John Wiley, 2004.

Bohan, L. 'Contextual History: A Framework for Re-Placing Women in the History of Psychology'. *Psychology of Women Quarterly* 14, no. 2 (1990): 213–27.

Bolton, P. *Education: Historical Statistics*. London: House of Commons Library, 2012.

Bones, series 4, episode 18, 'The Science in the Physicist'. Directed by Brad Turner. Aired 9 April 2009, Fox.

Bradley, L., and P. Bryant. 'Categorizing Sounds and Learning to Read – A Causal Connection'. *Nature* 301 (1982): 419–21.

Brady, S. 'The Role of Working Memory in Reading Disability'. In *Phonological Processes in Literacy: A Tribute to Isabelle Y. Liberman*, edited by S. Brady and D. Shankweiler, 129–51. New York: Lawrence Erlbaum Associates, 1991.

Brady, S., D. Shankweiler, and V. Mann. 'Speech Perception and Memory Coding in Relation to Reading Ability'. *Journal of Experimental Child Psychology* 25, no. 2 (1983): 345–67.

Bramwell, B. 'Illustrative Cases of Aphasia'. *The Lancet* (3 April 1897): 950–3.

British Dyslexia Association. 'Neurodiversity and Co-Occurring Differences'. Accessed 18 November 2021. https://www.bdadyslexia.org.uk/dyslexia/neurodiversity-and-co-occurring-differences.

– 'Teaching for Neurodiversity'. Accessed 18 November 2021. https://www.bdadyslexia.org.uk/advice/educators/teaching-for-neurodiversity.

Bibliography

British Medical Journal. 'William Pringle Morgan, M.B. D.P.H'. *British Medical Journal* (31 March 1934): 604.

Broadbent, W. 'Note on Dr Hinshelwood's Communication on Word-Blindness and Visual Memory'. *The Lancet* (4 January 1896): 18.

Broca, P. 'Remarks on the Seat of the Faculty of Articulated Language, Following an Observation of Aphemia (Loss of Speech)'. *Bulletin de la Société Anatomique* 6 (1861): 330–57.

Brown, B. 'Foreword'. In *Dyslexia: An Appraisal of Current Knowledge*, edited by A. Benton and D. Pearl, v–vii. New York: Oxford University Press, 1978.

Bruland, I. 'Edith Norrie (1889–1960)'. *Danish Female Biographical Lexicon*. 2003. https://www.kvinfo.dk/side/597/bio/1130/origin/170/query/edith%20norrie/.

Brunswick, N., E. McCrory, C. Price, C. Frith, and U. Frith. 'Explicit and Implicit Processing of Words and Pseudowords by Adult Developmental Dyslexics'. *Brain* 122, no. 10 (1999): 1901–17.

Bryant, P. 'Comments on the Design of Developmental Studies of Cross-Modal Matching and Cross- Modal Transfer'. *Cortex* 4, no. 2 (1968): 127–37.

– 'Cross-Modal Development and Reading'. In *Reading, Perception and Language: Papers from the World Congress on Dyslexia*, edited by D. Duane and M. Rawson. Baltimore, MD: York Press, 1975.

Bryant, P., and U. Goswami. 'Strengths and Weaknesses of the Reading Level Design: A Comment on Backman, Mamen, and Ferguson'. *Psychological Bulletin* 100, no. 1 (1986): 101–3.

Burt, C. *The Causes and Treatment of Backwardness*. London: University of London Press, 1957.

– 'Counterblast to Dyslexia'. *AEP Newsletter*, 5 (1966): 2–6.

– 'The Definition and Diagnosis of Mental Deficiency'. *Studies in Mental Inefficiency* 1, no. 3 (1920): 49–54.

– 'Experimental Tests of General Intelligence'. *British Journal of Psychology* 2, nos. 1–2 (1909): 94–177.

– 'The Inheritance of Mental Ability'. *American Psychologist* 13, no. 1 (1958): 1–15.

Burt, C., and C. Banks. 'A Factor Analysis of Body Measurement for British Adult Males'. *Annals of Eugenics* 13, no. 1 (1946): 238–56.

Burt, C., and R. Lewis. 'Teaching Backward Readers'. *British Journal of Educational Psychology* 16, no. 3 (1946): 116–32.

Byrne, B. 'The Learnability of the Alphabetic Principle: Children's Initial Hypotheses about How Print Represents Spoken Language'. *Applied Psycholinguistics* 17, no. 4 (1996): 401–26.

Call Me Fitz, series 2, episode 3. Directed by Jason Priestly. Aired 2 October 2011, HBO Canada.

Cameron, C. 'Bodies'. In *Disability Studies: A Student's Guide*, edited by C. Cameron, 16–18. London: SAGE, 2014.

– 'The Disabled People's Movement'. In *Disability Studies: A Student's Guide*, edited by C. Cameron, 39–42. London: SAGE, 2014.

Campbell, J., and M. Oliver. *Disability Politics: Understanding Our Past, Changing Our Future*. London: Routledge, 1996.

Campbell, R., and B. Butterworth. 'Phonological Dyslexia and Dysgraphia in a Highly Literate Subject: A Developmental Case with Associated Deficits of Phonemic Processing and Awareness'. *Quarterly Journal of Experimental Psychology* 39, no. 3 (1985): 435–75.

Campbell, T. *Dyslexia: The Government of Reading*. Basingstoke, UK: Palgrave Macmillan, 2013.

– 'From Aphasia to Dyslexia, a Fragment of a Genealogy: An Analysis of the Formation of a "Medical Diagnosis"'. *Health Sociology Review* 20, no. 4 (2011): 450–61.

Capshew, J. *Psychologists on the March: Science, Practice, and Professional Identity in America, 1929–1969*. Cambridge: Cambridge University Press, 1999.

Caravalos, M. 'The Nature and Causes of Dyslexia in Different Languages'. In *The Science of Reading: A Handbook*, edited by M.J. Snowling and C. Hulme, 336–55. Oxford: Blackwell, 2005.

Caravalos, M., A. Lervåg, P. Mousikou, C. Efrim, M. Litavský, et al. 'Common Patterns of Prediction of Literacy Development in Different Alphabetic Orthographies'. *Psychological Science* 23, no. 6 (2012): 678–86.

Castles, A., H. Datta, J. Gayan, and R. Olson. 'Varieties of Developmental Reading Disorder: Genetic and Environmental Influences'. *Journal of Experimental Child Psychology* 72 (1999): 73–94.

Castles, A., K. Rastle, and K. Nation. 'Ending the Reading Wars: Reading Acquisition from Novice to Expert'. *Psychological Science in the Public Interest* 19, no. 1 (2018): 5–51.

Castles, A., K. Wheldall, and M. Nayton. 'Should We Do Away with "Dyslexia"'. *The Conversation*. 19 March 2014. https://theconversation.com/should-we-do-away-with-dyslexia-24027.

Catts, H., S. Adlof, T. Hogan, and S. Weismer. 'Are Specific Language Impairment and Dyslexia Distinct Disorders?' *Journal of Speech, Language, and Hearing Research* 48, no. 6 (2005): 1378–96.

Bibliography

Catts, H., M. Fey, X. Zhang, and J. Bruce Tomblin. 'Language Basis of Reading and Reading Disabilities: Evidence from a Longitudinal Investigation'. *Scientific Studies of Reading* 3, no. 4 (1999): 331–61.

Chance, B. 'Developmental Alexia: Two Cases of Congenital Word Blindness'. *New York Medical Journal* 97 (1913): 697–9.

Charity Organisation Society. *The Feeble-Minded Child and Adult: A Report on the Investigation of the Physical and Mental Condition of 50,000 School Children, with Suggestions for the Better Education and Care of the Feeble-Minded Children and Adults.* London: Charity Organisation Society, 1893.

Chasty, H. 'What Is Dyslexia?' In *Children's Written Language Difficulties: Assessment and Management*, edited by M.J. Snowling, 11–27. London: Routledge, 1985.

Chien, C. 'Graceful Advocacy'. International Dyslexia Association. 2018. https://dyslexiaida.org/graceful-advocacy/.

Chinn, S. 'A Brief History of Dyslexia: Links Across 'the Pond''. *Perspectives on Language and Literacy* 38, no. 3 (2012): 21–3.

Clarke, P. *Hope and Glory: Britain 1900–2000.* London: Penguin, 1997.

Clay, M. *The Early Detection of Reading Difficulties: A Diagnostic Survey.* London: Heinemann, 1972.

Clemensha, J. 'Congenital Word Blindness or Inability to Learn to Read'. *Journal of Ophthalmology and Otolaryngology* 9, no. 1 (1915): 1–6.

Closer. 'Television Ownership in Private Domestic Households'. Accessed 18 November 2021. https://www.closer.ac.uk/data/television-ownership-in-domestic-households/.

Collinson, C. 'Dyslexics in Time Machines and Alternate Realities: Thought Experiments on the Existence of Dyslexics, "Dyslexia" and "Lexism"'. *British Journal of Special Education* 39, no. 2 (2012): 63–70.

Coltheart, M. 'Acquired Dyslexias and Normal Reading'. In *Dyslexia: A Global Issue*, edited by R. Malatesha and H. Whitaker, 357–73. Dordrecht, Netherlands: Springer, 1984.

– 'In Defence of Dual-Route Models of Reading'. *Behavioral and Brain Sciences* 8, no. 4 (1985): 709–10.

Coltheart, M., J. Masterson, S. Byng, M. Prior, and J. Riddoch. 'Surface Dyslexia'. *Quarterly Journal of Experimental Psychology* 35, no. 3 (1983): 469–95.

Conn, R., and D. Bhugra. The Portrayal of Autism in Hollywood Films. *International Journal of Culture and Mental Health*, 5, no. 1 (2012): 54–62.

Copeland, I. 'The Establishment of Models of Education for Disabled Children'. *British Journal of Educational Studies* 43, no. 2 (1995): 179–200.

Cornubian and Redruth Times. 'Word Blindness'. 14 February 1902: 5.
Critchley, E. 'Reading Retardation, Dyslexia and Delinquency'. *The British Journal of Psychiatry* 114, no. 517 (1968): 1537–47.
Critchley, M. *Developmental Dyslexia*. London: William Heinemann, 1964.
– *The Dyslexic Child*. London: William Heinemann, 1970.
Dalton, P. *Dyslexia and Dyscalculia*. London: Parliamentary Office of Science and Technology, 2004.
Danforth, S. *The Incomplete Child: An Intellectual History of Learning Disabilities*. New York: Peter Lang, 2009.
Davis, R. *The Gift of Dyslexia: Why Some of the Brightest People Can't Read and How They Can Learn*. New York: Pedigree, 1994.
DeFries, J., M. Alarcon, and R. Olson. 'Genetics and Dyslexia: Developmental Differences in the Etiologies of Reading and Spelling Deficits'. In *Dyslexia: Biology, Cognition, and Intervention*, edited by M.J. Snowling and C. Hulme, 20–37. London: Whurr, 1997.
DeFries, J., D. Fulker, and M. LaBuda. 'Evidence for a Genetic Aetiology in Reading Disability'. *Nature* 329, no. 6139 (1987): 537–9.
Dejerine, J. 'Sur un Cas de Cécité Verbale avec Agraphie Suivi D'Autopsie'. *Mémoires de la Société de Biologie* 3 (1891): 197–201.
Derbyshire, E. 'Virtual Teaching for Children with Dyslexia: The Realities and Disturbing Absence of Research'. *British Educational Research Association*. 26 June 2020. https://www.bera.ac.uk/blog/virtual-teaching-for-children-with-dyslexia-the-realities-and-disturbing-absence-of-research.
Dewey, J. *Democracy and Education: An Introduction to the Philosophy of Education*. New York: Macmillan, 1916.
Dispatches. 'The Myth of Dyslexia'. Produced by David Mills. Aired 8 September 2005, Channel 4.
Dittmer, J. *Popular Culture, Geopolitics, and Identity*. Lanham, MD: Rowman and Littlefield, 2010.
Dodds, K., and P. Kirby. 'It's Not a Laughing Matter: Critical Geopolitics, Humour and Unlaughter'. *Geopolitics* 18 (2013): 45–59.
Douglas, J. *The Home and the School: A Study of Ability and Attainment in the Primary School*. London: Macgibbon and Kee, 1964.
Dover Express. 'Science Notes'. 4 December 1896.
Draper, I. 'Assessment and Teaching of Dyslexic Children' [book review]. *Journal of Neurology, Neurosurgery and Psychiatry* 34, no. 2 (1971): 205–6.

Bibliography

Dyslexia Daily. 'Famous and Dyslexic – A Tom Cruise Story'. Accessed 18 November 2021. https://www.dyslexiadaily.com/blog/famous-and-dyslexic-a-tom-cruise-story/.
Edwards, J. *The Scars of Dyslexia: Eight Case Studies in Emotional Reactions*. London: Cassell, 1994.
Elliot, J. 'Dyslexia: Beyond the Debate'. In *Dyslexia: Developing the Debate*, edited by A. Davis, 73–116. London: Bloomsbury, 2016.
Elliott, J., and E. Grigorenko. *The Dyslexia Debate*. Cambridge: Cambridge University Press, 2014.
– 'The End of Dyslexia?' *The Psychologist* 27 (2014): 576–81.
European Dyslexia Association. 'About EDA: What Is the European Dyslexia Association?' Accessed 18 November 2021. https://eda-info.eu/about-the-eda/index.html.
Evans, B. *The Metamorphosis of Autism: A History of Child Development in England*. Manchester: Manchester University Press, 2017.
Evans, R.J.W. 'A Pioneer in Context: T. R. Miles and the Bangor Dyslexia Unit'. *Oxford Review of Education* 46, no. 4 (2020): 439–53.
– 'Tim Miles'. *Oxford Dictionary of National Biography*. 2021. https://doi.org/10.1093/odnb/9780198614128.013.100932.
Evening Telegraph. 'A Strange Case of Word-Blindness'. 11 February 1902.
Exley, S., and S. Ball. 'Neo-Liberalism and English Education'. In *Neo-Liberal Educational Reforms: A Critical Analysis*, edited by D. Turner and H. Yolcu, 13–31. New York: Routledge, 2014.
Feinstein, A. *A History of Autism: Conversations with the Pioneers*. Malden, MA: Wiley-Blackwell, 2010.
Felicity, series 4, episode 19, 'The Power of the Ex'. Directed by Lawrence Trilling. Aired 8 May 2002, The WB.
Fildes, L. 'A Psychological Inquiry into the Nature of the Condition Known as Congenital Word-Blindness'. *Brain* 44, no. 3 (1921): 286–307.
Fischer, F., I. Liberman, and D. Shankweiler. 'Reading Reversals and Developmental Dyslexia, a Further Study'. *Cortex* 14, no. 4 (1978): 496–510.
Fischer, S. *A History of Reading*. London: Reaktion, 2003.
Fisher, S., and J. DeFries. 'Developmental Dyslexia: A Genetic Dissection of a Complex Cognitive Trait'. *Nature Reviews: Neuroscience* 3, no. 10 (2002): 767–80.
Fitzpatrick, K. 'Hinshelwood, James'. *Oxford Dictionary of National Biography*. 2021. https://doi.org/10.1093/odnb/9780198614128.013.90000369384.

Foerster, R. 'Beiträge zur Pathologie des Lesens und Schreibens (Congenitale Wortblindheit bei einem Schwachsinnigen)'. *Neurologisches Zentralblatt* 24 (1905): 235.

Foucault, M. *The Birth of the Clinic: An Archaeology of Medical Perception*. Abingdon, UK: Routledge, 2003.

– *The History of Sexuality: Volume I: An Introduction*. New York: Pantheon, 1978.

– *Madness and Civilization: A History of Insanity in the Age of Reason*. Abingdon: Routledge, 2001.

Frederickson, N., and R. Reason. 'Discrepancy Definitions of Specific Learning Difficulties'. *Educational Psychology in Practice* 10, no. 4 (1995): 195–205.

Frith, U. 'Beneath the Surface of Developmental Dyslexia'. In *Surface Dyslexia*, edited by K. Patterson, J. Marshall, and M. Coltheart, 301–30. London: Erlbaum, 1985.

– ed. *Cognitive Processes in Spelling*. London: Academic Press, 1980.

Frith, U., J. Morton, and A. Leslie. 'The Cognitive Basis of a Biological Disorder: Autism'. *Trends in Neurosciences* 14, no. 10 (1991): 433–8.

Funnell, E., and M. Davison. 'Lexical Capture: A Developmental Disorder of Reading and Spelling'. *The Quarterly Journal of Experimental Psychology* 41, no. 3 (1989): 471–87.

Galaburda, A., and T. Kemper. 'Cytoarchitectonic Abnormalities in Developmental Dyslexia: A Case Study'. *Annals of Neurology* 6, no. 2 (1979): 94–100.

Galaburda, A., G. Sherman, G. Rosen, F. Aboitiz, and N. Geschwind. 'Developmental Dyslexia: Four Consecutive Patients with Cortical Anomalies'. *Annals of Neurology* 18, no. 2 (1985): 222–33.

Gallagher, A., U. Frith, and M.J. Snowling. 'Precursors of Literacy Delay among Children at Genetic Risk of Dyslexia'. *Journal of Child Psychology and Psychiatry, and Allied Disciplines* 41, no. 2 (2000): 203–13.

Gallagher, D., D. Connor, and B. Ferri. 'Beyond the Far Too Incessant Schism: Special Education and the Social Model of Disability'. *International Journal of Inclusive Education* 18, no. 11 (2014): 1120–42.

Galton, F. *Inquiries into Human Faculty and Its Development*. London: Macmillan, 1883.

Galuschka, K., E. Ise, K. Krick, and G. Schulte-Körne. 'Effectiveness of Treatment Approaches for Children and Adolescents with Reading Disabilities: A Meta-Analysis of Randomized Controlled Trials'. *PLoS One* 9, no 2 (2014): e89900.

Gelb, S. 'Social Deviance and the 'Discovery' of the Moron'. *Disability, Handicap and Society* 2, no. 3 (1987): 247–58.

Bibliography

Geschwind, N. 'Why Orton Was Right'. *Annals of Dyslexia* 32 (1982): 13–30.

Gillingham, A., and B. Stillman. *Remedial Training for Children with Specific Disability in Reading, Spelling, and Penmanship*. Cambridge, MA: Educators Publishing Service, 1946.

Gladwell, M. *David and Goliath: Underdogs, Misfits and the Art of Battling Giants*. London: Penguin, 2014.

Globe. 'Literary Gossip'. 18 August 1900: 6.

Goldacre, B. 'Dyslexia "Cure" Fails to Pass the Tests'. *The Guardian*. 4 November 2006. https://www.theguardian.com/science/2006/nov/04/badscience.uknews.

Goswami, U. 'Phonological Representations, Reading Development and Dyslexia: Towards a Cross-Linguistic Theoretical Framework'. *Dyslexia* 6, no. 2 (2000): 133–51.

– 'Phonology, Reading Development, and Dyslexia: A Cross-Linguistic Perspective'. *Annals of Dyslexia* 52 (2002): 139–63.

Goulandris, N., ed. *Dyslexia in Different Languages: Cross-Linguistic Comparisons*. London: Whurr, 2003.

Graff, H., ed. *Literacy and Social Development in the West: A Reader*. Cambridge: Cambridge University Press, 1982.

Grayson, K., M. Davies, and S. Philpott. 'Pop Goes IR? Researching the Popular Culture–World Politics Continuum'. *Politics* 29 (2009): 155–63.

Gregory, R. 'Zangwill, Oliver Louis'. *Oxford Dictionary of National Biography*. 2004. https://doi.org/10.1093/ref:odnb/39981.

Guardiola, J. 'The Evolution of Research on Dyslexia'. *Anuario de Psicología* 32, no. 1 (2001): 3–30.

Gvarmathy, E., and E. Vassné Kovács. 'Dyslexia in Hungary'. In *The International Book of Dyslexia*, edited by I. Smythe, J. Everatt, and R. Salter, 116–21. Chichester, UK: John Wiley, 2004.

Haker. 'Asperger Syndrome – A Fashionable Diagnosis?' *Praxis* 103, no. 20 (1994): 1191–6.

Hall, R. 'Word Blindness: Its Causes and Cure'. *British Journal of Ophthalmology* 29, no. 9 (1945): 467–72.

Hallgren, B. 'Specific Dyslexia (Congenital Word-Blindness): A Clinical and Genetic Study'. *Acta Psychiatrica Scandinavia* 65 (1950): 1–287.

Hampshire, S. *Every Letter Counts*. London: Bantam, 1990.

– *Susan's Story: An Autobiographical Account of My Struggle with Words*. London: Corgi, 1990.

Hampshire Telegraph. 'All Very Curious'. 2 January 1897: S12.

Hargrave-Wright, J. 'Dyslexia Journey: As Travelled by Joyce Hargrave-Wright'. *Dyslexia Contact* 32, no. 1 (2013): 13–17.

Hatcher, P. 'Reading Intervention: A "Conventional" and Successful Approach to Helping Dyslexic Children Acquire Literacy'. *Dyslexia* 9, no. 3 (2003): 140–5.

– 'Sound Links in Reading and Spelling with Discrepancy – Defined Dyslexics and Children with Moderate Learning Difficulties'. *Reading and Writing* 13 (2000): 257–72.

Hatcher, P., C. Hulme, and A. Ellis. 'Ameliorating Early Reading Failure by Integrating the Teaching of Reading and Phonological Skills'. *Child Development* 65, no. 1 (1994): 41–57.

Havegal, C. 'Government Confirms Cuts to Disabled Students' Allowance. *Times Higher Education*. 2 December 2015. https://www.timeshighereducation.com/news/government-confirms-cuts-disabled-students-allowance.

Heaton, T. 'Access'. In *Disability Studies: A Student's Guide*, edited by C. Cameron, 1–2. London: SAGE, 2014.

Heitmuller, G. 'Cases of Developmental Alexia or Congenital Word Blindness'. *Washington Medical Annals* 17 (1918): 124–9.

Henshaw, C. 'Council Attacked for Saying Dyslexia "Questionable"'. *TES*. 31 October 2018. https://www.tes.com/news/council-attacked-saying-dyslexia-questionable.

Hermann, K. *Reading Disability: A Medical Study of Word-Blindness and Related Handicaps*. Springfield, IL: C.C. Thomas, 1959.

Hermann, K., and E. Norrie. 'Is Congenital Word-Blindness a Hereditary Type of Gerstmann's Syndrome?' *Monatsschrift für Psychiatrie und Neurologie* 136, nos. 1–2 (1958): 59–73.

Heseltine, D. *Misunderstood: Living with Dyslexia*. PublishNation, 2017.

Hewitt-Main, J. *Dyslexia behind Bars: Final Report of a Pioneering Teaching and Mentoring Project at Chelmsford Prison – 4 Years On*. Benfleet, UK: Mentoring 4U, 2012.

Heywood, C. *A History of Childhood: Children and Childhood in the West from Medieval to Modern Times*. Cambridge: Polity Press, 2018.

Hinshelwood, J. 'A Case of Dyslexia: A Peculiar Form of Word-Blindness'. *The Lancet* (21 November 1896): 1451–4.

– 'A Case of "Word" without "Letter" Blindness'. *The Lancet* (12 February 1898): 422–5.

– 'Congenital Word-Blindness'. *The Lancet* (26 May 1900): 1506–8.

Bibliography

– *Congenital Word-Blindness*. London: H.K. Lewis, 1917.
– 'Congenital Word-Blindness' [Letter]. *The Lancet* (29 December 1917): 980.
– 'Four Cases of Word-Blindness'. *The Lancet* (8 February 1902): 358–63.
– '"Letter" without "Word" Blindness'. *The Lancet* (14 January 1899): 83–6.
– *Letter-, Word- and Mind-Blindness*. London: H.K. Lewis, 1900.
– 'Word-Blindness and Visual Memory'. *The Lancet* (21 December 1895): 1564–70.
– 'Word-Blindness and Visual Memory' [Letter]. *The Lancet* (18 January 1896): 196.
Hitchens, P. 'Dyslexia Is Not a Disease. It Is an Excuse for Bad Teachers'. *Mail Online*. 2 March 2014. https://www.dailymail.co.uk/debate/article-2570977/PETER-HITCHENS-Dyslexia-not-disease-It-excuse-bad-teachers.html.
Hogenson, D. 'Reading Failure and Juvenile Delinquency'. *Bulletin of the Orton Society* 24 (1974): 164.
Hook, D. *Foucault, Psychology and the Analytics of Power*. Basingstoke, UK: Macmillan, 2007.
Howell, J. 'Dyslexia: A History of the Term and Current Challenges'. 17 April 2019. https://www.dyslexiacommentary.com/single-post/Dyslexia-A-History-of-the-Term-and-Current-Challenges.
Hoyles, A., and M. Hoyles. *Dyslexia from a Cultural Perspective*. Hertford, UK: Hansib, 2007.
– 'Race and Dyslexia'. *Race, Ethnicity and Education* 13, no. 2 (2010): 209–31.
Hughes, A. 'Dyslexia in Ireland'. In *The International Book of Dyslexia*, edited by I. Smythe, J. Everatt, and R. Salter, 132–5. Chichester, UK: John Wiley, 2004.
Hughes, B., and K. Paterson. 'The Social Model of Disability and the Disappearing Body: Towards a Sociology of Impairment'. *Disability and Society* 12, no. 3 (1997): 325–40.
Hulme, C. 'The Effects of Manual Tracing on Memory in Normal and Retarded Readers: Some Implications for Multi-Sensory Teaching'. *Psychological Research* 43 (1981): 179–91.
– 'Mind the (Inferential) Gap'. *Psychological Science* 30, no. 7 (2019): 1097–8.
– *Reading Retardation and Multi-Sensory Teaching*. London: Routledge, 1981.
Hulme, C., and M.J. Snowling. 'Deficits in Output Phonology: An Explanation of Reading Failure?' *Cognitive Neuropsychology* 9, no. 1 (1992): 47–72.
– eds. *Developmental Disorders of Language and Cognition*. Oxford: Wiley-Blackwell, 2008.
– eds. *Dyslexia: Biology, Cognition and Intervention*. London: Whurr, 1997.
Hulme, C., C. Bowyer-Crane, J. Carroll, F. Duff, and M.J. Snowling. 'The Causal

Role of Phoneme Awareness and Letter-Sound Knowledge in Learning to Read'. *Psychological Science* 23, no. 6 (2012): 572–7.

Hulme, C., M.J. Snowling, G. West, A. Lervåg, and M. Melby-Lervåg. 'Children's Language Skills Can Be Improved: Lessons From Psychological Science for Education Policy'. *Current Directions in Psychological Research* 29, no. 4 (2020): 372–7.

Humphries, E. 'Edward Humphries, Page-Boy'. In *Useful Toil: Autobiographies of Working People from the 1820s to the 1920s*, edited by J. Burnett, 209–14. Abingdon, UK: Routledge, 1974.

Huston, P. *The Iowa State Psychopathic Hospital*. Iowa City: State Historical Society of Iowa, 1974.

Illustrated London News. 'Science Jottings'. 8 March 1902: 358.

Indian Express. 'The Early Years: Demystifying Dyslexia'. 4 March 2019. https://indianexpress.com/article/parenting/learning/early-childhood-decoding-dyslexia-5448265/.

International Dyslexia Association. 'History of IDA'. Accessed 18 November 2021. https://dyslexiaida.org/history-of-the-ida/.

Irish News and Belfast Morning News. 'Word Blindness and Visual Memory'. 31 December 1895: 7.

Jackson, E. 'Developmental Alexia (Congenital Word-Blindness)'. *American Journal of Medical Science* 131 (1906): 843–9.

James, L. *The Middle Class: A History*. London: Abacus, 2008.

Jenkins, J. *Women in the Labour Market: 2013*. London: Office for National Statistics, 2013.

Johnson, D., and H. Myklebust. *Learning Disabilities: Educational Principle and Practices*. New York: Grune and Stratton, 1967.

Jones, K., and K. Williamson. 'The Birth of the Schoolroom'. *Ideology and Consciousness* 5, no. 1 (1979): 5–6.

Kale, S. 'The Battle over Dyslexia'. *The Guardian*. 17 September 2020. https://www.theguardian.com/news/2020/sep/17/battle-over-dyslexia-warwickshire-staffordshire.

Kamhi, A. 'A Meme's Eye View of Speech-Language Pathology'. *Language, Speech, and Hearing Services in Schools* 35, no. 2 (2004): 105–11.

Keenan, J., R. Betjemann, S. Wadsworth, J. DeFries, and R. Olson. 'Genetic and Environmental Influences on Reading and Listening Comprehension'. *Journal of Research in Reading* 29, no. 1 (2006): 75–91.

Bibliography

Kellmer Pringle, M., and S. Naidoo. *Early Child Care in Britain*. London: Routledge, 1975.
Kerr, D. 'Beheading the King and Enthroning the Market: A Critique of Foucauldian Governmentality'. *Science and Society* 63, no. 2. (1999): 173–202.
Kerr, J. 'School Hygiene, in Its Mental, Moral, and Physical Aspects'. *Journal of the Royal Statistical Society*, 60 (1897): 613–80.
Kinsbourne, M., and E. Warrington. 'The Developmental Gerstmann Syndrome'. *Archives of Neurology* 8, no. 5 (1963): 490–501.
Kirby, P. 'Dyslexia Debated, Then and Now: A Historical Perspective on the Dyslexia Debate'. *Oxford Review of Education* 46, no. 4 (2020): 472–86.
– 'Gift from the Gods? Dyslexia, Popular Culture and the Ethics of Representation'. *Disability and Society* 34, no. 9 (2019): 1573–94.
– 'Literacy, Advocacy and Agency: The Campaign for Political Recognition of Dyslexia in Britain (1962–1997)'. *Social History of Medicine* 33, no. 4 (2020): 1306–26.
– 'What's in a Name? The History of Dyslexia'. *History Today* 68, no. 2 (2018): 48–57.
– 'White Franklin, Alfred'. *Oxford Dictionary of National Biography*. 2021. https://doi.org/10.1093/odnb/9780198614128.013.90000369547.
– 'Worried Mothers? Gender, Class and the Origins of the "Dyslexia Myth"'. *Oral History* 47, no. 1 (2019): 92–104.
Kirby, P., K. Nation, M.J. Snowling, and W. Whyte. 'The Problem of Dyslexia: Historical Perspectives'. *Oxford Review of Education* 46, no. 4 (2020): 409–13.
Kirby, P., and M.J. Snowling. *Refuting the Dyslexia Myth: Answering FAQs about Dyslexia's Existence*. Bracknell, UK: British Dyslexia Association, 2019.
Kudlick, C. 'Comment: On the Borderland of Medical and Disability History'. *Bulletin of the History of Medicine* 87, no. 4 (2013): 540–59.
Kussmaul, A. Chapter XXVII. In *Cyclopaedia of the Practice of Medicine: Vol. XIV: Disease of the Nervous System and Disturbances of Speech*, edited by H. von Ziemssen, 770–78. New York: William Wood, 1877.
LaBuda, M., and J. DeFries. 'Genetic and Environmental Etiologies of Reading Disability: A Twin Study'. *Annals of Dyslexia* 38 (1988): 131–8.
The Lancet. 'Congenital Word Blindness'. *The Lancet* (9 September 1905): 774.
– 'Ophthalmological Society'. *The Lancet* (14 May 1910): 1348–9.
Landerl, K., F. Ramus, K. Moll, H. Lyytinen, P. Leppänen, et al. 'Predictors of Developmental Dyslexia in European Orthographies with Varying Complexity'.

Journal of Child Psychology and Psychiatry, and Allied Disciplines. 54, no. 6 (2013): 686–94.

Landerl, K., H. Wimmer, and U. Frith. 'The Impact of Orthographic Consistency on Dyslexia: A German-English Comparison'. *Cognition* 63 (1997): 315–34.

Lawlor, C. *From Melancholia to Prozac: A History of Depression.* Oxford: Oxford University Press, 2012.

Lawrence, D. *Understanding Dyslexia: A Guide for Teachers and Parents.* Berkshire, UK: Open University Press, 2009.

Lefly, D., and B. Pennington. 'Longitudinal Study of Children at Family Risk of Dyslexia: The First Two Years'. In *Towards a Genetics of Language*, edited by M. Rice, 49–75. New York: Lawrence Erlbaum Associates, 1996.

Lemann, N. 'The Reading Wars'. *The Atlantic* (November 1997): 84.

Lervåg, A. 'Correlation and Causation: To Study Causality in Psychopathology'. *The Journal of Child Psychology and Psychiatry* 60, no. 6 (2019): 603–5.

Liberman, A., F. Cooper, S. Shankweiler, and M. Studdert-Kennedy. 'Perception of the Speech Code'. *Psychological Review* 74, no. 6 (1967): 431–61.

Liberman, I., D. Shankweiler, F. William Fischer, and B. Carter. 'Explicit Syllable and Phoneme Segmentation in the Young Child'. *Journal of Experimental Psychology* 18, no. 2 (1974): 201–12.

Liddle, R. 'Dyslexia Is Meaningless. But Don't Worry – So Is ADHD'. *The Spectator.* 15 March 2014. https://www.spectator.co.uk/article/dyslexia-is-meaningless-but-don-t-worry-so-is-adhd.

Literacy Task Force. *Implementation of the National Literacy Strategy.* London: Department for Education and Employment, 1997.

Little, C., R. Haughbrook, and S. Hart. 'Cross-Study Differences in the Etiology of Reading Comprehension: A Meta-Analytical Review of Twin Studies'. *Behavioral Genetics* 47, no. 1 (2017): 52–76.

Lloyd, B., and C. Burt. *Report of an Investigation upon Backward Children in Birmingham.* Birmingham: City of Birmingham Stationery Department, 1921.

Logan, J. 'Dyslexic Entrepreneurs: The Incidence; Their Coping Strategies and Their Business Skills'. *Dyslexia* 14, no. 4 (2009): 328–46.

London Councils. *Representation to Government: Autumn Budget 2017.* London: London Councils, 2017.

Lopes, J. 'Biologising Reading Problems: The Specific Case of Dyslexia'. *Contemporary Social Science* 7, no. 2 (2012): 215–29.

Loucks, N. *No One Knows: Offenders with Learning Difficulties and Learning Disabilities.* London: Prison Reform Trust, 2007.

Bibliography

Love, Mary. Directed by Robert Day. Aired 8 October 1985, CBS.
Lowe, R. *The Welfare State in Britain since 1945*. Basingstoke, UK: Palgrave Macmillan, 2005.
Lowenstein, L. 'Dyslexia: Fad and Fashion or Specific Diagnostic Category?' *School Psychology International* 4, no. 3 (1983): 159–67.
Lubs, H., M. Rabin, E. Feldman, B. Jallad, A. Kushch, et al. 'Familial Dyslexia: Genetic and Medical Findings in Eleven Three-Generation Families'. *Annals of Dyslexia* 43 (1993): 44–60.
Lyytinen, H., T. Ahonen, K. Eklund, and T. Guttorm. 'Developmental Pathways of Children with and without Familial Risk for Dyslexia'. *Developmental Neuropsychology* 20, no. 2 (2001): 535–54.
Macdonald, S. 'Biographical Pathways into Criminality: Understanding the Relationship between Dyslexia and Educational Disengagement'. *Disability and Society* 27, no. 3 (2012): 427–40.
– *Crime and Dyslexia: A Social Model Approach*. Saabrücken, Germany: V.D.M. Verlag, 2002.
– 'Towards a Social Reality of Dyslexia'. *British Journal of Learning Disabilities*. 38 (2009): 271–9.
– *Towards a Sociology of Dyslexia*. Saabrücken, Germany: V.D.M. Verlag, 2009.
– 'Windows of Reflection: Conceptualizing Dyslexia Using the Social Model of Disability'. *Dyslexia* 15 (2009): 347–62.
Mackintosh, N., ed. *Cyril Burt: Fraud or Framed?* New York: Oxford University Press, 1995.
Malmquist, E. 'A Decade of Reading Research in Europe, 1959–1969: A Review'. *The Journal of Educational Research* 63, no. 7 (1970): 309–29.
Man Alive. 'Could Do Better: 1'. Directed by Shirley Fisher. Aired 12 January 1972, BBC Two.
Man Alive. 'Could Do Better: 2'. Directed by Simon Wadleigh. Aired 19 January 1972, BBC Two.
Mantle, A. 'Motor and Sensory Aphasia – (Word Blindness, Word Deafness, Mind Blindness)'. *British Medical Journal* 6, no 1. (1884): 325–8.
Marazzi, C. 'Dyslexia and the Economy'. *Angelaki: Journal of the Theoretical Humanities* 16, no. 3 (2011): 19–32.
Marshall, J., and F. Newcombe. 'Patterns of Paralexia: A Psycholinguistic Approach'. *Journal of Psycholinguistic Research* 2 (1973): 175–99.
Matti, J. 'Marion Welchman'. *Independent*. 9 June 1997. https://www.independent.co.uk/incoming/marion-welchman-5563833.html.

Mazumdar, P. 'Burt, Sir Cyril Lodowic'. *Oxford Dictionary of National Biography*. 2012. https://doi.org/10.1093/ref:odnb/30880.

McAnally, K., and J. Stein. 'Auditory Temporal Coding in Dyslexia'. *Proceedings of the Royal Society B: Biological Sciences* 263, no. 1373 (1996): 961–5.

McClelland, J. 'Gillingham: Contemporary after 76 Years'. *Annals of Dyslexia* 39 (1989): 34–49.

McDonagh, P. *Idiocy: A Cultural History*. Liverpool: Liverpool University Press, 2008.

McGowan, D., C. Little, W. Coventry, and R. Corley. 'Differential Influences of Genes and Environment across the Distribution of Reading Ability'. *Behavior Genetics* 49, no. 2 (2019): 425–31.

McLeod, J. 'Prediction of Childhood Dyslexia'. *Bulletin of the Orton Society* 16, no. 1 (1966): 14–23.

Mean Creek. Directed by Jacob Aaron Estes. Paramount, 2004. DVD.

Melby-Lervåg, M., S.-A. Halaas Lyster, and C. Hulme. 'Phonological Skills and Their Role in Learning to Read: A Meta-Analytic Review'. *Psychological Bulletin* 138, no. 2 (2012): 322–52.

Miles, T. *The Bangor Dyslexia Test*. Wisbech, UK: Learning Development Aids, 1983.

– *Fifty Years in Dyslexia Research: A Personal Story*. Oxford: Wiley, 2006.

Miles, T., and E. Miles. *Dyslexia: A Hundred Years On*. Buckingham: Open University Press, 1999.

Millard, C. 'Concepts, Diagnosis and the History of Medicine: Historicising Ian Hacking and Munchausen Syndrome'. *Social History of Medicine* 30, no. 3 (2017): 567–89.

Millfield School. 'Our History'. Accessed 18 November 2021. https://www.millfieldschool.com/discover-brilliance/our-history.

A Mind of Her Own. Directed by Owen Carey Jones. Carey Films, 2006. DVD.

The Mindy Project, series 3, episode 1, 'We Are A Couple Now, Haters!' Directed by Michael Spiller. Aired 16 September 2014, Fox.

Mold, A. *Making the Patient-Consumer: Patient Organisations and Health Consumerism in Britain*. Manchester: Manchester University Press, 2015.

Moll, K., M.J. Snowling, and C. Hulme. 'Introduction to the Special Issue: Comorbidities between Reading Disorders and Other Developmental Disorders'. *Scientific Studies of Reading* 24, no. 1 (2020): 1–6.

Monroe, M. *Children Who Cannot Read: The Analysis of Reading Disabilities and*

Bibliography

the Use of Diagnostic Tests in the Instruction of Retarded Readers. Chicago: University of Chicago Press, 1932.

Montgomery, D. *Dyslexia and Gender Bias: A Critical Review*. London: Routledge, 2019.

Mortimore, T. *Dyslexia and Learning Style: A Practitioner's Handbook*. London: John Wiley, 2008.

Morton, J., and U. Frith. 'Causal Modeling: A Structural Approach to Developmental Psychology'. In *Manual of Developmental Psychopathology*, 357–90. New York: Wiley, 1995.

Moss, S. 'Half of Britain's Prisoners are Functionally Illiterate. Can Fellow Inmates Change That?' *The Guardian*. 15 June 2017. https://www.theguardian.com/inequality/2017/jun/15/reading-for-freedom-life-changing-scheme-dreamt-up-by-prison-pen-pals-shannon-trust-action-for-equity-award.

Mukerji, C., and M. Schudson. *Rethinking Popular Culture: Contemporary Perspectives in Cultural Studies*. Berkeley, CA: University of California Press, 1991.

Munafò, M., B. Nosek, D. Bishop, K. Button, C. Chambers, et al. 'A Manifesto for Reproducible Science'. *Nature Human Behaviour* 1 (2017): no. 0021.

Muri, A. *The Enlightenment Cyborg: A History of Communications and Control in the Human Machine, 1660–1830*. Toronto: University of Toronto Press, 2007.

Murray, S. *Representing Autism: Culture, Narrative, Fascination*. Liverpool: Liverpool University Press, 2008.

Nadesan, M. *Constructing Autism: Unravelling the 'Truth' and Understanding the Social*. Abingdon, UK: Routledge, 2005.

Nag, S., and M.J. Snowling. 'Reading in an Alphasyllabary: Implications for a Language Universal Theory of Learning to Read'. *Scientific Studies of Reading* 16, no. 5 (2011): 404–23.

Naidoo, S. *Specific Dyslexia*. London: Pitman, 1972.

Nation, K. 'Naidoo [*née* Basu, Bose], Sandhya'. *Oxford Dictionary of National Biography*. 2021. https://doi.org/10.1093/odnb/9780198614128.013.90000369382.

Nelson, H., and E. Warrington. 'Developmental Spelling Retardation and its Relation to Other Cognitive Abilities'. *British Journal of Psychology* 65, no. 2 (1974): 265–74.

— 'An Investigation of Memory Functions in Dyslexic Children'. *British Journal of Psychology* 71, no. 4 (1980): 487–503.

Newton, M., and M. Thomson. *Aston Index: A Classroom Test for Screening and Diagnosis of Language Difficulties, Age from 5 to 14 Years*. Wisbech, UK: Learning Development Aids, 1976.

Nicolson, R. 'Developmental Dyslexia: The Bigger Picture'. In *Dyslexia: Developing the Debate*, edited by A. Davis, 5–72. London: Bloomsbury, 2016.
– 'Dyslexia and Dyspraxia: Commentary'. *Dyslexia* 6, no. 3 (2000): 203–4.
Nicolson, R., and A. Fawcett. 'Automaticity: A New Framework for Dyslexia Research'. *Cognition* 35, no. 2 (1990): 159–82.
Nicolson, R., Fawcett, A., and P. Dean. 'Developmental Dyslexia: The Cerebellar Deficit Hypothesis'. *Trends in Neurosciences* 24, no. 9 (2001): 508–11.
Noddings, N. *Philosophy of Education*. New York: Routledge, 2015.
Oldham, J. 'Dyslexic Boy's Heartbreaking Diary Documents His Desperate Struggle at Mainstream School'. *Mirror*. 24 June 2015. https://www.mirror.co.uk/news/uk-news/dyslexic-boys-heartbreaking-diary-documents-5938002.
Olivardia, R. 'Book Review: Coping with Dyslexia, Dysgraphia and ADHD'. International Dyslexia Association. 2019. https://dyslexiaida.org/book-review-coping-with-dyslexia-dysgraphia-and-adhd-a-global-perspective/.
Olson, R., B. Byrne, and S. Samuelsson. 'Reconciling Strong Genetic and Strong Environmental Influences on Individual Differences and Deficits in Reading Ability'. In *How Children Learn to Read*, edited by K. Pugh and P. McCardle, 213–33. New York: Lawrence Erlbaum Associates, 2009.
Olson, R., B. Wise, F. Conners, J. Rack, and D. Fulker. 'Specific Deficits in Component Reading and Language Skills: Genetic and Environmental Influences'. *Journal of Learning Disabilities* 22 (1989): 339–48.
Olson, R., B. Wise, and J. Rack. 'Dyslexia: Deficits, Genetic Aetiology and Computer-Based Remediation'. *The Irish Journal of Psychology* 10, no. 4 (1989): 494–508.
ONE. Lost Potential Tracker. 13 July 2021. https://lostpotential.one.org/.
Oram, A. 'A Master Should Not Serve under a Mistress: Women and Men Teachers 1900–70'. In *Teachers, Gender and Careers*, edited by S. Acker, 21–34. Lewes, UK: Falmer Press, 1989.
Orton, C. 'Dyslexia in England'. In *The International Book of Dyslexia*, edited by I. Smythe, J. Everatt, and R. Salter, 86–91. Chichester, UK: John Wiley, 2004.
Orton, S. *Reading, Writing and Speech Problems in Children*. London: Chapman and Hall, 1937.
– 'Word-Blindness in School Children'. *Archives of Neurology and Psychiatry* 14, no. 5 (1925): 581–615.
Orton Society. 'Facts about the Orton Society'. *Bulletin of the Orton Society* 23 (1973): 219.

Bibliography

Oxford English Dictionary. 'Dyslexia'. Oxford: Oxford University Press, 2010.

Palmer, R. 'Dyslexia in the Caribbean'. In *The International Book of Dyslexia*, edited by I. Smythe, J. Everatt, and R. Salter, 43–7. Chichester, UK: John Wiley, 2004.

Paradice, R. 'An Investigation into the Social Construction of Dyslexia'. *Educational Psychology in Practice* 17, no. 3 (2001): 213–25.

Patoss. 'Dyslexia No Longer Being Diagnosed by Councils Who Called the Disorder "Scientifically Questionable"'. 16 January 2019. https://www.patoss-dyslexia.org/news/Page-3/dyslexia-no-longer-being-diagnosed-by-councils-who-called-the-disorder-scientifically-questionable-/.

Paulesu, E., J. Démonet, F. Fazio, E. McCrory, V. Chanoine, et al. 'Dyslexia: Cultural Diversity and Biological Unity'. *Science* 16 (2001): 165–7.

Paulesu, E., U. Frith, M.J. Snowling, A. Gallagher, J. Morton, et al. 'Is Developmental Dyslexia a Disconnection Syndrome? Evidence from PET Scanning'. *Brain* 119 (1996): 143–57.

Pearl Harbor. Directed by Michael Bay. Touchstone, 2001. DVD.

Penfield, W., and L. Roberts. *Speech and Brain-Mechanisms.* Princeton, NJ: Princeton University Press, 1959.

Pennington, B. 'From Single to Multiple Deficit Models of Developmental Disorders'. *Cognition* 101, no. 2 (2006): 385–413.

– 'The Genetics of Dyslexia'. *The Journal of Child Psychology and Psychiatry* 31, no. 2 (1990): 193–201.

– 'Using Genetics to Understand Dyslexia'. *Annals of Dyslexia* 39, no. 1 (1989): 81–93.

Pennington, B., and D. Bishop. 'Relations among Speech, Language, and Reading Disorders'. *Annual Review of Psychology* 60 (2009): 283–306.

Pennington, B., L. McGrath, and R. Peterson. *Diagnosing Learning Disorders: From Science to Practice.* New York: The Guilford Press, 2019.

Percy Jackson and the Lightning Thief. Directed by Chris Columbus. Twentieth Century Fox, 2010. DVD.

Percy Jackson: Sea of Monsters. Directed by Thor Freudenthal. Twentieth Century Fox, 2013. DVD.

Perfetti, C. 'Reading Ability: Lexical Quality to Comprehension'. *Scientific Studies of Reading* 11, no. 4 (2007): 357–83.

– 'The Universal Grammar of Reading'. *Scientific Studies of Reading* 7, no. 1 (2003): 3–24.

Perlman Lorch, M. 'The Unknown Source of John Hughlings Jackson's Early Interest in Aphasia and Epilepsy'. *Cognitive and Behavioural Neurology* 17, no. 3 (2004): 124–32.

The Pest. Directed by Paul Miller. Sony, 1997. DVD.

Peters, A. 'Über Kongenitale Wortblindheit'. *Münchner Medizinische Wochenschrift* 55 (1908): 1116.

Pickstone, J. 'Ways of Knowing: Towards a Historical Sociology of Science, Technology and Medicine'. *The British Journal for the History of Science* 26, no. 4 (1993): 433–58.

Plowden, B. *Children and Their Primary Schools: A Report of the Central Advisory Council for Education (England)*. London: H.M. Stationery Office, 1967.

Pollard, S. *David Blunkett*. London: Hodder and Stoughton, 2004.

Pons, D. 'Dyslexia Education in the Age of COVID-19'. *Smart Brief*. 24 June 2020. https://www.smartbrief.com/original/2020/06/dyslexia-education-age-covid-19.

Positive Dyslexia. 'What Is Dyslexia?' Accessed 18 November 2021. https://www.positivedyslexia.co.uk/about-dyslexia/.

Preston Herald. 'Education of the Brain in Sections'. 12 July 1902: 11.

Prince, R. 'In for a Penny: The New Paymaster General on Dyslexia, Defence and Making a Difference'. *Politics Home*. Accessed 18 November 2021. https://www.politicshome.com/thehouse/article/penny-mordaunt-dyslexia-women-brexit-interview-profile.

The Princess and the Cabbie. Directed by Glenn Jordan. Aired 3 November 1981, CBS.

Pringle Morgan, W. 'A Case of Congenital Word Blindness'. *The British Medical Journal* 2, no. 1871 (1896): 1378.

Pritchard, D. *Education and the Handicapped, 1760–1960*. London: Routledge, 1963.

Quinnell, S. *The Hardest Test*. Cardiff: Accent Press, 2008.

Rack, J. 'The Incidence of Hidden Disabilities in the Prison Population'. *Dyslexia Review* 15, no. 2 (2005): 10–22.

Ramus, F. 'Developmental Dyslexia: Specific Phonological Deficit or General Sensorimotor Dysfunction?' *Current Opinion in Neurobiology* 13, no. 2 (2003): 212–18.

– 'Neurobiology of Dyslexia: A Reinterpretation of the Data'. *Trends in Neurosciences* 27, no. 12 (2004): 720–6.

Ramus, F., S. Rosen, S. Dakin, B. Day, J. Casellote, et al. 'Theories of Developmental Dyslexia: Insights from a Multiple Case Study of Dyslexic Adults'. *Brain* 126, no. 4 (2003): 841–65.

Bibliography

Ramus, F., S. White, and U. Frith. 'Weighing the Evidence between Competing Theories of Dyslexia'. *Developmental Science* 9, no. 3 (2006): 265–9.

Ranschburg, P. *Die Leseschwäche (Legasthenie) und Rechenschwäche (Arithmasthenie) der Schulkinder im Lichte des Experiments*. Berlin: Springer, 1916.

Rayner, K., B. Foorman, C. Perfetti, D. Pestsky, and M. Seidenberg. 'How Psychological Science Informs the Teaching of Reading'. *Psychological Science in the Public Interest* 2, no. 2 (2001): 31–74.

Reading Well. 'Famous People with Dyslexia'. Accessed 18 November 2021. https://www.dyslexia-reading-well.com/famous-people-with-dyslexia.html.

Reason, R., K. Woods, N. Frederickson, M. Heffernan, and C. Martin. *Dyslexia, Literacy and Psychological Assessment: A Report of a Working Party of the British Psychological Society Division of Educational and Child Psychology*. Leicester: British Psychological Society, 1999.

Rehnberg, V., and E. Walters. 'The Life and Work of Adolph Kussmaul 1822–1902: "Sword Swallowers in Modern Medicine"'. *Journal of Intensive Care Society* 18, no. 1 (2017): 71–2.

Reid, G. *Dyslexia: A Practitioner's Handbook*. Oxford: Wiley, 2016.

Reisman, J. *A History of Clinical Psychology*. New York: Brunner-Routledge, 1991.

Riddick, B. 'Dyslexia and Inclusion: Time for a Social Model of Disability Perspective?' *International Studies in Sociology of Education* 11, no. 3 (2001): 223–36.

Rifkin, J. *The Third Industrial Revolution: How Lateral Power Is Transforming Energy, the Economy, and the World*. New York: Palgrave Macmillan, 2011.

Riordan, R. *The Battle of the Labyrinth*. London: Puffin, 2008.

– *The Last Olympian*. London: Puffin, 2009.

– *Percy Jackson and The Lightning Thief*. London: Puffin, 2005.

– *The Sea of Monsters*. London: Puffin, 2006.

– *The Titan's Curse*. London: Puffin, 2007.

Robertson, S. '"Remaking the World": Neoliberalism and the Transformation of Education and Teachers' Labor'. In *The Global Assault on Teaching, Teachers, and Their Unions*, edited by M. Compton and L. Weiner, 11–27. New York: Palgrave Macmillan, 2008.

Robinson, S. 'The Voice of a Gifted Black Male with Dyslexia Represented through Poetry: An Auto-Ethnographic Account'. *Journal of Poetry Therapy* 30, no. 2 (2017): 113–19.

Rose, J. *Identifying and Teaching Children and Young People with Dyslexia and Literacy Difficulties*. London: Department for Children, Schools and Families, 2009.

Rose, N. *The Psychological Complex: Psychology, Politics and Society in England 1869–1939*. London: Routledge, 1985.
Rothbard, M. *Education, Free and Compulsory*. Auburn, AL: Ludwig von Mises Institute, 1999.
Royal Commission on the Blind, Deaf and Dumb. *Report of the Royal Commission on the Blind, Deaf and Dumb*. London: H.M. Stationery Office, 1889.
Rutter, M., and W. Yule. 'The Concept of Specific Reading Retardation'. *The Journal of Child Psychology and Psychiatry* 16, no. 3 (1975): 181–97.
Rutter, M., J. Tizard, W. Yule, P. Graham, and K. Whitmore. 'Isle of Wight Studies, 1964–1974'. *Psychological Medicine* 6 (1976): 313–32.
Saksida, A., S. Iannuzzi, C. Bogliotti, Y. Chaix, J.-F. Démonet, et al. 'Phonological Skills, Visual Attention Span, and Visual Stress in Developmental Dyslexia'. *Developmental Psychology* 52, no. 10 (2016): 1503–16.
Savage, R., N. Frederickson, R. Goodwin, U. Patni, N. Smith, et al. 'Relationships among Rapid Digit Naming, Phonological Processing, Motor Automaticity, and Speech Perception in Poor, Average, and Good Readers and Spellers'. *Journal of Learning Disabilities* 38, no. 1 (2005): 12–28.
Scarborough, E. 'Mrs Ricord and Psychology for Women, circa 1840'. *American Psychologist* 47, no. 2 (1992): 274–80.
Scarborough, H. 'Very Early Language Deficits in Dyslexic Children'. *Child Development* 61, no. 6 (1990): 1728–43.
Schmitt, C. 'Developmental Alexia: Congenital Word-Blindness, or Inability to Learn to Read'. *The Elementary School Journal* 18, no. 9 (1918): 680–700.
Schulte-Körne, G., and J. Bruder. 'Clinical Neurophysiology of Visual and Auditory Processing in Dyslexia: A Review'. *Clinical Neurophysiology* 121, no. 11 (2010): 1794–809.
Schuyler, M. *A Short History of Government Taxing and Spending in the United States*. Washington, DC: Tax Foundation, 2014.
Science Daily. 'US Dyslexia Policies "Ignore Scientific Evidence", Expert Says'. 5 March 2018. https://www.sciencedaily.com/releases/2018/03/180305093024.htm.
Scotsman. 'Science and Nature: Word Blindness'. 14 June 1910: 11.
– 'Scottish News'. 25 April 1919: 4.
Scrubs, series 2, episode 22, 'My Dream Job'. Directed by Bill Lawrence. Aired 17 April 2003, NBC.
Seidenberg, M. *Language at the Speed of Sight: How We Read, Why So Many Can't, and What Can Be Done About It*. New York: Basic, 2017.

Bibliography

– 'The Science of Reading and Its Educational Implications'. *Language Learning and Development* 9, no. 4 (2013): 331–60.
Seymour, P., M. Aro, and J. Erskine. 'Foundation Literacy Acquisition in European Orthographies'. *British Journal of Psychology* 94, no. 2 (2003): 143–74.
Shakespeare, T. 'The Social Model of Disability'. In *The Disability Studies Reader*, edited by L. Davis, 214–21. New York: Routledge, 2013.
Shakespeare, T., and N. Watson. 'The Social Model of Disability: An Outdated Ideology?' *Research in Social Science and Disability* 2 (2002): 9–28.
Shaw, S. 'History of Education'. In *Professional Studies in Primary Education*, edited by H. Cooper, 3–17. London: SAGE, 2012.
Shaywitz, B., T. Holford, J. Holahan, J. Fletcher, K. Stuebing, et al. 'A Matthew Effect for IQ but Not for Reading: Results from a Longitudinal Study'. *Reading Research Quarterly* 30, no. 4 (1995): 894–906.
Shu, H., X. Chen, R. Anderson, N. Wu, and Y. Xuan. 'Properties of School Chinese: Implications for Learning to Read'. *Child Development* 74, no. 1 (2003): 27–47.
Silberman, S. *Neurotribes: The Legacy of Autism and the Future of Neurodiversity*. New York: Avery, 2015.
The Simpsons, series 19, episode 9, 'Eternal Moonshine of the Simpson Mind'. Directed by Chuck Sheetz. Aired 16 December 2007, Fox.
Singer, J. '"Why Can't You Be Normal for Once in Your Life?" From a "Problem with No Name" to the Emergence of a New Category of Difference'. In *Disability Discourse*, edited by M. Corker, and S. French, 59–67. Buckingham, PA: Open University Press, 1999.
Sladen, B. 'Inheritance of Dyslexia'. *Bulletin of the Orton Society* 20 (1970): 30–40.
Smith, K. *The Government of Childhood: Discourse, Power and Subjectivity*. London: Palgrave Macmillan, 2014.
Smith, M. 'Hyperactive around the World? The History of ADHD in Global Perspective'. *Social History of Medicine* 30, no. 4 (2017): 767–87.
– *Hyperactive: The Controversial History of ADHD*. London: Reaktion, 2012.
Smith, S., W. Kimberling, B. Pennington, and H. Lubs. 'Specific Reading Disability: Identification of an Inherited Form through Linkage Analysis'. *Science* 219 (1983): 1345–7.
Smythe, I., J. Everatt, and R. Salter, eds. *International Book of Dyslexia*. Chichester, UK: John Wiley, 2004.
Snowling, M.J. 'The Comparison of Acquired and Developmental Disorders of Reading'. *Cognition* 14, no. 1 (1983): 105–18.

- 'The Development of Grapheme-Phoneme Correspondence in Normal and Dyslexic Readers'. *Journal of Experimental Child Psychology* 29, no. 2 (1980): 294–305.
- *Dyslexia*. Oxford: Blackwell, 2000.
- *Dyslexia: A Very Short Introduction*. Oxford: Oxford University Press, 2019.
- 'Early Identification and Interventions for Dyslexia: A Contemporary View'. *Journal of Research in Special Educational Needs* 13, no. 1 (2013): 7–14.
- 'Hornsby [née Hodges; Other Married Names Barley, Buckham], Beryl, [Known as Bevé Hornsby]'. *Oxford Dictionary of National Biography*. 2021. https://doi.org/10.1093/odnb/9780198614128.013.90000369381.
- 'Phonemic Deficits in Developmental Dyslexia'. *Psychological Research* 43 (1981): 219–34.
- 'Reach for the Stars: A Tribute to Bevé Hornsby'. *Dyslexia Review* 16, no. 2 (2005): 4–9.

Snowling, M.J., J. Adams, C. Bowyer-Crane, and V. Tobin. 'Levels of Literacy among Juvenile Offenders: The Incidence of Specific Reading Difficulties'. *Criminal Behaviour and Mental Health* 10, no. 4 (2000): 229–41.

Snowling, M.J., D. Bishop, and S. Stothard. 'Is Preschool Language Impairment a Risk Factor for Dyslexia in Adolescence?' *Journal of Child Psychology and Psychiatry* 41, no. 5 (2000): 587–600.

Snowling, M.J., P. Bryant, and C. Hulme. 'Theoretical and Methodological Pitfalls in Making Comparisons Between Developmental and Acquired Dyslexia: Some Comments on A. Castles and M. Coltheart (1993)'. *Reading and Writing* 8, no. 5 (1996): 443–51.

Snowling, M.J., N. Goulandris, N. Bowlby, and P. Howell. 'Segmentation and Speech Perception in Relation to Reading Skill: A Developmental Analysis'. *Journal of Experimental Child Psychology* 41, no. 3 (1986): 489–507.

Snowling, M.J., and C. Hulme. 'A Longitudinal Case Study of Developmental Phonological Dyslexia'. *Cognitive Neuropsychology* 6, no. 4 (1989): 379–401.

- *The Science of Reading: A Handbook*. Oxford: Blackwell, 2005.

Snowling, M.J., and M. Melby-Lervåg. 'Oral Language Deficits in Familial Dyslexia: A Meta-Analysis and Review'. *Psychological Bulletin* 142, no. 5 (2016): 498–545.

Snowling, M.J., H. Nash, D. Gooch, M. Hayiou-Thomas, C. Hulme, et al. 'Developmental Outcomes for Children at High Risk of Dyslexia and Children With Development Language Disorder'. *Child Development* 90, no. 5 (2019): 548–64.

Bibliography

Snyder, T. *120 Years of American Education: A Statistical Portrait*. Washington, DC: National Center for Education Statistics, 1993.

Solvang, P. 'Developing an Ambivalence Perspective on Medical Labelling in Education: Case Dyslexia'. *International Studies in Sociology of Education* 17, nos. 1–2 (2007): 79–94.

Sonday, A. 'The Road to Reading: Basic Skills to College Allowances'. In *Dyslexia: Integrating Theory and Practice*, edited by M.J. Snowling and M. Thomson, 283–92. London: John Wiley, 1991.

South London Press. 'South London Police Courts'. 22 May 1908: 4.

St James's Gazette. 'Children Who Are Letter Blind'. 8 July 1904: 10.

Stanovich, K. 'Annotation: Does Dyslexia Exist?' *The Journal of Child Psychology and Psychiatry* 34, no. 4 (1994): 549–95.

— 'Explaining the Differences between the Dyslexic and the Garden-Variety Poor Reader'. *Journal of Learning Disabilities* 21, no. 10 (1988): 590–604.

— 'The Right and Wrong Places to Look for the Cognitive Locus of Reading Disability'. *Annals of Dyslexia* 38 (1988): 154–77.

Start, K., and B. Wells. *The Trend of Reading Standards*. Slough, UK: National Foundation for Educational Research, 1972.

Stein, J., and V. Walsh. 'To See but Not to Read; The Magnocellular Theory of Dyslexia'. *Trends in Neurosciences* 20, no. 4 (1997): 147–52.

Stewart, J. *Child Guidance in Britain, 1918–1955: The Dangerous Age of Childhood*. London: Pickering and Chatto, 2013.

Stone, L. 'Literacy and Education in England 1640–1900'. *Past and Present* 42, no. 1 (1969): 69–139.

Strange, M. *War Baby: A Dyslexic Life*. CreateSpace, 2018.

Streeter, M. 'People: Dyslexic Successfully Sues Education Authority'. *Independent*. 24 September 1997. https://www.independent.co.uk/news/people-dyslexic-successfully-sues-education-authority-1240836.html.

Studio 60 on the Sunset Strip, series 1, episode 4, 'The West Coast Delay'. Directed by Timothy Busfield. Aired 9 October 2006, NBC.

Sussex Express. 'Why Argentina Remembers an Unsung Sussex Hero'. 4 April 2007. https://www.sussexexpress.co.uk/news/why-argentina-remembers-unsung-sussex-hero-1294288.

Sutherland, G. *Ability, Merit and Measurement: Mental Testing and English Education 1880–1940*. New York: Clarendon Press, 1984.

Swain, J., S. French, and C. Cameron, eds. *Controversial Issues in a Disabling Society*. Buckingham, UK: Open University Press, 2003.

Swan, D., and U. Goswami. 'Phonological Awareness Deficits in Developmental Dyslexia and the Phonological Representations Hypothesis'. *Journal of Experimental Child Psychology* 66, no. 1 (1997): 18–41.

Talcott, J., P. Hansen, E. Assoku, and J. Stein. 'Visual Motion Sensitivity in Dyslexia: Evidence for Temporal and Energy Integration Deficits'. *Neuropsychologia* 38, no. 7 (2000): 935–43.

Taylor, J., K. Rastle, and M. Davis. 'Can Cognitive Models Explain Brain Activation during Word and Pseudoword Reading? A Meta-Analysis of 36 Neuroimaging Studies'. *Psychological Bulletin* 26, no. 4 (2013): 766–91.

Temple, C., and J. Marshall. 'A Case Study of Developmental Phonological Dyslexia'. *British Journal of Psychology* 74, no. 4 (1983): 517–33.

The Thick Of It, series 4, episode 2. Directed by Billy Speddon. Aired 15 September 2012, BBC Two.

Thom, D. 'Wishes, Anxieties, Play and Gestures: Child Guidance in Interwar England'. In *In the Name of the Child: Health and Welfare*, edited by R. Cooter, 200–19. London: Routledge, 1992.

Thomson, D. *England in the Twentieth Century (1914–79)*. London: Penguin, 1981.

Thomson, M. *Psychological Subjects: Identity, Culture, and Health in Twentieth-Century Britain*. Oxford: Oxford University Press, 2006.

Times. 'Obituary: Dr Alfred White Franklin'. 4 October 1984: 16.

Tizard, B. 'Pringle, Mia Lilly Kellmer'. *Oxford Dictionary of National Biography*. 2007. https://doi.org/10.1093/ref:odnb/31569.

Tizard, J. *Children with Specific Reading Difficulties*. London: H.M. Stationery Office, 1972.

Tizard, P. 'Sheldon, Sir Wilfrid Percy Henry'. *Oxford Dictionary of National Biography*. 2011. https://doi.org/10.1093/ref:odnb/31674.

Tomlinson, S. *Education in a Post-Welfare State*. Buckingham, UK: Open University Press, 2001.

– 'The Irresistible Rise of the SEN Industry'. *Oxford Review of Education* 38, no. 3 (2012): 267–86.

Tosto, M., M. Hayiou-Thomas, N. Harlaar, E. Prom-Wormley, P. Dale, et al. 'The Genetic Architecture of Oral Language, Reading Fluency, and Reading Comprehension: A Twin Study from 7 to 16 Years'. *Developmental Psychology* 53, no. 6 (2017): 1115–29.

Tucker, W. 'Burt's Separated Twins: The Larger Picture'. *Journal of the History of the Behavioural Sciences* 43, no. 1 (2007): 81–6.

Bibliography

Turner, R., A. Howseman, G. Rees, O. Josephs, and K. Friston. 'Functional Magnetic Resonance Imaging of the Human Brain'. *Experimental Brain Research* 123 (1998): 5–12.

UK Department for Education and Employment. *Education for All*. London: Department for Education and Employment, 2001.

– *Excellence in Schools*. London: Department for Education and Employment, 1997.

UK Department for Education and Skills. *Schools: Building on Success*. London: Department for Education and Skills, 2001.

UK Government. *Chronically Sick and Disabled Persons Act*. London: H.M. Stationery Office, 1970.

– *Education Act of 1872*. London: H.M. Stationery Office, 1872.

– *Education Act of 1981*. London: H.M. Stationery Office, 1981.

– *Education Reform Act of 1988*. London: H.M. Stationery Office, 1988.

– *Elementary Education Act of 1870*. London: H.M. Stationery Office, 1870.

– *Elementary Education (Blind and Deaf Children) Act of 1893*. London: H.M. Stationery Office, 1893.

– *Elementary Education (Defective and Epileptic Children) Act of 1899*. London: H.M. Stationery Office, 1899.

– *Equality Act of 2010*. London: H.M. Stationery Office, 2010.

– *Gender Recognition Act of 2004*. London: H.M. Stationery Office, 2004.

UK House of Commons Education and Skills Committee. *Special Educational Needs*. London: House of Commons, 2006.

UK House of Lords. Judgments – Phelps (A.P.) v. Mayor Etc. of The London Borough of Hillingdon Anderton (A.P.) (By Her Mother and Next Friend) v. Clywd County Council in Re G (A.P.) (A Minor) (By His Next Friend) Jarvis (A.P.) v. Hampshire County Council. https://publications.parliament.uk/pa/ld 199900/ldjudgmt/jd000727/phelp-1.htm.

UK Office for National Statistics. *Long-Term Trends in UK Employment: 1861 to 2018*. London: Office for National Statistics, 2019.

UK Parliament. 'The 1870 Education Act'. Accessed 18 November 2021. https://www.parliament.uk/about/living-heritage/transformingsociety/livinglearning/school/overview/1870educationact/.

UK Select Committee on Education and Skills. *Third Report*. London: The Stationery Office, 2006.

Valdois, S., M.-L. Bose, B. Ans, S. Carbonnel, M. Zorman, et al. 'Phonological and

Visual Processing Deficits Can Dissociate in Developmental Dyslexia: Evidence from Two Case Studies'. *Reading and Writing* 16 (2003): 541–72.

Valentine, E. '"A Lady of Unusual Ability and Force of Character"'. *The Psychologist* 32 (2019): 76–8.

Valtin, R. *Legasthenie – Theorien und Untersuchungen*. Weinheim, Germany: Beltz, 1973.

van Gijn, J. 'The Pathology of Sensory Aphasia, with an Analysis of Fifty Cases in Which Broca's Centre Was Not Diseased. By M. Allen Starr, MD. *Brain* 1889: 12; 82–99; *with* A Remarkable Case of Aphasia. Acute and Complete Destruction by Embolic Softening of the Left Motor-Vocal Speech Centre (Broca's Convolution), in a Right-Handed Man: Transient Motor Aphasia, Marked Inability to Name Objects and Especially Persons, Considerable Agraphia and Slight Word-Blindness. By Byron Bramwell, MD. *Brain* 1898: 21; 343–73; *and* Recent Work on Aphasia. By James Collier, MD. *Brain* 1909: 31; 523–49'. *Brain* 130, no. 5 (2007): 1175–7.

Vellutino, F. *Dyslexia: Theory and Research*. Cambridge, MA: MIT Press, 1979.

Vellutino, F., J. Fletcher, M.J. Snowling, and D. Scanlon. 'Specific Reading Disability (Dyslexia): What Have We Learned in the Past Four Decades'. *The Journal of Child Psychology and Psychiatry* 45, no. 1 (2004): 2–40.

Vellutino, F., R. Pruzek, J. Steger, and U. Meshoulam. 'Immediate Visual Recall in Poor and Normal Readers as a Function of Orthographic-Linguistic Familiarity'. *Cortex* 9, no. 4 (1973): 370–86.

Wagner, R. 'Rudolf Berlin: Originator of the Term Dyslexia'. *Bulletin of the Orton Society* (1973): 57–63.

Walsh, R, T. Teo, and A. Baydala. *A Critical History and Philosophy of Psychology*. Cambridge: Cambridge University Press, 2014.

Waltz, M. *Autism: A Social and Medical History*. Basingstoke, UK: Palgrave Macmillan, 2013.

Warnock, M. *Special Educational Needs: Report of the Committee of Enquiry into the Education of Handicapped Children and Young People*. London: H.M. Stationery Office, 1978.

Welchman, M. 'A Personal Reflection'. In *1966–1991: An Account of Events and Achievements during the Twenty Five Years since the Foundation of the First Local Dyslexia Association*, edited by the British Dyslexia Association, 5–7. Bracknell, UK: British Dyslexia Association, 1991.

White, S. 'Some General Outlines of the Matrix of Developmental Changes between Five and Seven Years'. *Bulletin of the Orton Society* 20 (1970): 41–57.

Bibliography

White, S., E. Milne, S. Rosen, P. Hansen, J. Swettenham, et al. 'The Role of Sensorimotor Impairments in Dyslexia: A Multiple Case Study of Dyslexic Children'. *Developmental Science* 9, vol. 3 (2006): 237–55.

White Franklin, A., ed. *Word-Blindness or Specific Developmental Dyslexia: Proceedings of a Conference Called by the Invalid Children's Aid Association 12 April, 1962 and Held in the Medical College of St. Bartholomew's Hospital, London, E.C.1*. London: Pitman, 1962.

White Franklin, A., and S. Naidoo. *Assessment and Teaching of Dyslexic Children*. London: Invalid Children's Aid Association, 1970.

Whyte, W. 'Class and Classification: The London Word Blind Centre for Dyslexic Children, 1962–72'. *Oxford Review of Education* 46, no. 4 (2020): 414–28.

– 'Welchman [*née* Eves], (Elsie) Marion'. *Oxford Dictionary of National Biography*. 2021. https://doi.org/10.1093/odnb/9780198614128.013.66232.

Wilcutt, E., L. McGrath, B. Pennington, J. Keenan, J. DeFries, et al. 'Understanding Comorbidity between Specific Learning Disabilities'. *New Directions for Child and Adolescent Development* 2021, no. 176 (2021): 91–109.

Wilsher, C. 'Is Medicinal Treatment of Dyslexia Advisable?' In *Dyslexia: Integrating Theory and Practice*, edited by M.J. Snowling, and M. Thomson, 204–12. London: Whurr, 1992.

Wimmer, H. 'Characteristics of Developmental Dyslexia in a Regular Writing System'. *Applied Psycholinguistics* 14, no. 1 (1993): 1–33.

Wolf, M. 'Dyslexia and the Brain That Thinks Outside the Box'. *Dyslexia Review* 19, no. 2 (2008): 30–1.

– 'Naming, Reading, and the Dyslexias: A Longitudinal Overview'. *Annals of Dyslexia* 34 (1984): 87–115.

– 'Rapid Alternating Stimulus Naming in the Developmental Dyslexias'. *Brain and Language* 27, no. 2 (1986): 360–79.

Wood, A. 'Congenital Word-Blindness'. *The Lancet* (20 April 1921): 935.

Wood, B. *Patient Power? The Politics of Patients' Associations in Britain and America*. New York: McGraw Hill Education, 2000.

Wooldridge, A. *Measuring the Mind: Education and Psychology in England, c.1860–c.1990*. Cambridge: Cambridge University Press, 2010.

Wootton Bridge Historical. Miss Lucy May (Maisie) Holt 1900–2003. http://woottonbridgeiow.org.uk/holtlm.php.

Writing Lives. 'Edward S. Humphries: Reading and Writing'. 7 March 2017. http://www.writinglives.org/reading-and-writing/edward-s-humphries-reading-writing.

YouTube. 'Dyslexia Diagnosis, Scientific Understandings, and Belief in a Flat Earth'. 31 January 2019. https://www.youtube.com/watch?v=Q0Sc5Z64B98.

Yule, W. 'Differential Prognosis of Reading Backwardness and Specific Reading Retardation'. *British Journal of Educational Psychology* 43, no. 3 (1973): 244–8.

Yule, W., and M. Rutter. 'Neurological Aspects of Intellectual Retardation and Specific Reading Retardation'. In *Education, Health and Behaviour*, edited by M. Rutter, J. Tizard, and K. Whitmore, 54–74. London: Longman, 1970.

Ziegler, J., and U. Goswami. 'Becoming Literate in Different Languages: Similar Problems, Different Solutions'. *Developmental Science* 9, no. 5 (2006): 429–36.

– 'Reading Acquisition, Developmental Dyslexia, and Skilled Reading Across Languages'. *Psychological Bulletin* 131, no. 1 (2005): 3–29.

Ziegler, J., C. Perry, A. Ma-Wyatt, D. Ladner, and G. Schulte-Körne. 'Developmental Dyslexia in Different Languages: Language-Specific or Universal?' *Journal of Experimental Child Psychology* 83, no. 3 (2003): 169–93.

Zweiniger-Bargielowska, I. *Women in Twentieth-Century Britain: Social, Cultural and Political Change*. Abingdon, UK: Routledge, 2014.

Index

activism. *See* advocacy and lobbying
adults with dyslexia, 58–9, 95
advantages and disadvantages of dyslexia, 181
advocacy and lobbying: for disability rights, 132; by local associations, 123–4; of middle-class mothers, 127–8; for patients' rights, 123; for political recognition, 134, 137–8, 159, 179; for state funding, 182
aetiology, 16, 36, 92
All-Party Parliamentary Group on Dyslexia and Specific Learning Difficulties, 158
Alpha to Omega (Hornsby and Shear), 121
Amess, David, 148–9, 151
Anderson, Peggy, 22
Annals of Eugenics, 53
aphasia, 22, 26, 42, 51–2, 89
Appeals Court, 155, 157
applied research, 49, 86–7, 89–90, 101, 107–8, 111
Arkell, Emil, 57
Arkell, Helen: founding Helen Arkell Dyslexia Centre, 41, 49, 117; as leader in dyslexia teaching, 83; personal dyslexia of, 57–8, 120; support of Sandhya Naidoo, 75
Ashley, Jack, 143
assessment: in case of Phelps, 154–5; criteria for, 153–4; in Education Act 1981, 149; importance of, 181; in Naidoo's research process, 74–5; by Orton, 42–4; by the Word Blind Centre for Dyslexic Children, 64, 80, 86–7, 89

Assessment and Teaching of Dyslexic Children (Naidoo), 82
Aston Index, 116
Aston Language Development Unit, 116
Athenaeum Club, 80
Atkinson, Colin, 118
attention deficit hyperactivity disorder (ADHD), 7, 107, 166, 174
Attlee, Martin, 58, 118
austerity policies, 169
autism, 123, 135, 164, 166, 174, 175
awareness, public: of middle-class families, 78; supported by organisations, 64, 83, 86, 113, 116; through television, 151, 167–9

Backwards: The Riddle of Dyslexia (1984), 165
Balls, Ed, 157
Bangor Dyslexia Test, 70, 83
Bangor Dyslexia Unit, 70, 116, 117, 121, 122, 126
Bannatyne, Alex, 72, 73, 74, 82, 121
Barber, Michael, 153
Barrington Stoke, 131
Bartie, Louise, 58–9
Barts Dyslexia Clinic, 121
Barts Hospital, London, 68, 121
Bath Association for the Study of Dyslexia, 115
Bath Technical College, 115
BBC, 84, 165
behaviour genetics, 96–7

Belgium, 83
'Beneath the Surface of Developmental Dyslexia' (Frith), 95
Bennett, Tom, 170, 173
Bennett, Tony, 3
Berkhan, Oswald, 26
Berlin, Rudolf, 5, 10, 23, 35
Beveridge report 1942, 112
Bideford College, 118
biological causes of dyslexia, 104. *See also* brain-imaging studies; genetics
biopower, 17
Birkbeck College, London, 95
black experiences with dyslexia, 130
Blair, Tony, 152
Blunkett, David, 152–3
Boies, David, 167
Bones (2009), 168
'boosterism', 179
Bradley, Lynette, 101, 102, 126
brain-imaging studies, 102–4
Branson, Richard, 3, 167
Brazil, 116
Brewis, Henry, 140
British Association for the Study and Prevention of Child Abuse and Neglect, 81
British Dyslexia Association (BDA): awareness-raising work of, 64, 68; creation of, 5–6, 11, 83; endorsing neurodiversity, 176; lobbying of, 134, 137, 146, 151; Marion Welchman as founder of, 63, 114; neurodiversity endorsement of, 176; role in founding other organisations, 112, 116
British Library's British Newspaper Archive, 31–2
British Medical Journal, 24
British Ophthalmological Society, 30
British Psychological Society, 80, 153
British Rose review of dyslexia, 3, 7
Broadbent, William, 27–8, 68–9, 171–2
Broca, Paul, 22
Brunel University, 31
Bryant, Peter, 94, 101, 102
Bulgaria, 83
Bulletin of the Orton Society, 63, 142
Bullock report 1975, 128

Burnett Archive, 31
Burt, Cyril, 40, 50–5, 65, 70, 173

Call Me Fitz (2011), 167
campaigns, media, 151
Campbell, Tom, 7, 16–17, 37, 135–6
Canada, 5, 96, 104
capitalism, late modern, 17, 135–6. *See also* economics; neoliberalism
Caravolas, Marketa, 105
'Carl', 58. *See also* case studies
Carrey, Jim, 3, 167
'Case of Congenital Word Blindness, A' (Morgan), 24
case studies: Helen Arkell, 57–8; Louise Bartie, 58–9; 'Carl', 58; Percy F., 28–9; Ronald Hall, 56–7; 'Margaret', 77–78; 'Martin', 77; M.P., 42; M.R., 43–4; Robert Payne, 84; of physicians, 124; in popular media, 165; as research method, 106; revealing life challenges, 131; 'Simon', 78
Cass Business School, 180
causal hypotheses, 99–102
celebrity campaigners for dyslexia, 3, 130, 167
cerebellum brain region, 104
Charity Organisation Society, 20
Chasty, Harry, 117
Chautauqua Academy, 119
children and childhood: association with education, 36; changing understandings of, 54–5; child abuse prevention, 81; child-centred approaches to teaching, 141, 177; child development, 54–5, 69; child guidance clinics, 54–5, 78, 154–5; early focus on in dyslexia research, 29; focus of psychology on, 54–5; poor treatment of those with dyslexia, 38; unreached children with dyslexia, 128
Children and Their Primary Schools, 141
Children Who Cannot Read (Monroe), 47
Children with Specific Reading Difficulties, 84, 144, 146. *See also* Tizard report
Childs, Sally, 63, 115
Chinn, Steve, 119
Chronically Sick and Disabled Persons Act, 83–4, 142–3, 150

Index

class bias, 65–6, 123–8
Clay, Marie, 102
Code of Practice, 150
cognition: cognitive abilities, 38–9; cognitive differences, 19, 135, 136, 164, 178; cognitive neuropsychology, 89, 95; cognitive research, 88–89. *See also* neurodiversity
Collinson, Craig, 8
Colorado research group, 97–9, 106
Coltheart, Max, 95
comedy, 167–8
Committee of Enquiry, 145
complexity of dyslexia, 163, 169, 178
compulsory state education: dyslexia support in, 142–3, 147, 149–150, 153, 179; expansion of, 36–7, 39–40, 59; experiences of dyslexia in, 129, 154–6; funding for dyslexia in, 137; lack of reading provisions in, 66; psychology and, 54; widened access to, 59. *See also* Education Acts
concordance rates, 97
condescension in psychology, 52–3
conferences, 64, 67–72, 81–2, 116, 170
congenital alexia, 51
congenital aphasia, 51–2
congenital word-blindness, 34, 42, 51–2
Congenital Word Blindness (Hinshelwood), 34
consensus on dyslexia, lacking, 141, 169–70. *See also* skepticism of dyslexia
construction of learning disabilities, 135
'continuum of need', 147
Cooke, Ann, 121–2, 126
Coram, Thomas, 72
Coram's Fields, 72
Cotterell, Gill, 75, 83
Council for the Registration of Schools Teaching Dyslexic Pupils, 118
creativity, 180
criminality, 130–1, 180
Critchley, Eileen, 130–1
Critchley, Macdonald: in book *The Dyslexic Child* (1970), 142; definitions of dyslexia of, 82–3; on dyslexia history, 34–5; involvement with Word Blind Centre for Dyslexic Children, 64, 67–8, 90, 111; on

Word Blind Committee, 121; work with Elizabeth Warrington, 88
cross-modal coding, 88
Cruise, Tom, 3, 167
Czechoslovakia, 83, 115

Daily Mail, 170
Daniels, J.C., 70
David and Goliath (Gladwell), 167
David Copperfield (Dickens), 184
da Vinci, Leonardo, 167
Davis, Ron, 166
Dawn House School, 76, 118
day schools, 118
debate: about dyslexia in laws, 150; about word blindness and dyslexia terms, 26–9; contributions of psychology to, 37–8; current vs Victorian era, 171–2, 173; on defining dyslexia, 65; at the Word-Blindness Conference, 68–70
'defective' term, 43
definitions of dyslexia: ambiguity of, 173; British Rose review, 3–4, 106–7; considered too broad, 171; discrepancy, 96, 100; early versions of, 23–28; history informing, 184; Macdonald Critchley's, 83, 90; in popular culture, 168–9; in Rose report, 158, 170; Word Blind Centre lacking clear, 82; by World Federation of Neurology, 152
DeFries, John, 97, 98
demographics, 76–80, 128–32. *See also* middle class, the
Denmark, 48–9, 63–4, 67, 139–40, 151
Department for Education and Employment, 153, 156
Department of Children, Schools and Families, 157
Department of Education and Science, 140–1, 143–5, 148, 151
depression, 174
de Séchelles, Suzanne, 67
desirability and undesirability, 22
Developmental Dyslexia (Critchley), 83
developmental phonological dyslexia, 95
Dewey, John, 43

dextrad and sinistrad writing, 44
diagnosis: accepted as useful, 174; in adulthood, 130; avoiding, 132; case studies of, 28–30, 32–3, 43–4, 56; criteria for, 91, 106–7, 150, 171; differentiation from feeble-mindedness, 38–9; discrepancy diagnostic model, 29, 100; lack of, 128–30; over-diagnosis, 171, 173
diagraphs, 47
Dickens, Charles, 20
difference vs disability, 178
digital capitalism, 180
diphthongs, 47
disabilities: Disability Discrimination Act, 150; disability rights, 154–9; disability rights advocates, 132; 'disability' term, 8, 43; discrimination, 8; invisible, 174; in law, 142
disputes, intellectual, 26–9
Division of Educational and Child Psychology, 153
divisions in dyslexia work: academic vs applied, 49, 89, 107–8, 111; apparent at conferences, 68–71; among Word Blind Centre members, 65
documentaries, 84–5, 164
Dover Express, 32
Doyne, Robert Walter, 25
Dunn, Robert, 148, 149–50, 151–2
dyscalculia, 107, 178
dyslexia: acquired, 95; adapting to, 59; apathy from policy-makers toward, 135, 136; arguments against term, 171; attitudes of educational authorities toward, 71; brain-imaging studies of, 102–4; celebrities with, 3, 130, 167; children with categorized as different, 18; chronology of emergence, 26–30; cognitive aspects of, 88; community undermined by class and gender, 127; composition of community, 134; conceptualization of, 7–9, 23–4; context of emergence, 19–22; cynicism toward, 51; developmental phonological, 95; differences between languages, 105–6; diversity of views on, 163; early accounts of, 15–16, 24–9, 32–3, 42; first-hand accounts of, 56–9, 77–8; gaps in research about, 90; global interest and research, 67, 83, 108, 112; hereditary nature of, 96–7; ideas for overcoming, 34, 36; ignored in reports, 128–9, 137–8, 141, 143, 145; intelligence associations with, 27, 174; in legislation, 83–4, 142; numbers of children with, 143–4; as phonological awareness deficit, 94; phonological deficit hypothesis of, 98; popularity of topic, 3, 12; in popular press, 31–5, 163–4, 165–9; protections for people with, 154; psychological perspectives on, 93–4; public confusion about, 82; research on, 30–1, 74–5; research in twenty-first century, 104–8; sensitivity toward challenges of, 55; term origins, 23; two types, 89, 91; uncovering mechanisms of, 88; as verbal deficit, 94; women in community, 119–23
Dyslexia Debate, The (Elliott and Grigorenko), 164, 170, 173, 174–5
'Dyslexia Diagnosis, Scientific Understandings, and Belief in a Flat Earth' conference, 170
Dyslexia Institute: as a business enterprise, 117; founding of, 116; global influence of, 112, 114; Susan Hampshire as president of, 125; Literacy Programme, 116; lobbying of, 134; as a parent-led organisation, 6; Phelps's assessment at, 155, 156; social class and, 136; women in, 120
Dyslexia Myth, The (2005), 164
'Dyslexia, Where Now?' conference, 81–2
Dyslexic Child, The (Critchley), 83, 142
dyspraxia, 107, 178

East Court School, 118, 122
economics: economic arguments for dyslexia, 17, 135; economic change, 16–17, 113, 119–20; economic competitiveness, 39, 144–5, 151. *See also* neoliberalism
Edington School, 118
Edith Edwards House School, 72, 76, 118
Education (Handicapped Children) Act, 142
Education Act 1870, 19–22

Index

Education Act 1944, 59, 65, 113, 120, 155
Education Act 1981, 147–8, 149, 154, 155
Education Act 1993, 150
Education Act 1996, 150–1
educational psychology: critical of word-blindness, 52, 71, 82; Sandhya Naidoo working in, 74; rise of, 39–41; role in dyslexia assessment, 47, 153–4, 155; wariness of doctors and academic psychologists, 65, 69; women in, 120
educational records, 117
Eine Besondere Art der Wortblindheit (Dyslexie) (A Special Kind of Word-Blindness [Dyslexia]) (Berlin), 23
Einstein, Albert, 167
Elliott, Julian, 170–1, 172, 174–5
Ellis, Andrew, 101
emotional disturbance, 79–80
emotionality of dyslexia: children lacking self-confidence, 121–2; first-hand accounts of, 56–7; for mothers, 71; as part of scepticism, 139; relief of diagnosis, 44; stress of, 46, 157
employment struggles, 157, 180
English language, 29–30, 38, 44, 105–6
entrepreneurs, 180
environmental vs genetic factors, 92, 97–8. *See also* genetics
epidemiology, 90–3
Equality Act of 2010, 132, 154–9
Ethical Culture School, 45
Etlinger, George, 88
eugenics, 22, 50, 53
Eugenics Review, 53
European Dyslexia Association, 112, 151
Evans, Bonnie, 53
Every Letter Counts (Hampshire), 130
evidence for dyslexia, building, 89–90, 127, 142. *See also* research; scepticism of dyslexia
Excellence in Schools, 152
experiences of dyslexia: of diagnosis, 130; difficulties of, 157, 180; effects on self-confidence, 121–2; of Pamela Phelps, 154–5; portrayed in media, 84–5; profiles of, 55–8; in state schools, 129, 131–2

eyesight, 25

'Factors relating to Reading Disabilities in the First Grade of the Elementary School' (Malmquist), 91–2
Fairley House School, 118, 122, 131
family-risk study, 99–100
fathers, 29, 122, 124. *See also* mothers; parents and parenthood
Fawcett, Angela, 104
Feeble-Minded Child and Adult, The (1893), report, 20
feeblemindedness, 19–22, 38, 53
Felicity (2002), 168
female leadership, 119–23
Fildes, Lucy, 47
films and documentaries, 164, 165–8
Finland, 100
Fisher, F. Herbert, 25
Fisher, Wendy, 116, 120
Foucault, Michel, 17, 136
France, 5, 64, 67, 83, 151
Freeman mechanical puzzle box, 42
Frith, Uta, 94, 95
Fulker, David, 97, 98
funding: as advocacy priority, 182; through assessments, 181; for Bath Association for the Study of Dyslexia, 115; dependent on evidence, 108; end of for Word Blind Centre, 75, 80–1; fundraising, 118, 125; government for research, 153; for special education needs, 152; state, 137, 140; strategies for, 116–17

Galaburda, Al, 102
Gallagher, James Roswell, 67
Gallagher, Noel, 3
Galton, Francis, 22, 50
gender: in dyslexia diagnosis, 92; in dyslexia work, 119–23; inequalities, 49, 75, 76, 79
general reading backwardness, 91, 92
genetics: genetic approaches to dyslexia, 96–9, 104, 180–1; origins of dyslexia, 108
German language, 30, 105
Germany, 83, 112, 115

Index

Gerstmann syndrome, 89
Geschwind, Norman, 83
Gift of Dyslexia, The (1994), 166, 167
Gillingham, Anna, 10, 41, 45–8, 49, 55
Gladwell, Malcolm, 167, 179
Goulandris, Nata, 105
government: changes in structure and spending, 39–40; funding for research, 153; governmentality, 136; governmental logic, 135; resistance to supporting dyslexia, 17–18; role of supporting citizens, 113
Graham, Allen Dowdeswell, 64
Gray, Thomas, 32
Greater London Council, 130
Grigorenko, Elena, 170–1, 172, 174–5
Groening, Matt, 168

Hall, Ronald, 56
Hamilton-Fairley, Daphne, 118
Hampshire, Susan, 9, 125, 130, 151
Hampshire School, 125
Hampshire Telegraph, 32
handedness, 44
'handicapped' students, 147
Hargrave-Wright, Joyce, 79, 116, 126
Hart, David, 155
Harvard Medical School, 67, 83
Harvard University, 102
Haskins group, 93
Haskins Laboratories, 99
Hatcher, Peter, 101
Head, Henry, 42
Healy pictorial completion task, 42
Heath, Edward, 143
Helen Arkell Dyslexia Centre, 41, 49, 58, 117, 153
Henderson, Peter, 137
hereditary nature of dyslexia, 96–7, 98
Hertford College, 145
Hickey, Kathleen, 115, 116
High Court, 155, 156
Hillingdon Council, 155, 157
Hinshelwood, James: death of, 34–5; debate with William Broadbent, 27–8, 68–9, 171–2; descriptions of word-blindness by, 25–6, 29–30, 124; inspiration to Orton, 42;

introduction, 5, 10, 18, 23–4; as ophthalmologist, 24–5; research in newspapers, 34
history of dyslexia, brief, 5–6
Hitchens, Peter, 170
Hodgson, Helen, 123
Hodgson, Sharon, 158
Holt, Maisie, 68, 80, 121
Hopkins, Kelvin, 158
Horne, J.N., 137, 138, 139, 140
Hornsby, Bevé, 115, 116, 121, 127
Hornsby International Dyslexia Centre, 112, 121
House of Lords, 155, 157
Hoyles, Asher and Martin, 130
Hulme, Charles, 94, 101, 102
human operating systems, 164
humour, 32, 167–8
Humphries, Edward S., 31
Hungary, 30–1
hypotheses, causal, 99–102

idiocy, notions of, 19, 20. *See also* feeblemindedness
Illustrated London News, 32
impairment vs disability, 8
'imperialistic rationale' in psychology, 37, 38
income, 124
incongruity humour, 167, 168
infrastructure, organisational, 111–12
Ingram, Thomas, 67
Inquiries into Human Faculty and Its Development (Dalton), 22
Institute of Child Health, 72
insula brain region, 103
intelligence: dyslexia and, 27, 80, 171, 174; heritability of, 50–5; intelligence quotient (IQ) tests, 38–9, 42–3, 51, 59, 76, 88–9, 91. *See also* assessment
International Children's Aid Association (ICAA), 64, 66, 67, 71–2, 75–6, 80–1
International Dyslexia Association, 112, 152, 176. *See also* Orton Society
Invalid Children's Aid Association, 85, 115, 138, 140
Invergowrie, Lord, 169–70
'invisible disabilities', 174

Index

Isle of Wight study, 90–3
Italy, 115

Jaarsma, Pier, 178
Jackson, Percy, 166
James, Lawrence, 124
John Horniman School, 72, 76, 118
Johns Hopkins University, 119
jokes, 32, 167–8
Joseph, Keith, 148
juvenile delinquents, 130–1. *See also* criminality; life outcomes

Kellmer Pringle, Mia, 74, 76, 121
Kerr, James, 5, 23–4, 33, 35, 41
Knightley, Keira, 3, 167
Korean language, 105
Kussmaul, Adolph, 5, 10, 22–3, 26, 35, 172

labels: campaigns for, 8–9, 136–7; in contrast to neurodiversity approach, 164, 175, 178; impacts of use, 172; Orton's views on, 43; stance of Warnock report on, 147
Lancet journal, 27, 32, 57, 69, 139
language difficulties, 88, 90, 92, 100, 106
Lathan, Dorothy, 57
Latin America, 83
law and lawsuits, 142, 154–9. *See also* Education Acts
learning difficulties: assessments for, 41–2; conceptualization of, 40; conflated with dyslexia, 172–3; interest in, 16–17; need for treatment of, 181–2; social context of, 176–7
legal provision, 154–9
Leicester School Board, 21
letter-knowledge, 101, 102
lexical quality theory, 105
Lexism, 8
Liberman, Isabelle, 93
Liddle, Rod, 170, 172
life outcomes, 87, 113–14, 128, 131–2, 158. *See also* criminality; *Phelps vs London Borough of Hillingdon*
linguistics, 93
literacy: expansion of, 7, 15; new importance of, 16, 35, 37, 39, 49; New Labour

party's emphasis on, 152; rates of in 1972 in Britain, 128; role in society, 30, 113, 135, 178–9, 184; as a social product, 8
lobbying. *See* advocacy and lobbying
local organisations, 116
Logan, Julie, 180
London Barts Dyslexia Clinic, 116
London County Council, 51
London Foundling Hospital, 72
London Globe, 32
London Remand Home and Classification Centre, 130
London School Board, 21, 33
'look and say' approaches to reading, 45
Lordat, Professor, 15–16, 22
Love, Mary (1985), 165
Lyttinen, Heikki, 100

Macmillan, Harold, 137, 140
Magee, William Richard, 32–3
Malmquist, Eve, 91–2
Man Alive series, 84–5, 165
Manchester Metropolitan University, 153
Maple Hayes School, 118
Marazzi, Christian, 179–80
'Margaret', 77–8. *See also* case studies
Margaret, Princess, 66, 72
Mark College, 118, 119
Marshall, John, 95
'Martin', 77. *See also* case studies
Matthew effect in reading, 96
McDougall, William, 50
media coverage, 30–5, 84–5, 163–4, 165–9
medical perspectives on dyslexia, 38, 86, 181. *See also* physicians
Meier-Hedde, Regine, 22
Mellow Lane School, 155
memes, 173
memory processes, 94–5, 103
Meredith, George, 67, 121, 139, 141
meta-analyses, research, 171
Meyer, Jack, 58
middle class, the: middle-class expansion, 113, 124; middle-class families, 78, 82, 113; middle-class myth, 126, 164, 170, 171, 172; middle-class parents, 123–4
Miles, Elaine, 126

Miles, Tim: as leader of Bangor Dyslexia Unit, 116, 126; as psychologist at University College of North Wales, 68, 70; reasons for interest in dyslexia, 122; Word Blind Centre involvement of, 64, 85, 89; work on Bangor Dyslexia Test, 71, 83
Millfield School, 58, 118, 145
Mindy Project, The (2014), 168
Ministry of Education: as a lobbying target, 134, 137; rebuffing Word Blind Centre, 156–7; views on dyslexia of, 12, 127, 139, 140–1
Monroe, Marion, 47
Moor House, 118
moral panics, 151
Mordaunt, Penny, 3
mothers, 119–23, 124, 125, 127. *See also* fathers; parents and parenthood
M.P., 42. *See also* case studies
M.R., 43–4. *See also* case studies
myth of dyslexia, 164, 169–74. *See also* debate; scepticism of dyslexia

Nadesan, Majia, 135
Naidoo, Sandhya: as applied researcher, 89; as director of Word Blind Centre, 85, 121; as a foundational researcher, 111; on J.C. Daniels, 70; personal background and work of, 73–6; research at Word Blind Centre for Dyslexic Children, 76–80; views on Word Blind Centre closure, 81; Word Blind Centre involvement of, 64
naming deficits, 27, 94–5, 96, 104, 105
narratives of dyslexia, 163–4, 165–9
Nation, Kate, 74
National Archives, 137
National Assistance Act, 112
National Association of Head Teachers, 155
National Children's Bureau, 75–6
National Curriculum of 1988, 151
National Education League (NEL), 19
National Health Service, 123
National Health Service Act, 112
National Hospital for Nervous Diseases, 68, 88
National Institute of Health, 67

National Insurance Act, 112
National Literacy Strategy, 152
natural variation, 175, 176
neoliberalism, 144–5, 151–4
Nettleship, Edward, 25
neurodiversity, 164, 175–8
neuropsychology, 88, 102; cognitive, 89
New Labour party, 152, 153
newspapers, 31–2. *See also* media coverage
Newton, Margaret, 89, 116
New York Neurological Institute, 46
Nicolson, Rod, 104
non-governmental organisations. *See* organisational infrastructure
normal vs abnormal, 176. *See also* neurodiversity
Norrie, Edith: founding Ordblinde Instituttet, 10, 58, 63, 120; impact on perceptions of dyslexia, 40, 55; Norrie letter-case, 48–9
North Surrey Dyslexia Association, 116

Oliver, Jamie, 3
Olson, Richard, 98
Ontario Institute for Studies in Education, 96, 104
ophthalmology, 25, 31, 37
oral histories, 4, 9. *See also* case studies
Ordblinde Instituttet, 48–9, 58, 63, 67, 139. *See also* Norrie, Edith
organisational infrastructure, 111–12, 115–16, 120, 134
orthographies, 16, 87, 105
Orton, June, 63
Orton, Samuel: alignment with lexical quality theory, 105; as American leader in dyslexia research, 10, 40; benefits to children with dyslexia, 43–4; as dyslexia pioneer, 112; genetic components to dyslexia, 99; impact on perceptions of dyslexia, 55; as a physician, 31; research on dyslexia by, 41–2, 43; reversal errors observed by, 88; understanding of dyslexia, 44–5; views of treatment of dyslexic children, 38; working with Gillingham and Stillman, 46–8

Index

Orton Dyslexia Society, 64
Orton-Gillingham-Stillman method, 45, 52, 115
Orton Society: founding of, 40–1, 63; Marion Welchman connected to, 114–15; as a model organisation, 6, 112; working with Chautauqua Academy, 119
Oxford Dictionary of National Biography (ODNB), 6
Oxford Dyslexia Archive, 4, 9, 125, 131, 137, 169
Oxford University, 145

paediatrics, 67
parents and parenthood: changing understandings of, 54–5; defensiveness of, 78–9; middle-class, 78–9; parent groups and associations, 49, 113, 115, 118, 122–4; parenthood, 124, 172; requests for support from, 84; worried about dyslexia, 29, 52–3, 57, 71, 78
pathologization, 17, 70
Patients Association, 123
patients' rights, 123
Payne, Robert, 84, 165
Pearson, Karl, 50
Pennington, Bruce, 106
perceptual deficits, 88
Percy F., 24, 25, 28–9, 32, 96, 173. *See also* case studies
Percy Jackson series (Riordan), 166–7
Perfetti, Charles, 104–5
performance vs competence, 43
Pest, The (1997), 168
Phelps, Pamela, 154–5
Phelps vs London Borough of Hillingdon, 154–7
phonology: phonemes, 44, 94; phonetic language, 29–30; phonics, 44–5, 48, 52, 57, 101; phonograms, 47; phonological awareness, 98, 101, 102, 107; phonological deficit hypothesis of dyslexia, 98, 99, 106, 108, 152; 'phonological dyslexia', 95–6; phonological memory, 94–5; phonological processing, 29–30, 93, 94–6, 103
physicians: case studies of, 42, 124, 165, 173; concern with congenital rather than acquired dyslexia, 30–1; disputes of, 139; as early dyslexia researchers, 5, 10, 18, 21–5; as men, 119, 122; views compared to psychologists, 37
Pintner-Patterson performance test, 42
Plowden report, 141–2, 177
poetry, 32
political recognition, 134–6, 142, 148–54, 156, 159, 179
Pollock, Joy, 117
popular culture, dyslexia in, 163–4
population studies, 90
power, 65–6, 136
Princess and the Cabbie, The (1981), 165
Pringle, Mia Kellmer, 74
Pringle Morgan, William: case studies of, 96, 124, 173; case studies of in newspapers, 34, 165; with first account of dyslexia, 10, 23–4, 28–9; influence on Samuel Orton, 42; as prominent dyslexia researcher, 5
prison populations, 128, 130, 131, 180
Prison Reform Trust, 131
Pritchard, David, 16
processing speed, 98
progressive educators, 43
psychology: as an administrative technology, 51, 54; assessments, 42–3; condescension in, 52–3; educational, 39, 40, 52, 121; emergence as leading dyslexia field, 31; focus on children, 36–7, 54–5; history of Western, 37; perspectives on dyslexia, 93–4; two-tiered labour market in, 49; work on reading, 87–8
psychometric testing, 42–3
public awareness and acceptance. *See* awareness, public
public spending, 113. *See also* funding

racism, 130
Rain Man (1988), 166
Ramus, Franck, 106
Ranschburg, Paul, 30–1
rapid naming tests, 105
Rattenbury, Grace, 75

reading: ability as a continuous trait, 97; age matched design, 94; becoming widespread, 16, 18, 39; comprehension, 98; difficulties, 21–3, 27–8, 128, 130–1, 143–4; fluency of, 105; lack of experience in, 96; learning to, 18; methods for addressing difficulties in, 41; process of learning, 29–30; reading disability instead of dyslexia, 170; reading wars, 63–4; research on, 93; specific reading retardation, 91, 92; tests of, 91; as 'via regia' of psychology, 87–8

recognition of dyslexia, 6, 136, 147–50, 156, 157

Registrar General for England and Wales, 76, 124

regression analysis, 91

Remedial Education Centre, 121

remedial instruction: child guidance clinics struggling to provide, 72; development of, 45–8; formal studies of, 100–2; as goal of research, 41; guides for, 82; ideas for, 34, 36; methods for, 51–2, 57, 107, 171, 181; Orton developing, 44–5; as primary goal of dyslexia organisations, 121; progressive specialist schools for, 58; testing efficacy of, 101

Remedial Training for Children with Specific Disability in Reading, Spelling and Penmanship (Orton, Gillingham, and Stillman), 46

representations of dyslexia. See narratives of dyslexia

reproducibility agenda, 171

research: applied, 49, 86–7, 89–90, 101, 107–8, 111; case studies, 106; community, 63, 111; conferences, 64, 67–72, 81–2, 116, 170; meta-analyses, 171; methods (more), 94, 99–100; perceived lack of, 139, 141; for remedial techniques, 41; retrospective analyses, 99; rigour, 89, 108; rivalries, 69–70; in twenty-first century, 104–8

reversal errors, 88

rhyme processing, 103

rights, dyslexia, 156, 169

Riis-Vestergaard, Ingrid, 67

Riordan, Rick, 166

rivalries in research, 69–70

Romania, 83

Rose, Nikolas, 37

Rose review, 3, 7, 107, 157–9, 170

Royal Commission on the Care and Control of the Feeble-Minded, 20

Royal Commission on the Factory Acts 1876, 20

Royal Household of Queen Elizabeth II, 80

Royal Society, 80

Rutter, Michael, 6, 90, 91

Salter, Jennifer, 127, 129

Scarborough, Hollis, 99–100

scepticism of dyslexia: by J.N. Horne, 138–40; male cynicism toward dyslexia, 49; peak of in 1960s and 1970s, 164; renewed, 170; of Graham Stringer MP, 158–9; of Thatcher's Department of Education and Science, 143–4, 149, 152; UK government letting go of, 153; because of women's advocacy, 127. See also debate; myth of dyslexia

Schmidt, Johannes, 15

school boards, creation of, 19–20

'School Hygiene, in Its Mental, Moral and Physical Aspects' (Kerr), 24

schooling, elementary. See compulsory state education

science: academic vs applied, 107–8; debate in, 174; foundations of in dyslexia research, 86–90; on speech and linguistics, 93; to validate dyslexia, 111. See also research

Science and Technology Committee, 158

Scotsman, 34

screening tests for dyslexia. See assessment; diagnosis

Scrubs (2003), 168

self-confidence, 121–2. See also emotionality of dyslexia; experiences of dyslexia

semantic categorization, 101

Shankweiler, Donald, 67, 83, 93, 111

Shapwick School, 118, 119

Shear, Frula, 115, 121

Sheldon, Wilfrid, 67, 80

Short, Edward, 143

Silberman, Steve, 164

'Simon', 78. See also case studies

Simpson, Jessica, 3

Index

Simpsons, The (2007), 168
Singapore, 115, 116
Singer, Judy, 175–7
Smith, Jacqui, 156
Smith, Matthew, 135
Snowling, Maggie, 94, 121
social class: dyslexia associated with privilege, 27, 32; hierarchies, 53; impact on dyslexia support, 180, 182; intelligence and, 50–1; intersections with dyslexia, 21–2; middle-class bias of dyslexia community, 123–8; mobility, 158; of researchers, 80; Word Blind Centre and, 65–6, 76–80. *See also* middle class, the
social constructionist approaches, 135–6
social Darwinism, 50
social development models, 53
social justice, 66, 158, 175, 178
social media, 179
social model of disability, 175
societal shifts, 15–17, 39, 113, 119–20. *See also* economics
Society for the Scientific Study of Reading, 104
Solvang, Per, 9
Sorkin, Andy, 167
South Africa, 115
South London Press, 32
Spain, 83
Spearman, Charles, 50
special education and schools: emerging need for, 20–1; emerging private schools, 58; expansion of, 117–19; lack of support at state schools, 131–2; needs industry, 181–2; provisions for, 142, 147; as realm of educational psychologists, 65; for speech and language problems, 72; varied access to, 129
'specific dyslexia', 139
Specific Dyslexia (Naidoo), 74, 76, 79, 81, 142
'specific learning difficulties', 146, 154
specific reading retardation, 91, 92. *See also* reading
Spectator, 170
spectrum of abilities, 175–7, 181. *See also* neurodiversity
speech and linguistic sciences, 93
speech therapists, 72

spelling, 95
standardised testing, 54–5, 74
Stanford-Binet IQ test, 42
Stanovich, Keith, 96, 104
state education. *See* compulsory state education; special education and schools
statementing, 117, 129, 147, 149, 150, 159
State Psychopathic Hospital, 41
statistical analysis and research, 91, 97–8
St David's College, 118
Stein, John, 104
Stenquist mechanical assembly test, 42
Stephenson, Sydney, 25
stigma, 132
Stillman, Bessie, 10, 40, 41, 45–7, 55
St James Gazette, 33
St John's College, Oxford, 4
strephosymbolia, 44, 141
Stringer, Graham, 158
St Teresa of Ávila, 15, 22
Studio 60 on the Sunset Strip (2006), 167
Stuttgart, Germany, 23
"sub-normal" learners, 21. *See also* feeble-mindedness
subskills of reading, 98. *See also* reading
subtraction in brain-imaging, 103. *See also* brain-imaging studies
superiority humour, 167–8. *See also* humour
surface dyslexia, 95, 99
Surrey, England, 126
Sustainable Development Goals of United Nations, 179
syllables, 93. *See also* phonology

Taiwan, 83
teachers: learning about dyslexia, 82, 115; teaching profession, 47–8, 120
'Teaching Backward Readers' (Burt), 51–2
Teather, Sarah, 158
television, 84–5, 151, 167–8
Temple, Christine, 95
testing accommodations, 131
Thatcher, Margaret, 143–4, 151
Thick of It, The (2012), 168
Thompson, Kenneth, 140
Thomson, Mike, 116
Thomson, Patience, 122, 131

Tizard, Jack, 143, 144
Tizard report, 84, 144, 145, 146
Tomlinson, Sally, 181–2
Tory Reform Group, 148
transparent languages, 105
Treacher Collins, Edward, 25, 30, 38, 44, 176
Tunbridge Wells Group, 81
twenty-first-century dyslexia research, 104–8
twin studies, 97–8

United States, 73, 83, 93, 112, 115. See also Orton Society
University College London, 88, 95, 170, 172
University College of North Wales, 68, 70, 83
University of Albany, 83, 93
University of Birmingham, 121
University of Connecticut, 83
University of Glasgow, 73
University of Illinois, 73
University of Montpellier, 15–16
University of Oxford, 95, 101, 104
University of Sheffield, 104

van Straubenzee, William, 143
Vellutino, Frank, 6, 83, 93
verbal memory, 98, 107
visual memory, 25, 93
visual perception research, 87

wages at dyslexia centres, 126
Walker, Alex, 172
Walker, Peter, 148
Waller, Elisabeth, 117
Warnock, Mary, 127, 145–6, 147
Warnock report 1978: disability statements in, 149; impact of, 146–7, 152, 157; mention of dyslexia in, 128–9; social class in, 172–3; use of continuum concept, 177
Warrington, Elizabeth, 88–9
Warwickshire County Council, 169
Watkins, Bill, 122
Wechsler Intelligence Scale for Children, 76
Welchman, Marion: influenced by Orton Society, 63; reasons for interest in dyslexia, 120, 127; work with British Dyslexia Association, 11, 83, 114, 115–16

welfare state, 59, 112–13
Welin, Stellan, 178
White Franklin, Alfred, 66–8, 71–2, 80–2, 83, 115, 137–8
'whole-word' approaches to reading, 45
Whyte, William, 64, 69, 79
Williams, Steve, 129
Wilson, Harold, 140, 143
Wolff, Agnes, 115
women, contributions of, 45–8, 49, 75, 119–24. See also gender; mothers
Wooldridge, Adrian, 69
Word Blind Centre for Dyslexic Children: as case study of dyslexia movement, 64–6; closure of, 80–5, 113, 114, 116; creation of, 5, 10–11, 71–6; demographics of children at, 76–80, 125–6; Mrs Devon at, 124–5; as early specialist centre, 85, 112; increasing public awareness, 82; lobbying of, 12, 134, 137–8; patient records at, 125; research conducted at, 86–7; role in increasing public awareness, 86; women in leadership at, 121
Word Blind Committee, 68, 72–4, 88, 121, 139
word-blindness: concept of, 139–40; congenital, 26–30, 31, 42, 51–2; definitions of, 26–8, 68–9; introduction, 4, 5, 22–6; as a mental defect, 51; in popular press, 30–5
'Word-Blindness and Visual Memory' (Hinshelwood), 27
Word-Blindness Conference, 67, 69–72
'"Word-Blindness" in School Children' (Orton), 41, 42, 46
'Word-Blindness or Specific Developmental Dyslexia' (White Franklin). See Word-Blindness Conference
World Federation of Neurology, 82–3, 90, 96, 152
writing systems, 105. See also orthographies
Wundt, Wilhelm, 37

Yale University, 93, 99
Yule, William, 6, 90, 91

Zangwill, Oliver, 74, 80, 88, 121
Zephaniah, Benjamin, 130